Nameless Faceless People

Ten Years With The Free Burma Rangers

David Small

NAMELESS FACELESS PEOPLE: Ten Years With The Free Burma Rangers

Contents

For Mom and Dad.
I love you.

A Note From The Author

"Every night in my dreams, I see you, I feel you..."

Can you name the movie this song is from? If you said *Titanic,* you're correct.

Growing up, I loved movies. They transport you to other worlds, other galaxies, other stories. The soundtracks to those movies are nearly as important and memorable as the films themselves. I've always thought books should have soundtracks too.

Well, now they do.

For many of the chapters in this book, I took the main themes and lessons and wrote a song. I was fortunate to have talented friends take the lyrics and create melodies, then sing and produce the songs.

You can find the full book soundtrack on Spotify, Apple Music, and other streaming platforms. I encourage you—when you finish a chapter—to listen to the song based on that chapter. Just search Nameless Faceless People on any streaming platform.

It adds another layer to the story.

Enjoy!

David Small

Foreword

Nameless Faceless People is a wonderful book. May God bless you as you read it.

David Small is a man led by God, serving God, and doing his best to love and speak as God leads him. It's been an honor to know him for over 20 years. We have known him since he was an earnest, capable young teenager to an adult serving with us in many capacities in the Free Burma Rangers.

The Free Burma Rangers is a humanitarian relief organization, started over 30 years ago to bring help, hope, and love to people under attack in Burma. We've gone on to also work in Iraq and Syria, Sudan, Tajikistan and Afghanistan, and Ukraine. Our primary work is still in Burma, and along with humanitarian relief, the foundation of all we do is to share the saving love of Jesus. We want to be ambassadors for Jesus, and when David Small joined us, he also wanted the same.

He did that so well while he was with us. First, as a young volunteer carrying heavy loads and leading Good Life Club programs as well as coordinating relief. And then later on, as an instructor, then finally running complete trainings for new Rangers.

He has a gift of administration, coordination and instruction. He has a deep love for the people and they love him back. He has a special way of connecting that brings out the best in the people he's training. He was able to bring unity and organization and excellent training to ethnic men and women from over 18 different ethnic groups from all over Burma, as well as many religions. He did all this while keeping a focus on Jesus and proclaiming his word sweetly and boldly.

From morning devotions during the training, throughout the training and into the night, he worked to ensure that the Rangers had the highest quality of training, were fed well, and most importantly, were in an environment of love and pointing to God. After training missions were completed, he accompanied the new Rangers on missions with us, and I knew I could always depend on him to be calm, cool, God-centered, and loving to everyone around us. He also conducted missions on his own with relief teams working in conflict-torn areas.

Our children, Sahale, Suuzanne and Peter all grew up in Burma going on missions and when David Small joined us he was like an older brother or extra uncle to them. They love and trust him and always thought he was fun to be around. They could see his love and care for the ethnic people that they love so much. David Small is a man of love, desirous of serving God above all else, and always wanting to put other people first. He is a friend, and someone I can count on. Whenever we have difficult decisions, I stop and pray and ask David for his thoughts and advice.

He carefully prays and chooses his words, and helps us make the right decisions. As you read this book, you will get to know him better, as well as others in Burma and the situation here.

Burma has the longest running civil war in the world at 75 years, and the last four years have been the worst when the military clamped down even more. And, as a result of that, the Burman people, who comprise about half the country rose up. Right now, we have two things happening concurrently. One is the Burma dictatorship response to that uprising, which is the most brutal attacks that we've ever seen in our 32 years of service here.

This is the heaviest fighting since World War II. This is because the dictators are very afraid to lose the country, and now with support from China and Russia in the form of jet fighters, bombers, attack helicopters, armored vehicles, and artillery and drones—the Burma military is coming with a speed and a force we've never seen.

Over four and a half million people have been displaced in the last four years alone, and that's on top of millions more before that. Thousands have been killed at a rate we've never seen, and to date, 77 of our own Rangers have been killed, as well as over 200 Rangers wounded. That is representative of what's happening in Burma.

At the same time, the good news is that the Burman majority and the ethnic minorities are united in a way they never have been before and are working together at the grassroots level to build a new country. In the face of daily and nightly attacks, they are uniting to serve and help each other. They want an end to the dictatorship and some form of federal democracy.

Please pray for them that they will have that, and more importantly, that they will follow Jesus and love and forgive each other. Please pray also for the dictators of Burma and the army to change their hearts so that there could be forgiveness, reconciliation, and the birth of a new country.

David Small's mission has gone on now to build up young people to follow Jesus through the Jungle Discipleship School and he continues to serve in Burma. He is part of that changing of hearts.

Thank you for all you do to help us and for your prayers and love. May God bless you,

Dave and Karen, Sahale, Suu, Peter, and all the Free Burma Rangers.
December 2025
Karen State, Burma
www.freeburmarangers.org

Introduction

Growing up in a small town in Canada, I had never had a gun pointed in my face—let alone someone ready to kill me. I grew up with the quintessential Canadian childhood: a log cabin in the forest by a frozen lake where we played pond hockey. Mom would have a big pot of chili on the stove, CBC radio humming in the background, and a wood fire warming the home. But over the past decade, I've snuck across borders, met with potential terrorists, tiptoed through landmine fields, hidden in jungles while being hunted, and endured furious bombings—all while being far more Mr. Bean than James Bond.

You may know Burma as Myanmar, but for this book, I'll call it Burma—the name most of its people still use. It's home to the world's longest-running civil war. For nearly a hundred years, Burma has known conflict, made bloodier still after the coup on February 1, 2021. Most people hear little about Burma, partly because journalists can't easily reach it, and partly because the world has sympathy fatigue. Israel. Ukraine. Africa. The headlines blur together. Our hearts can only hold so much grief.

I served with the Free Burma Rangers (FBR), an international humanitarian organization, for nearly a decade—training Ranger teams and joining missions deep in the conflict zones. I've suffered more loss than I thought a heart could bear, though not nearly as much as the people of Burma. The jungle tests everything—your patience, your body, and your faith. I learned there not to be led by comfort or fear. We must be led by something higher: love.

Love alone can lead us into uncomfortable and dangerous places —and sustain us there. It shields us from the exhaustion of war. Over the years I've learned that the reward isn't in solving big problems or meeting important people. It's in loving the ones the world overlooks. Most people in Burma will never have their stories told—entire generations erased without justice or home. But when we start to notice the forgotten, the ones who carry our burdens and wash our dishes, we find strength to love the nameless, faceless people.

I never set out to be a missionary. I wasn't ready, trained, or qualified—I was following God. Growing up in that small Canadian town, I thought following God meant going to church on Sundays.

Boring.

I was wrong. Following God is the greatest adventure imaginable. And he's faithful not to leave us where he finds us. He's shaping us into people who will follow him anywhere—even when a terrorist puts a gun to your head.

Chapter 1

Terrorists

He waved the gun back and forth between my boss's face and mine. At the time I was calm; I was more surprised that despite all the tight security around the refugee camps, this man had snuck a gun in. It wasn't until days later that I realized he was 100% ready and willing to kill me. At that moment and in the moments afterward, it didn't occur to me that if this guy had gotten spooked, he would have taken my life. He had taken many lives; I wouldn't be the first—but maybe I'd be the first foreigner he'd kill.

My boss and I were possibly the first foreigners he had met in a long time. He had been in hiding for many years, slowly building an army. He was on terrorist watch lists, and every journalist I knew would kill to have an interview with him, but no one could find him. I hadn't believed we would get to meet with him until we walked into his compound a few minutes ago and he stepped out. From behind his back, he pulled a handgun and pointed it at us before placing it on the table.

After getting the call, I flew to Bangladesh to prepare for the meeting. I consulted with my boss, and he consulted with old friends who work in the FBI and State Department. One of our team members at headquarters put together a briefing binder with everything she could find about this guy and the army he was leading. I spent hours poring through anything I could find about ARSA, the Arakan Rohingya Salvation Army, and its leader.

He was born in Burma, a Rohingya himself. He moved to Saudi Arabia, where he grew up and studied to become an imam. After that, he went to Pakistan, where he studied guerrilla warfare tactics. Then he went back to Burma, where he started an army.

It was attacks by ARSA that led up to the ferocious Burma Army response of August 2017. ARSA killed six or seven Burma Army soldiers and afterwards just disappeared. The Burma Army was furious with these attacks and used them as an excuse to conduct genocide on the Rohingya people, attacking them with fury and disproportion, killing 10,000 men, women, and children. This led to a massive flight of the Rohingya people from Burma into Bangladesh. They streamed out as fast as they could, and by October over 800,000 Rohingya had fled from the steady, planned cleansing the Burma Army was conducting. Three weeks after the initial attacks, I stood in the middle of this sea of Rohingya refugees. And two years after that, I stood in front of one of the leaders of ARSA while he yelled in Arabic and waved a gun around.

When I arrived in Bangladesh to prepare for the meeting, we called our contact to let him know we were there. He said he would call us when the meeting was ready. We sat around the hotel for two days waiting. I assumed they were watching the hotel and watching us. We get spied on and followed quite a bit, but we had nothing to hide, so I figured it was okay if they wanted to observe us for a few days. After two days, we got the call. He said, "Rent a car tomorrow morning at 8:00 a.m. I want you driving north from your hotel along the Teknaf Road. I'll call you once you're on the road with more instructions." Then he hung up. Without us telling him, he already knew which hotel we were staying at, confirming my suspicions we were being watched.

As he'd instructed, we hired a car and, after a quick prayer, jumped in and started driving north at 8:00 a.m. sharp. We drove for about twenty minutes when the phone rang. It was our guy. He asked to speak to the driver. We passed the phone over, and the driver listened for a few minutes, said okay, and hung up. He turned the car around, drove back about a mile, and pulled over. An inconspicuous guy came over to our vehicle and, without knocking or saying anything, opened the side door and got in.

He looked just like any other Rohingya refugee who mills around the camp areas. Smiling at us, he shook our hands and began directing our driver. After guiding us for about ten minutes, he instructed our driver to pull over. Again, without saying anything, he opened the door, jumped out, and another guy jumped in. This guy repeated the same procedure. He shook our hands and guided the driver. We pulled off onto a tiny road that weaved through one of the refugee camps. These makeshift roads are barely wide enough for a vehicle to fit, and we were constantly brushing past people and refugee huts as we made our way through the overcrowded camp. He guided us as far as the road could take us, then we got out on foot.

There was another guy waiting for us. They handed us off, and the guy told us to follow him. He walked quickly through the trails that wound through the camp. It was a maze. We went down side roads, into someone's house, out the back door onto a little footpath. Back onto a main trail, around and in circles. After walking with us for about ten minutes, we met another guy at what I assumed was a predetermined meeting place.

These lower-ranking "foot soldiers" didn't know where the boss was hiding; they only knew enough to bring us to the next guy, who would know enough to bring us to the next guy. I think we were handed off five or six times. I could see they had a disciplined security plan in place as we made our way to meet the leader.

In the past, whenever I've been in the camps, I've been swarmed with people everywhere I go. Literally from the moment I step out of the vehicle, I'm surrounded by at least 20 or 30 people. And they follow me around. But this time it was different. This time people would notice the white people walking, then they'd see who our guides were, and they would turn around and pretend like they hadn't noticed us. The refugees literally sit for hours on end in the doorway to their huts, and when we would pass with our guides, they would either turn around or go inside their houses, disappearing into the darkness. As we approached the compound where the boss would meet us, we got handed off three or four times within a few minutes and then ushered quickly into an enclosed compound with high walls. We were now way out at the back end of the refugee camp, where the camp butts up against the mountain range that runs like a spine down the Teknaf peninsula.

We were quickly ushered into the house and told to sit at a small table with plastic chairs around it. We sat and our latest guide disappeared into a back room. It wasn't more than a couple of minutes later that I was looking at the gun in the hand of the leader as he waved it around, proving to us that he was the real deal and that he was in charge.

It's a funny thing when someone is ready to kill you. It's funny—the thoughts that go through your mind and your reactions and instincts that kick in. Many people talk about our response to fear by activating the "fight or flight" response—but some people also freeze. They don't run away (flight) and they don't pounce (fight); they freeze in a place of total uselessness. It's like their muscles turn to cement and, despite their brains trying to talk some sense into them, they're stuck. I've seen this unfold in people.

But at this moment, when I had a gun waving in my face, I found my thoughts wondering how on earth did I wander into this situation? What choices in my life led me to this moment?

Chapter 2

Initiation

I am sitting at a homemade picnic table in Burma at our Free Burma Rangers (FBR) training camp. I'm watching the five-foot-long banana tree leaves dance with God in the wind. The white noise of the rushing river below. Dozens of butterflies float through camp. Behind me, 120 young men and women are being put through the paces, learning what it means to become a Free Burma Ranger.

Our training camp, also known as Tah U Wah Camp, which translates to White Monkey Camp, has grown over the years into a bustling village that houses our Ranger families year-round. We have the Jungle School of Medicine Kawthoolei (JSMK) where we train some of the best medics I've ever worked with at a small wooden teaching hospital. Villagers will walk or carry their loved ones sometimes up to five days to get treatment at JSMK.

The Ranger side of the camp is across the small, rushing river that runs through camp. This is where we conduct our annual servant leadership and relief team training. Young men and women come from all across Burma, some traveling for up to a week to attend our three-month training program. They all have the same goal: to go back and help their people, who are being killed and oppressed by the Burma Army.

In 2014, I agreed to give up six months of my life to volunteer with the Free Burma Rangers. When that six months ended and I went back to Canada to try to find a "real job," I sensed in my spirit that I should give up the job search and call Free Burma Rangers home. The Headquarters (HQ) staff had become my family, our ethnics inside Burma had become my brothers and sisters, aunts and uncles, and somehow, I had become familiar with things that used to terrify me.

I must start this book about adventures with the Free Burma Rangers by explaining that I am a weak, timid, and fearful person. I don't say this out of false humility, but brutal honesty. I don't know why, but for some reason when I was maybe ten or eleven years old I watched the movie *Arachnophobia*. It had never occurred to me that spiders could amass an army and maliciously come after humans. I was suddenly terrified of anything that crawled, especially spiders. My family had a beautiful camp on a lake, one of the most amazing places in the world for me, yet as a child and teenager, I would dread going there because of the giant furry dock spiders that would hide in the dark cracks on the dock, waiting and calculating the exact moment they should come and attack.

It was a fear that was paralyzing. The kind of fear where all breath leaves your body, your vocal cords seem to dry and shrivel up instantly, and no sound comes except maybe a slight croak and whine. You cannot run, cannot move. Fear would totally grip my heart in the presence of those spiders.

Fears give birth to doubt and self-consciousness. Because I didn't want to show others how scared I was, I would avoid situations that might leave me vulnerable to my fear surfacing. I stopped seeking adventures. I dreamed of an office job in a big city. I didn't want to have any grass to cut, or plants to water—places that bugs or spiders might make their home. I doubted my ability to survive in the wilderness if I ever had to. I was self-conscious about my fear and wimpiness.

As my fears grew, so did my love of reading stories about young boys who didn't have the same kind of fears I did. I envied the characters I would read and reread in books like *Hatchet* by Gary Paulsen. I would picture myself being like Brian, surviving in the wilderness after a plane crash. Relying on my instincts and brain to build a shelter and survive. I read *Where the Red Fern Grows* and would picture myself being brave enough to be out alone for days and nights, just me and the dogs; competent enough in the wilderness to fend off mountain lions and hunt raccoons. I read stories of young boys racing the Iditarod, and would imagine myself commanding a dogsled team out in the Alaskan frontier. All the stories I read had two powerful themes: a young boy trying to become a man, and wilderness pushing him to the limit. But despite all the reading, I felt more and more like a boy, and less and less like I wanted anything to do with the wilderness.

My insecurities carried on through my teens. The only place I found solace for my insecurities was on the hockey rink. It seemed to be the only place I could fit in and belong. I would go camping with friends, as long as it was in a semi-controlled environment. It started with camping in my backyard, then moved onto camping on a lake somewhere, as long as one or more of my other friends was familiar with the area and could "take care of me" if something bad happened to us.

One evening, some neighborhood boys and I decided to camp out in my backyard. We had a large family-sized tent that we set up, then threw a bunch of mattresses down and all piled in on sleeping bags. It wasn't much as far as "camping" goes—but for me, even though my parents' house was only 50 meters away, it seemed like the forest was going to swallow the tent up.

There was a strange series of events that took place that night.

First it was the rabbits—the damn rabbits.

My neighbor had rabbits and wanted to bring them camping with us. They were allowed, but the rabbits had to sleep in the cage outside the tent. I was sleeping in the middle of the tent. I didn't want to be anywhere near the edge of the tent for fear that a bear or wolf might tear through the tent and drag me away into the forest. The rabbit cage was outside the tent, just above where my head was—the only thing between me and the rabbit cage was a thin nylon tent wall.

I woke up in the middle of the night to the sound of something hitting the rabbit cage. I could hear the rabbit scurrying around in panic, and then I heard a sniffing noise. My heart was racing. Fear instantly grabbed hold of me. I pictured a pack of wolves surrounding the tent, drooling over the rabbits. I thought we were so stupid to leave the rabbits out there—it was baiting wolves or bears to come and find a tent full of dinner. Stupid.

I seemed to be the only one who was awake, and I didn't know what to do. Sleeping next to me was an older neighborhood boy. I knew him a little, but he was a lot older than I was. I silently shuffled over towards where he was sleeping and nudged him, hoping he'd wake up and hear the noises and do something. He eventually woke up. By this time the noises outside the tent had stopped, but in my imagination I was expecting the wolves to pounce at any minute. The older neighborhood boy seemed a bit annoyed that I had woken him up, but he could also see the fearful look in my eyes. He reached out and put his hand on me. First, I believe, to comfort me. Then, he slowly started to slide his hand down my body, and eventually stopped just above the waistband of my pajamas, only momentarily.

My brain didn't know how to handle the sexual assault that took place that night. I blamed myself for it. I knew it was wrong. I knew what he did was wrong, but it was my fault. If I weren't so afraid, if I had some more courage, I wouldn't have needed to wake him up. If I could have gotten up and shooed away whatever was freaking the rabbit out, then I could have solved the problem myself. But instead, I was paralyzed by my fear. I felt so embarrassed and ashamed.

Shame.

Shame entered my life that night. I was maybe only ten or eleven years old, and up until that point, had no memory of shame. But after that, shame entered my life. Every part of me seemed shameful. My cowardice was shameful; my sexuality was now shameful; my fear was shameful. I had to hide. Exposing my fear and weakness was almost as terrifying as spiders. It became my full-time job to avoid being exposed for who and what I really was—a shameful, abused coward.

Frederick Buechner once wrote, "The world sets in to making us what the world would like us to be, and because we have to survive after all, we try to make ourselves into something that we hope the world will like better than it apparently did the selves we originally were. That is the story of all our lives." I was trying to survive middle school and high school. Just survive. I was getting good at making myself into something that I thought the world would like more than the original self I was slowly forgetting. I told no one about the trauma and abuse of that night in the tent; I went on quietly surviving.

The original self that I was slowly losing was being replaced by a poser. In situations where I wasn't sure if I had the skills or competency or courage to survive, I would either run away from them or fake it. I had a natural gift for leadership and would rely on this into my early adult years, taking a place of leadership instead of having to be tested to see if I had what it takes.

Life has a way of circling back to the places we've tried to bury. What I once hid behind confidence and control began to surface years later, halfway around the world.

It had been decades since the night in the tent when I was sexually assaulted, and although I hadn't let it define my life, I now found the memory resurfacing. I was in another tent, this time in Bangladesh, and the thoughts of my own trauma slowly surfaced as I listened to a story from a newly arrived Rohingya refugee. It felt like my traumatic experience, which I hadn't thought about in years, was standing quietly on the sidelines watching and listening to a woman share her own story of being raped by the Burma Army before they executed her husband in front of her. Another woman told me that the Burma Army gathered up all the "pretty, younger women in the village" and locked them in a barn. The soldiers took turns raping them, sometimes multiple times, then locked the door to the barn and lit it on fire, burning everyone alive.

I knew that I couldn't do anything to help them, so I listened. I held their hand as they wept and recounted their story. I prayed with them. I understood their feelings of losing control. When you're in that moment of paralyzed fear or oppression from someone or something bigger and stronger than you, and you can't control the situation, you feel so helpless. I hate not being able to control things in my life. My poser had become so entwined with my real self that sometimes I couldn't tell the difference. I was so good at acting out of my poser, so good at hiding my insecurities and fears. Buechner continued to say, "The original, shimmering self gets buried so deep that most of us hardly end up living out of it at all. Instead, we live out all the other selves that we are constantly putting on and taking off like coats and hats against the world's weather."

I have a friend who is a logger. He has a skidder that is really old. One day a friend of mine was working with him, and they were using the skidder when suddenly an oil line blew and it started to spray oil all over the place. My friend said, "We need to fix that oil leak!" and his boss said, "If you don't look at it, then it's not broken."

I so often live this way in my life. My truck starts to make a funny noise, and the poser in me knows that I don't know how to fix it, that I don't have enough money for something serious to need attention on my truck, so I turn the music up so that I can't hear the noise anymore. If you don't look, if you can't hear it, it's not broken.

If you don't look, it's not broken.

So often, I take that attitude towards my own heart. If I don't look at it, if I don't listen to it, if I turn up the music, arrange my life so that it's so full and busy, then I won't need to see what's broken in my heart. I won't need to see that there are some old wounds and traumas that I might need to work through. My poser is a reflex of self-protection—but what am I trying to protect myself from? Old wounds, traumas, abuses, discomfort, fear, my uninitiated self—I could go on and on.

In the Bible, we see Jesus delivering people from demons and healing them from illnesses. But a broken heart is different from spiritual warfare. We don't "deliver" a broken heart, or cast out the brokenness. We need healing in our hearts. But I often hide my heart away.

A mentor of mine challenged me to pray and ask God to "show me my heart, what is going on in my heart?" So, I prayed and then sat quietly. Almost right away my brain went to scripture, to Genesis, at the very beginning, when Adam and Eve had eaten from the wrong tree, sinned, and realized that they were naked, so they hid in the bush. Shame. God comes walking through the garden looking for them, calling out to them, "Adam, where are you?" (as if he doesn't know). And as this image unfolded in my imagination, I sensed in my spirit that God was saying, "Your heart is so full of shame, hiding in the bush, hiding from Me." He was calling out, "David, where are you?" not as a question *to* me because he doesn't know where I am, but as a question *for* me, to ask myself, where am I in the story of my life? Is this how I want to live? In fear? In hiding behind a poser? Is this the kind of man that I want to be—one that is constantly afraid, constantly hiding, full of shame? Jesus was telling me to come out of hiding, to stop living a small story, to stop living a mediocre life.

I have lost so many friends to mediocrity. Friends that had so much potential, such great hearts, so many gifts, yet chose to lead such small lives. I am so tired of losing people I love to mediocrity. Despair. Hopelessness. Why can't we spend more time living our lives ambitiously, without fear? The only way to find out is to take your heart, leap out of your comfort zone with a parachute of grace, and take an adventure.

This is a story about a young boy becoming a man. This is a story about the wilderness pushing him to the limit.

Chapter 3

Uranium

I had roughly 30 pounds of uranium in my backpack and nearly a hundred miles to walk until we reached the border. Pure uranium is not more than a rock, so, basically, I had added a bunch of rocks to our gear. My pack weighed close to 80 pounds as I inched my way through the jungle towards the border. The mountains that I knew were coming along the trail would not be easy.

We were out on a mission deep in Burma, along the border of Karen State and Karenni State, when we came across the mine. At first pass, we were told that it was a tin mine, and we thought little of it. Later we learned it wasn't a tin mine, but a uranium mine. A couple of our Rangers went in for a closer look and met some of the mine workers. They noticed some Chinese people around the mine and asked what they were doing. The workers said they sell the uranium they collect from the mine to China, and sometimes hear Russian spoken too. I was the team leader on this mission, and as I listened to this report, I wondered what our response should be, if any.

The Free Burma Rangers (FBR) has two primary missions: to help the people and to get the news out. We help people in various ways, limited only by our creativity. It could look like standing with villagers who are being attacked; it might be rescuing a little girl trapped by ISIS sniper fire; or it could be responding with medicine to a malaria outbreak. Sometimes helping people can look like a building project in a village or a food distribution project to provide some staples needed to survive.

Helping the Burmese people is how it all started for FBR. In the very beginning Dave Eubank, the founder of FBR and a former US Special Forces officer, would fill a backpack with as much medicine as would fit, and take any money he could find, then walk into the jungle until he found the front line. There, he would help people in need.

The other thing we do is get the news out. For over 75 years, the Burma Army has been waging a civil war against its own people. They want the 184 ethnic groups within the current boundaries of Burma to all speak the same language (Burmese), and have the same religion (Buddhism). Any ethnic group, village, or person who wants to speak in their own dialect or have freedom of religion becomes an enemy of the state. When FBR gets the news out, we shine a light on what is happening on the ground in the conflict zone. We want to put a spotlight on the Burma Army which is oppressing people or committing human rights violations. We want to paint a picture for people to understand what life is really like living in the places where FBR serves: Burma, Iraq, Sudan, and Syria. Often, because we are willing to walk for weeks through the jungle to get to people in the conflict, we can tell stories and report on things that a journalist can't get to.

Sometimes getting the news out means telling a story about a secret uranium mine where workers earn next to nothing, and China and maybe Russia receive the uranium.

But that story is only good if we can get ourselves some evidence —like, say, a chunk of uranium stolen from the mine.

Early in the morning, two of our team members dressed like villagers who would go to work in the mine. They went and linked up with the mine worker they had met previously, and he got them into the mine so they could film and take photos. Then he led them back into a mine shaft, where they walked for nearly an hour deep into the mountainside. The conditions were horrible. I had asked them if it was possible to get me a small piece of uranium about the size of my fist. Inside the mineshaft, they hammered away at the ground and eventually pried free a chunk of uranium about the size of a basketball. They knocked away some of the other rock from around the jet black uranium, and they began their hour walk back to the mouth of the cave.

Drinking coffee and watching the sunrise, I saw the two return from the mine. I couldn't help but feel a bit like I was some sort of mob boss, sending his two mobsters to steal uranium while I sat in my headquarters drinking coffee. I asked them how things had gone, and, honestly, I was relieved that they were alive and not in jail. With a heavy thud, they clunked the chunk of uranium down on the table in front of me. My jaw dropped. For those not familiar with uranium, it is one of the heaviest materials you can find.

My excitement about their successful mission was quickly thwarted once I lifted the rock and realized how far I had to walk with that rock in my backpack. We hammered off more of the excess rock so that our sample was mostly uranium. It was a beautiful rock, dark black and shiny, with lines of gold littered throughout. I bagged the rocks and put them at the bottom of my pack. Two of my team members helped me lift the pack onto my back, and we made our way towards the border.

• • •

Walking is not the work of FBR, although sometimes it feels that way. We walk a lot—sometimes even when it's possible to take a truck, tractor, or motorcycle, we still walk.

But the work of FBR really begins when the walking ends, at the end of a long day, when we finally arrive at our destination. We meet with village leaders and sort out places for the team to stay. The medics need a place to set up their pop-up clinic, and the team needs a place to put on their children's program, the Good Life Club. If walking to the destination takes everything you've got, and you collapse into a useless pile of sweat once you reach the village, then you're no good to the team.

I also constantly remind myself that we're walking through an active war zone. Often, the Burma Army is only a ridge away. What would happen if the Burma Army started shooting at us or chasing us? If I'm so exhausted that I can't help my team get out of the way—or worse, one of my nightmares, my team has to slow down for me to keep up with them—someone could end up dead. It's absolutely essential to keep going, even when you think you have nothing left.

There is an old saying in the army that I learned: "When you think you're done, you're only 40% done." We are far stronger than we think we are. In his book *War*, Sebastian Junger writes this about our ability to do more than we think we can: "It starts with pain, of course, but that pain is at the edge of what I thought of as a deep, dark valley. At the bottom of the valley is true incapacitation, but it might take hours to get down there." In the army, I learned I could push myself beyond what I thought I could do. We did an exercise once in our basic officer training course where we had to stay awake for five days, digging a trench line, defending it at night, conducting patrols and section attacks during the day. I never thought I could stay awake for five days, let alone function and lead a section of troops in contact, but I learned I could. Junger goes on in his writing to say, "The most valuable thing I knew from all that running was that when you start hurting, you're not even close to the bottom of the valley, and that if you don't panic at the first agonies, there is much much more of yourself to give."

This was true of the nearly hundred-mile walk back to the border. We made progress step by slow step. Each day would inevitably have at least two or three mountains to cross, changing thousands of meters of elevation. The tropical heat was intense, and the narrow jungle trails often went straight up the mountains. This would not be a simple walk.

I sweat profusely. I'm the guy that no one enjoys playing basketball with because I slime everyone. This profuse sweating, coupled with the moist tropical heat, makes it very hard for me to stay hydrated.

While I knew I could push myself physically and mentally—that my body could withstand more abuse, and that pain was only the beginning of a long slow descent—I also knew that there was one variable that could totally take someone out: dehydration. On a mission like this, you are in a constant state of dehydration. We walk for a minimum of six hours a day, but sometimes up to 12 or 14 hours for several consecutive days, in order to reach the areas we want to serve.

At the end of the day when we peel our socks off our feet—being careful not to pull off blisters or scabs with the socks—and wash ourselves in a cold mountain stream, we also start the process of rehydration. It doesn't seem possible to drink enough water or electrolytes before going to bed to rehydrate ourselves. On many occasions, I have woken up in the middle of the night to excruciating muscle cramps in my calf or foot. I sit up from a dead sleep, gasping with pain as I see my calf muscle seizing up into a ball. Commercial electrolyte packs, while tasty, don't do much to help. On long days, we load our canteens with spoonfuls of salt and spoonfuls of sugar, the only way to curb the effects of dehydration and cramping.

A friend of mine in Finland is a great doctor, and he explained some of the science of water loss to me. He said, when you exercise, you lose between one half-liter and one liter of sweat per hour, and in every liter of sweat is approximately one teaspoon of salt. We average about eight hours of hiking per day, not in cool, dry Finnish climates, but in hot tropical jungles where the humidity is always extremely high. That means that during a walking day I sweat out at least eight liters of water a day, along with at least eight teaspoons of salt. As I come back to civilization after a long mission, my field hat and backpack have often turned white from all the salt that has soaked through them during the mission.

I had silver-dollar-sized blisters on the back of both my feet, and my knees and shoulders hurt from the heavy load on my back. But I started repeating a mantra to myself. With each agonizing step up the mountains, I would tell myself, don't ask for it to be easier; ask to be stronger. My friends and teammates would ask if they could help carry some of the rocks, but I knew their packs were already nearly as heavy as mine, so I declined and kept repeating this mantra over and over in my head.

Don't ask for it to be easier; ask to be stronger.

Each time I asked for strength, I could feel more energy going into my legs, despite the pain. Sweat poured off me in a constant stream, but I knew the signs of heat exhaustion very well. If I completely stopped sweating, that was when I needed to worry. As long as that steady stream of sweat was pouring off me, I knew I still had some water in me.

There have been several times when I've "bonked" from heat exhaustion. When walking in the jungle, you have to balance how much water you want to carry in your pack with how much that water weighs. You don't want to carry too much water, which makes your pack heavier, which makes you have to work harder to get up the hills, which makes you sweat more. At the same time, you don't want to carry too little water, which lightens your load but also increases the risk that you'll run out and become dehydrated.

The sun in the jungle is ferocious. Stepping out of the shade of the jungle into direct sunlight, I can literally feel my heart rate increase almost instantly. It is almost painful to walk in the direct sunlight. Instant nausea and weakness. A few times I have miscalculated my water supply and ended up in direct sunlight, which pushed my body to a state of dehydration I had never experienced before. I felt like vomiting, but there was nothing inside me. Black spots were dancing in front of my eyes, making it difficult to see. My skin was dry; there was no more moisture inside my body to sweat out. I could walk about five or ten meters before my heart rate would skyrocket, and I'd need to stop and sit down. Then my throat started to dry and close. I couldn't get any words out—there was no moisture left in my throat. What should have been a 15-minute hike turned into a dreadful hour, inching my way up the mountainside, hugging tight to any sliver of shade I could find.

In moments like these, I can easily begin to whine and complain to God that I want things to be easier—help me with this, bless that, heal this. But the thing is, the mountains, heat, and humidity aren't going anywhere. If I am unwilling to face them, then I shouldn't go on a mission there. I've realized that it will never get easier. Life will never get easier. But I will get stronger.

One of my favorite verses in the Bible comes from the prophet Isaiah. He writes, "[God] gives power to the weak and strength to the powerless. Even young people will become weak and tired and young men will fall in exhaustion. But those who trust in the Lord will find new strength. They will soar on wings like eagles. They will run and not grow weary. They will walk and not faint."

Those words take on a totally new meaning for me when I'm out in the jungle. As I slogged my way up the mountain under the weight of my uranium-filled backpack, asking to be stronger, I thought of these words. This strength comes from love. I want to be stronger so I can help the people I love, so I can tell their story, so I can shine a light on what's happening in their country. Easier isn't the right way.

I walked back to camp and then continued to the border with my backpack of uranium. Shortly after, I had a meeting with someone from the UN fact-finding team. She seemed to be green when it came to fieldwork, especially a fieldworker from FBR. She anxiously jotted down notes as she asked me about my time in Burma and what I'd like to share with her. The look on her face when I offered her a chunk of uranium was priceless. She stopped scribbling in her note-book and looked up at me, scanning my eyes, hoping I was joking.

"I've got it at my office if you want me to run and grab it for you," I said with a straight face. "You can have it."

"Wh-wh-what am I supposed to do with uranium? I can't accept a chunk of uranium from you at a coffee shop," she stammered back to me, looking around anxiously like she had suddenly found herself in the middle of a drug deal.

"I don't know, you can test it to see if it's actually uranium—which it is—then you can trace it, or read our reports, and take our GPS coordinates from where we collected it, and let people know that the Burma Army is selling their uranium to China?"

Her face suddenly looked as though she were involved in something way beyond her pay grade. I chuckled as she began asking more questions about the uranium and scribbling her anxiety into her notebook. I told her I didn't think it was enriched uranium, since I hadn't developed any superpowers from handling it. She didn't laugh at my joke.

Back at the HQ, I had actually started googling "how to enrich uranium" to make sure there was no way I could accidentally do it. I didn't get very far into my research before a co-worker came in and half-jokingly said, "I think that's the kind of Google search that gets flagged and ends up with you on some sort of watch list." I laughed, then glanced at the chunk of uranium on my desk and decided maybe it's better not to know.

The UN rep I met with that day did not take any uranium samples back with her. But she wrote about it in her next report, and the UN updated its maps of Burma to show the mines were not tin mines. A small victory. Sometimes you have to take whatever wins you can get.

A week later I flew to Finland for my friend Jesse's wedding. I left his wedding gift on the table with all the other toaster-shaped boxes wrapped in nice wrapping paper. My gift was in a small box stuffed into a brown paper bag; it weighed a lot more than its small size let on. What better gift for a newlywed couple than a small chunk of uranium with a little note attached to it, a motto for their new life as a married couple:

Don't ask for it to be easier; ask to be stronger.

Chapter 4

Genocide

On August 25th, 2017, a small group of Rohingya soldiers from the Arakan Rohingya Salvation Army (ARSA) attacked several Burma Army controlled checkpoints, killing a few soldiers. The Burma Army retaliated by coming into villages and opening fire. The numerous accounts I collected from many interviews in the months after this date painted a very graphic and clear picture: the Burma Army wanted to exterminate the Rohingya people.

The Burma Army would come into a village around dusk as the village was settling down for the night—farmers returning from their day's work in the fields or rivers. The army would then fire indiscriminately at the village. Houses made of bamboo or flimsy pieces of wood would disintegrate under the bullets. Soldiers would come to the huts and lock entire families in their homes, barricading the doors, then setting fire to the house, burning them alive.

The village would erupt in chaos and fear as people ran frantically, trying to find their family members and head into the jungle to hide. They would run until they made it to the next village, but eventually the Burma Army would come into that village as well and repeat the same horrific violence. It was a thorough and targeted effort by the military to get rid of all Rohingya people. Later, many accounts reported that they specifically targeted women and children in their attacks, aiming to eliminate future generations of Rohingya.

I can hear the screams in my mind—and sadly it pointed my heart towards the horrendous accounts of death and genocide found in the Bible. When Jesus was born, King Herod ordered the killing of all boys two years old and under. I can imagine the wailing and mourning of the parents as the soldiers stormed into their homes and killed their children.

As the slow and steady push by the Burma Army continued for days and into weeks, people quickly began pouring over the border from Burma into neighboring Bangladesh. The Naf River separates Bangladesh and Burma at the southernmost tip of Bangladesh, and this is directly across from where most of the attacks took place.

People fled however they could. If they could swim, they would try to get across. Since most couldn't swim, they walked for days northward until they could cross by land where the river narrowed, or if they could find some money, they could hire smuggler boats to bring them across. The smugglers moved in quickly and took advantage of the dire situation, charging huge amounts of money for a family to be boated across to Bangladesh.

Bangladesh is already a desperately poor country, and one of the top ten most densely populated countries in the world. Within a few weeks of August 25th, they suddenly found themselves with a half million newly arrived refugees crowding the Teknaf peninsula. They quickly called in the army to create some sort of order and sanity to the mass of humanity that had arrived and continued to arrive daily. In the coming months, Bangladesh would see over a million new refugees arrive into its already over-crowded country.

From the FBR headquarters (HQ) office, we were closely watching the situation and trying to connect with our teams in that area. We had tried a few years before to send an HQ team over to help the Rohingya, but the mission had failed. We could not get into the areas we wanted to and could not meet a Rohingya contact who would guide us. I felt a desire in my heart to help these people, but I had no idea how or why. I talked with my boss, who was busy planning for a mission into Iraq. He said to me, "If you can get there, pray and go." I found out that another NGO that we were friends with was planning a trip over to the camps to do some food distributions. I called their director and asked if I could come by and meet him.

Arriving at his office, he'd just come back from Sittwe, where many Rohingya lived. He had tears in his eyes as he recounted the situation and how it had changed. He told me that if I could get to Cox's Bazar, I was welcome to meet him, but I needed to book separate flights and arrange separate transportation. If I went there, he could arrange a driver and translator for us to go to the camps. I went back to my office and talked with a coworker, Larry, who also desperately wanted to help these people. We discussed the situation and then decided we should go. After booking our tickets for the following day, we immediately began researching security, immigration, and any available information to prepare.

We arrived in Dhaka around 2:00 a.m. I wasn't prepared for the chaos that is Dhaka, or Bangladesh for that matter. But it was nothing compared to what we were about to see in the camps.

The Dhaka airport is pure chaos. The environment was characterized by pandemonium, with individuals shouting and a noticeable absence of structure. To clear through immigration, you need to first line up at a small, unmarked window and pay exactly $51 USD for the visa fee. The man in the booth is very particular about getting very clean, crisp bills. On one trip, the man denied one of our team members because their bill was too crumpled. Thankfully, they had another dollar bill in their bag that was eventually good enough. Once you pay the visa fee, you wrestle your way to an immigration official and present a stack of paperwork to get the visa. Once stamped, you can go out and collect your bags and exchange money. The whole time you are being overwhelmed by people, smells, yelling, and chaos.

By 4:00 a.m. we arrived at our hotel where we got three hours of sleep, then returned to the airport to take a quick domestic flight down to Cox's Bazar.

Cox's Bazar is home to the world's longest unbroken beach, over a hundred miles of exquisite pristine beaches, often with no one in sight. It is definitely not a typical tourist destination. We took a taxi to the hotel that someone had recommended to us and then tried to contact Brad, from the other organization, who was supposedly already there. We got in touch with him, met him for dinner, and made plans to go with him down to the camps the next morning at 5:00 a.m.

Until this point in my life, I had never been in the middle of a major crisis or natural disaster. There wasn't anything that had happened in my life up to that point that would have prepared me for what we saw the next day when we went down into the camps. I still didn't have a clear idea or picture of why we were there or what we could do to help. From Cox's Bazar, it's about an hour and a half drive to the camps. The first part of the drive followed the beach and ocean along the western part of the peninsula, then about halfway down we cut across to the other side of the peninsula and drove into complete pandemonium. People were everywhere. We had a hard time driving because there were so many people lining the roads and filling every inch of available ground. Hundreds of thousands of people trying to find food, shelter, medicine, and help. Everyone had a look of total fear and panic on their face.

We stopped to walk into one of the new makeshift camps, and before we even got out of the vehicle, a mob of people were pressing up against the glass begging for food or water or anything. We got out of the vehicle and pressed our way through the crowd, but the crowd followed us everywhere we went. People constantly reaching out and touching your arm, putting their hands together to beg for something. I couldn't help but think about Jesus and the crowds that followed him when he was on the earth. The Bible talks about crowds that were so thick that people were pressing against him and touching him, desperate for something, desperate for life.

Our guide led us along the muddy path away from the road towards the camp. We came through a rice field, and as I looked out over the familiar green of the rice field, it reminded me of the many rice fields of Burma, but this time I could see people scattered throughout the rice field squatting down. I asked what they were doing, and our guide told us they were using it as a toilet. He said, "Right now they have one toilet for every 50,000 refugees." It didn't take long before these beautiful rice fields were totally decimated and destroyed, and eventually got swallowed up by the ever-expanding camps.

We walked up a hilltop through the crowds and eventually came to the top of the hill where we got a glimpse of the camp. I stood there with my jaw hanging limp, totally speechless as I scanned the horizon, seeing the camp sprawling out as far as I could see in any direction. I felt so small. So hopeless. I saw the spirit of fear and desperation on everyone's faces, and it overwhelmed me. It seemed like no one knew what to do or what had happened. People seemed in shock about the lost loved ones they left behind just days before, unable to bury, as they fled for their lives. Some still had bullets in them, some burns, some gashes from machetes. We stood silently on that hilltop for a few minutes, taking it in.

We eventually made our way back to our vehicle, constantly being harassed for food. There was a small shop near where our driver had parked, and the owner invited us in for a drink. I felt so guilty sitting there with a cold bottle of water and a bag of cookies in front of me while the crowd of people that had been following us stood around us watching us eat. I had no appetite and took only one drink of water to be polite. There was a small boy who had been following us since we got out of our car. He was wearing rags and looked totally shell-shocked and starving. I knew I couldn't give him my bag of cookies or bottle of water without causing an all-out riot. But it didn't seem right to leave this boy with nothing. I folded up some money in my pocket, and then before we left I went over to him and reached out to shake his hand and smile at him. He looked me in the eye and could feel that I was trying to give him something as I shook his hand, an old trick my grandfather used to pull to sneak his grandsons some money. I tried to tell him through my eyes to be careful with it as not to attract any unwanted extra attention, then I quickly let his hand go and started shaking other people's hands and saying goodbye. When I looked back, the boy had disappeared into the crowd.

Later that evening, Brad told me he had seen what I had done and that he liked it, but I needed to be careful; it could start a riot or get someone beaten. People were starving to death and would do anything for food.

We spent most of the day touring around the area and then eventually headed back to Cox's Bazar. The sun was setting over the ocean, and the beautiful, peaceful beach seemed like a different world from the chaos of the camps on the other side of the peninsula. Our van was silent as we drove back; we were all trying to process what we had seen. How could FBR be involved here or help here? I wondered as we drove back. We are just a small organization. We can't feed that many people; that's not even what we do. But then I remembered what my boss Dave would say when he talked about when he first started FBR in the late 90s.

He said he would go out to the people who were fleeing, and he'd try to help just one person, and they'd be happy and he'd be happy. And that was his goal for each day—just help one person. Make a difference in one person's life that day, and they'll be happy, and we'll be happy. Sounds simple. I made a difference in the little boy's life that day. I snuck him enough money for him to eat some food for a day or two. I'm not sure if he was happy, and I was so overwhelmed that happiness seemed like a distant memory, but I felt hopeful that we had a place there.

Cox's Bazar was swarming with NGOs. At one point, sources reported that over 400 different NGOs operated around the

Rohingya camps. The United Nations (UN) quickly arrived, and its convoys of white SUVs would stream through the streets of Cox's Bazar. Vans quickly got hired out, and NGOs slapped up stickers and magnets with their logos on the side; everyone was there. Every NGO and aid organization that you've ever heard of was there, as well as many you've never heard of. I had an old FBR t-shirt and a look of bewilderment on my face as we walked around the crowded streets of Cox's Bazar.

The next day we were heading down to a new arrivals camp to help with a food distribution that Brad had set up. They had three hundred bags of food that they were going to distribute. The food would last a family for a few weeks and contained rice, potatoes, oil, salt, and some dried fish. Before the sun came up, we were back on the highway following a large truck loaded with their 300 food bags.

We arrived at the camp, and their local contact had already preselected three hundred of the most desperate people, who were waiting in a line with a ticket they could exchange for a bag of food. As soon as the truck backed up with food, all hell broke loose. People started to push and yell and fight each other. The local contact quickly had to enlist some men to help keep things under control. They broke branches off of trees and started to beat people back away from the truck. I stood in the midst of the fighting, fearful and unsure of what I should do. I was totally out of my league. I did not know what I was doing or why I was there. I felt so out of place.

I pushed my way through the crowd and tried to walk away from the chaos of the food distribution. I wanted to find a quiet place where I wasn't surrounded by people. I walked to the other side of a little swamp and started to take photos. I eventually moved towards the back of the line and kept taking pictures. I snapped a picture of a woman's face that had a look of desperation in her eyes. I looked down into her hands and quickly realized that she didn't have a ticket in her hand. She was number 301, and wouldn't be getting any food that day. Her eyes told this story of desperation and sadness, like she knew that she wasn't going to get any food, but she had to stand in the line anyway, hoping that maybe there would be an extra bag, she had to do something, anything, to get some food for her family. The look in her eyes broke my heart.

When the food distribution ended, and the big truck drove away, the crowd slowly dispersed. We asked our translator if there was anyone there who had a story they could tell us. He said, "Ya sure," and then reached out to the next person who walked past us and said, "Tell them your story." We listened as he told us of his horrific experiences that led him to that camp, then he walked away and disappeared into the crowd. The translator stopped the next person who was walking past us and again said, "Tell them your story," and again we listened to a similar account of horrific violence. On and on it went. Person after person. He didn't need to set up any special interviews or find the right people; every person who walked past us told us a story that left us fighting back tears and shocked at the evils humans are capable of. I couldn't believe it.

The amount of grief and trauma that each of the new arrivals was walking around with was enough to sink the average person. But they didn't have time to let their grief destroy them. They had to keep living. They had to figure out how they could get a tarp so they could cut some bamboo and build a shelter. They had to figure out how to get some food, and clean water, and maybe some medicine. The shooting had stopped, but they still weren't safe. Many died in the weeks after the attacks from starvation, wounds, and illnesses.

Illnesses spread quickly through these camps. Everyone we met had some sort of fever, and many complained about diarrhea. No one was waiting in line for the toilets, and we were sometimes literally walking in muddy trails of human waste. The smells were sometimes unbearable, unlike anything I had ever smelled before—it was the smell of a slow rotting mass of human decay. As we left the food distribution that day, we drove down the eastern side of the peninsula and occasionally had views across the Naf River to where we could see Burma. Our guide pointed out plumes of smoke rising in the distance across the river. "The Burma Army is still burning down villages," he told us. We stopped for a moment to take in the sight. Black smoke rising in the air, too far away to make out any village or details, but the black smoke mixed with the stories we had heard from people that day was enough for my imagination to picture the scene across the river. I had never faced killing and death so close before. I had never stood on the banks of a river and looked across to see death unfolding before me. I shuddered, and my body ached with sadness.

On our third and final day, we went out on our own for part of the day and conducted some interviews. Brad said he could arrange a driver and translator for us, but first he needed to hand some money off to the translator, who was organizing another food distribution.

Bangladesh was crawling with police and military organizations. In the immediate aftermath, one "secret police" group followed Rohingya people around to ensure they did not travel outside of the contained camp areas. This secret police group later took on the mission of finding unregistered NGOs working illegally in Bangladesh, and our games of cat and mouse would begin. Since we were using Rohingya men as our translators and guides, we had to be careful when we were outside of the camps with them. We didn't want to put them at risk.

Brad had a backpack full of money that he was hoping to hand off to a young man named Aman, but before Brad could get close to Aman, he noticed Aman was being followed by secret police. He called Aman, who was keenly aware of the secret police following him, and asked him to get into a tuktuk and start heading south along the Teknaf highway, and Brad would get another tuktuk and come and meet him. So both men got separate tuktuks and headed south to find each other. Meanwhile, the secret police followed at a distance on their motorcycles, unsure of what Aman was up to.

Brad eventually caught up with Aman's tuktuk and pulled alongside it. Aman was smiling his giant smile, either calm in the face of being followed, or not concerned about the police following him. The two tuktuks zoomed down the road as the secret police followed on motorcycles, weaving in and out from behind cars. Brad started unloading the bricks of money from his backpack and handing them to Aman, all while driving down the road. The police could tell something was going on, but didn't know what. Aman smiled and put the money into his backpack. Then Brad sent him to meet with us, and he had his tuktuk turn around. When he drove past the secret police and they saw a foreigner was involved, they weren't sure what to do, and by the time they sped back up to catch up to Aman, he had already disappeared into a crowd of people and tuktuks.

In a separate vehicle, our driver had driven us to a camp, and it was only a few minutes after the handoff, with the secret police still searching for him, that Aman came and met us. He had never met us before but immediately gave us big hugs. I was taken aback by the amount of emotion he displayed and his level of English. I asked him how old he was; "I am 21 years running, brother," he replied with a smile. He had organized a few people that we could interview, so he jumped into our van and started guiding us to the Nayapara Refugee Camp.

Aman was born in this refugee camp. His mother was pregnant with him when the Burma Army forced her to run away over twenty years ago in similar oppression. Back then there weren't nearly as many Rohingya living in Burma as there are now, but the Burmese government always held that they didn't belong in Burma, but that they were Bengalis. Bangladesh and the Rohingya disagreed, saying their ancestors had been in Arakan state for centuries. Aman's mother fled from persecution, and a few months after arriving in Bangladesh gave birth to Aman, her second son. They registered with the UN, which was running the camps, and eventually settled into refugee living. They put aside money and eventually had enough to send Aman's older brother on a boat to Malaysia where he could find a job and send money back to the family. It was sad to say goodbye to their eldest son and Aman's big brother, but they knew it needed to happen in order for the family to survive. As Aman shared this story with me, the smile disappeared from his face for the first time since meeting him, and he continued to tell me, "My brother got on the boat, it was smugglers boat, you know, and so the boat was not a good boat... halfway across the ocean to Malaysia the boat sank and my brother could not swim. He drowned." Aman stoically looked off into the distance, before quickly returning to the present moment with a big smile returning to his face.

We were ushered through a refugee camp and eventually entered a small compound. They shooed out anyone who didn't belong in the compound and closed all the doors. They brought out chairs and water for us. We introduced ourselves to a man named Mohammad and interviewed him. As Larry was asking more questions of Mohammad, I was playing with the children in the compound and talking to some women who were standing watching. One of the young ladies shoved another woman forward and said, "You should talk to her; the Burma Army raped her."

The woman smiled shyly at me, her eyes fixed on the ground, only fluttering up to connect with my eyes for a brief second. I asked her if that was true. "Yes," she replied in a way that left me feeling like it isn't an uncommon thing. As Larry was wrapping up with Mohammad, I went over and told him I wanted to talk to the other woman, but then Aman got a phone call. A concerned look came over his face as he listened, and then, saying nothing, he hung up the phone. "Brother, we must go," he said quickly. "The police are coming, looking for us."

They ushered us through the house and out the back door of the compound. We weaved our way through the refugee camp, down back alleyways and through people's houses, until finally we ended up back on the main road. Aman called our driver and told him where to pick us up, and soon we were all back in the van. It seemed to be a normal part of Aman's life to be evading the police; he didn't seem overly concerned.

That evening I walked along the beach back in Cox's Bazar. The sun was setting, and our trip was ending. I wondered what our place was here? Then my heart shifted, and I wondered where God was in all this? I felt angry towards God for this whole situation and the unbelievable amount of evil that happened to these great people. I asked Jesus, "Where are you? What are you doing?" and then I got the answer. He whispered gently to my heart, "I am here. I am playing with the children. I am weeping with the widows. I am mourning the losses with them. I am helping them build homes. I am sitting with them and listening to them. I am here. I haven't abandoned them." I knew it was true. Even though these people were Muslims, I knew Jesus was here and had a plan for them. I didn't know what the plan was for myself or FBR, I was still trying to figure that out, but I knew Jesus was in it.

The next day we boarded our flight back home. Larry and I were both pretty quiet as we left. We were trying to process everything we had seen and done. It was overwhelming. We had made a new friend, Aman, and I had promised him I would return and see him again. He had come to the airport to say goodbye to us and given us both big hugs when we left and asked us not to forget him or his Rohingya people. I told him I wouldn't.

After getting back to HQ, we briefed the staff on what we had seen in the camps. We didn't have many conclusions or ideas about what was next, and it felt like the door to working with the Rohingya was closing. We aren't a big organization, so we can't do food distributions; we'd blow through our entire budget in a few months. It's also not what we do—we don't work in refugee camps; we help people get to refugee camps, but once they're there, we usually hand them off to the bigger NGOs and the UN to take care of them. No one seemed to have any ideas about the Rohingya and how we could be involved; everyone seemed to go back to focusing on other missions in Burma.

About a week after I got back, I was still reeling with the images and stories of the Rohingya going through my head when I got a phone call from Brad. I was surprised when he asked if I could meet him for coffee, so I said sure. When I sat down, he said, "I want to get right to it. I really liked the way you worked over there, and I'd like you to come work with us." I was shocked. I hadn't expected to come to the meeting and to be offered a job. He went on, "I will organize all the visas you need so you'll be legal, I'll offer you a very competitive US salary so you don't need to worry about fundraising anymore, and then I'll give you two million dollars that you can use however you want to help the Rohingya people." I was speechless. Not only was he giving me a way to go back and help the Rohingya people and make a difference in their lives, but he was also offering to take away the headaches of visa problems and fundraising. The cowboy in me who chases adventure was already thinking how I could clear my schedule so I could be back there right away, but the better man in me said, "Can I have some time to think about it and get back to you?"

"You can have the weekend then I need an answer," Brad replied.

It was Friday afternoon, and I decided to head home instead of going back to the office. That evening I had dinner with my friends and colleagues, Adam and Aimee, and shared with them about the offer. They seemed excited for me, but unsure if I should leave FBR. I was unsure too. Was this part of God's plan for me? I knew I wanted to do something with the Rohingya, but I wasn't sure if this was it.

The next day I met with my friend Mike, who was a pastor at a local church and who had originally put me in touch with Brad. I told him about the offer I had received. Mike thought about it for a moment and then he said, "I don't think you should take it. I'm not sure why, but I think this is a diversion from what God has for you." I was shocked. If anyone was going to be pushing me to take the offer, I thought it would be Mike. He was the one who connected us, and he was also considering working with Brad. I took his advice and chewed on it.

That night we had a gathering of FBR staff, and at one point Aimee came up to me and said, "I was praying about your decision, and I think it's a diversion." I looked at her, surprised. Why had she picked that word—diversion—to use? It was the same word Mike had used. She continued and said, "I think God has a plan and you're on the track right now, and if you accept this job, it's not a bad thing, but it's a diversion and will slow you down from achieving what God wants for you." That's difficult to swallow when you have no clue what God's plan for you is.

On Monday morning I met with Jesse, our Ops Director at FBR. I shared the offer with him. He said that if I felt strongly that God was calling me there, he would release me from my obligations to FBR, and I could leave with their blessing. Then he continued and said, "You'll be in the middle of the largest humanitarian crisis on the planet right now, but, digging toilets and doing food distributions quickly loses its charm."

It wasn't long after that Brad called, asking me when I could start. I hemmed and hawed and then told him I was very grateful for his offer, but I was not going to accept it. He seemed shocked, like he wasn't used to people turning him down. "If it's about the salary, we can negotiate a higher salary for you. And the two million I mentioned—it'll actually probably be more like four million by the time it's all said and done." He was trying to sweeten the deal, and there was a part of me that wanted so desperately to accept his offer and go with it.

"I'm sorry, Brad. I really think what you guys are doing is amazing there, and it's not about the money, I just don't think this is where God is calling me right now," I replied to him.

"It's hard to argue with that," he said and quickly ended the call.

I sat in my office wondering if I had made a huge mistake. Brad had offered me a huge budget to go and help these people. He'd offered to take away my financial problems and make my life easier by issuing me work visas. I had said no. I had decided that I'd rather stay at FBR, fundraise my own meager survival budget, play the visa game, making constant border runs, all while we had no plans to be involved with the Rohingya. What was I thinking?! Part of me wanted to pick up my phone and call Brad back and tell him I had made a mistake, but then I remembered something my boss, Dave Eubank, had said to me. He described faith as a highway, and he said, "On one side of the highway is a swamp of sin and bad things; if you veer off the highway into that swamp it will definitely slow you down.

And on the other side of the highway are good Christian things that you aren't called to. If you veer off onto that side, it'll slow you down too. Then there is what God called you to, and it's green lights as far as you can see. You can go as fast as you want; how much faith do you have?" What Brad was doing with the Rohingya was good Christian stuff, but it didn't seem I was called to it. I decided I wanted to stay in my lane and be ready for those lights to turn green when I figured out what God had for me.

Chapter 5

Love

It was just after 3:00 a.m. and I was up packing my gear, headlamps flashing around our makeshift camp. Within a few minutes we would eat, pray, and step off with me leading my first real FBR jungle mission. I felt totally unprepared, inexperienced, but also excited. I had a great ethnic leader who would co-lead with me named Ko Law Law Say (KLLS). He is a highly experienced Ranger and soldier. He doesn't say much, but commands respect every time he does speak. He has fought the Burma Army with the Karen National Liberation Army (KNLA) for many years and is a highly trusted member of our headquarters team. I was thankful they gave me such an experienced ethnic counterpart to help me on my first mission.

Before the sun came up, we wanted to be staged on a mountaintop, ready to cross a Burma Army-controlled car road. It was about a two-hour hike in the dark to our staging point, then at first light, someone would check the road for landmines, disable any mines and then we would cross. We had two teams leaving on mission. My team was going to head north through 5th Brigade of Karen State, and then into Karenni State. My boss's mission was going to stay in 5th Brigade where they would investigate IDPs that had recently fled due to the Burma Army building a new car road through their area. As I sat at the staging area waiting for the green light to cross, I watched the sun start to light up the beautiful mountains and valleys that surrounded us. I looked around at our team; I had about 30 Rangers coming with me, and my boss, Dave, had about 30 going with him. The Rangers were all smoking and joking; we had mules carrying loads of medicine and clothing for our village programs, and of course we had the FBR monkey bouncing around terrorizing people.

Once we got the green light, silence fell over the group, and everything happened rapidly. We hiked quietly and quickly for another 45 minutes until we reached the car road. We set up a security perimeter facing each direction down the road and then, single-file, made our way across the road, down the steep slope on the other side, and kept moving through a dried-up stream bed. We wanted to move quickly away from the car road; at any moment, a Burma Army patrol or resupply could come along the road, which would lead to them shooting at us.

I hurried through the jungle, trying to keep up with KLLS. The only thing he said during the whole walk was, "One time I was walking here"—he pointed into the jungle—"and came right in the middle of a Burma Army patrol that had stopped to take a nap. They woke up and started chasing me and shooting at me." Then he kept walking in silence. I didn't know what to make of that, but it was a sobering comment that reminded me we were in a war zone.

We were to cross the car road and keep walking for about an hour until we came to a predesignated fork in the trail, where my team would head right and Dave Eubank's team would head left. We reached the split; I was already sweating. It wasn't even 8:00 a.m. yet, and we had already walked for nearly four hours. We did a head count of both teams to make sure everyone was there and said goodbye to the other team, and then Dave gave a little speech and told my team, "Be a hero. Your country needs heroes. Be a hero." I remember thinking about that a lot. Unfortunately, it's a message that seems countercultural in the West. I remember when I lived in the UK and the government had a campaign called "Don't Be a Hero." On the London Underground and plastered all around London were signs that encouraged people not to be a hero. If something bad was happening, they didn't want people to get caught up in the middle of it; they wanted people to run away and get help and let someone else deal with it. What a sad campaign and message it is to our culture. We've gotten to where we're discouraging people from helping others in trouble or being a hero. And I believe Dave was right; the people here, and the people in the West, need a hero.

I definitely didn't feel like a hero. I was unprepared, inexperienced, out of shape, and still afraid of almost everything. What kind of hero is that? Until this point in working with FBR, I had done some smaller missions, and had worked quite a bit with the Rohingya, but this was going to be my first real, long jungle mission. We were going to walk a long way and spend a lot of time in the jungle, and be gone for at least a month. I had two other foreigners with me from our HQ team, both good guys, but both looking to me to lead the mission and lead them. I hoped I was up to the task.

Dave finished his speech, and the teams started walking in their respective directions. Dave and I waited until all our team was accounted for, heading the right direction down the right trail, and then he looked at me and said, "Brother, I trust you with my life. Have a good mission." Then he slipped into the jungle and disappeared.

I walked quickly to catch up with my team down the trail. We had a long day ahead, and I didn't want them slowed down by me. As I walked in silence, I thought about what Dave had said: "I trust you with my life." Who says that? It seemed like such a strange thing to say in my safe, Western-thinking brain. People don't meet up at a Starbucks for coffee and leave the other person by saying, "I trust you with my life." We don't live in an environment where we need to trust other people with our lives. And slowly we forget who we'd be willing to fight for, or die for. My boss spoke such encouragement to me with those simple words. He trusts me. Wow. He trusts my judgment and decision-making so much that he'd walk around a war zone with me. It's a pretty amazing thing to be entrusted with another person's life—and not out of obligation, but out of true brotherhood and sacrifice.

I had served in the military and spent most of my adult life up to this point working on sports teams. The feeling of brotherhood and sacrifice for others is more common in those places than in everyday work life in North America, but not to the level where people talk about trusting someone else with their life. Thinking through the who or what we're willing to die for helps us to figure out what's important in our life. Dave said he trusted me with his life, and suddenly I had a new sense of confidence and purpose on this mission. It's amazing what a little bit of encouragement can do.

I listened to a sermon once about encouragement and was convicted that I am not a very good encourager. The thing I found interesting about the word encouragement was that to encourage literally means that we "enter courage" into someone else. It's amazing that we can go into someone else's spirit and heart and take out fear, and doubt, and shame, and replace it with courage. I think in North America, and in the Western church, we have a severe courage drought right now. Maybe it could change if we would encourage one another instead of judging each other.

I walked all day thinking about what it means to be a hero and to trust someone else with your life. We walked for about twelve hours that day, and when we finally collapsed into a village for the night, I was exhausted. I had blisters on my feet; I was totally dehydrated, but my heart was full. I was excited to be on mission. Over the coming weeks, we'd walk a hundred miles through the jungle and put on several village programs, we'd steal some uranium from a mine, and we'd have a lot of laughs. I was learning and growing each day I spent in the jungle, and I felt like I was exactly where God wanted me to be.

As the mission drew to an end, we were going to part ways with most of our Rangers. They didn't need to return to the training camp, so our team numbers dropped down to just a few of us. On our final night together, we gathered everyone to give some speeches and say our goodbyes. I went first and gave a rousing speech telling them I was proud of them and loved them and trusted them with my life. I said, "If you guys ever need anything, please contact me at HQ. If you want to come back as Advanced Rangers next year, please contact me; I can help you. If your family needs help, I will try to help. If you want to become an FBR instructor, I'd like to help you. I am here for you." It was a very nice-sounding speech that received some head nods from the group.

When I finished, it was KLLS's turn to say something. He stood in front of the group and paused for a long minute and looked each of them in the eye and then he said to them softly, "If I have said or done something on this mission that has hurt or offended you I want to know and I'd like to ask your forgiveness." I was instantly humbled. KLLS led the mission with quiet thunder. He was serious and took his job and duty seriously. He kept the mission and team together and dealt with people fairly. I had so much fear, admiration, and respect for him as a leader, and here he stood in front of the team asking them for forgiveness.

I thought through what I had said, and I quickly realized how self-serving it was. My speech may have seemed like a gracious speech about helping them, but it was all about me and building me up. *I* can help you; *I* can help your family. If you need something, *I* will be the one to provide it. I am amazing. I felt so embarrassed. My nice speech was purely selfish, the false self wanting to be in control by having the team contact me if they need something. I wanted the nice feeling of being useful and needed and helpful. It wasn't about them at all, it was all about me—I was trying to make myself out to be a hero rather than quietly being one. Selfish. KLLS looked each man in the eye and from his heart asked them for forgiveness if he had wronged them. It wasn't a stunt or ploy; he genuinely wanted people to come forward publicly or privately and tell him how he had hurt them or offended them so he could ask for forgiveness. That was truly about them.

Lately, God has been showing me how selfish I am, and when my motives are driven from selfishness. It's kind of sickening how often I do something that, on the surface, might seem nice or caring, but is selfish. Sometimes my desire to help someone else isn't at all driven by a motive of loving them and caring for them but rather from wanting to seem like I am nice or can be the one who helps them.

I want God to create in me a truly selfless heart, and I believe it comes from taking the lowest seat at the table. One of my favorite authors and mentors is a guy named Morgan Snyder, who challenges men in their thirties to spend the decade of their thirties "taking the lowest seat at the table until God makes it impossible not to." For me, I've never been one to take the lowest seat. I've jumped to positions of leadership as quickly as I can because then I don't need to prove myself at the lower levels. Often I don't need to face my fears when I can jump over the hard stuff and become a leader. It's easier to stand at the top of the mountain and tell someone to rappel down instead of face your fear of heights and do it with them. My insecurities and shame fueled my desire to be in leadership. I didn't believe I had what it took in life or manhood, so I would pretend I knew what I was doing by jumping into leadership. Taking the lowest seat at the table is a daily challenge for me to serve others from a pure heart. The false self wants the seat of honor, but has a hard time functioning in the lowest seat.

I started this by doing the dishes at our office, but even there I realized that my motives were totally wrong. I thought to myself, I hope someone sees the Chief of Staff washing the dishes; that will motivate others to do their own dishes. I hoped people would think I was a humble servant, and hoped someone would walk in while I was washing the dishes. But this is a sick way to serve. I asked God to take my selfishness from me. I want to wash all the dishes and not have anyone know or see it. I want to serve, not because in my heart I think

I should or it's the right thing, but because it's my natural instinct. I want serving to be a reflex of my heart.

My job as the leader of a team on a mission, or at the HQ office, is to serve them. I try to ask myself, "How can I serve the staff today?" and it slowly changes the posture of my heart. When I enter a meeting or a room, instead of fighting for the seat of honor or importance that I am so used to doing, I try to ask myself what I can do to serve and how I can take the lowest seat in this situation. It's a humbling and difficult exercise that I fail at daily, but recognizing my selfishness is at least half the battle.

The next morning we gave last hugs to each other before we parted ways with our team. My backpack was full of uranium, and my heart was full of hope and love. Beh Reh, my Burmese little brother, waited until the very end to come over and give me a big hug and say goodbye. He hugged me and held on for a while. We had had an incredible past few months together, and little did I know it was just getting started. I told him I would try to come up and see him in his refugee camp as soon as I could. He smiled at me and nodded his head even though I knew he couldn't speak any English. He squeezed me tight again and then ran off to meet up with the rest of his team and head for home. It had been over four months since they had left home or seen their families, and they were all itching to get home. I was too.

Our walking pace back to camp was fast. We had a hundred miles and some monster mountains to cross before we would make it back to the car road we had crossed a month earlier. Our team of thirty had now dwindled down to only ten, and we could cover a lot of ground. We laughed a lot as we walked, and the battle rhythm of our team was now well entrenched; we all knew our place and role. Within a few days we were back at the edge of the Burma Army-controlled car road. We found out that there were some new landmines planted by the Burma Army right around where we needed to cross. A random guy walking through the jungle had told us about them. We asked him if he knew where they were and if he could disable them. He said he could do it, and we eventually agreed we'd pay him the equivalent of $50 to disable three landmines.

The man stashed his bag in the jungle, took his pants off so he was in his shorts and t-shirt, then he sat down and prepared some food. I was eager to get home and was getting antsy to get a move on. We all sat around waiting while he ate his meal and then sat on a stump and smoked a cigar. My frustration gave way to laughter as I thought of the absurdity of the situation. I was paying the guy less than a day's wage for most people in North America to potentially go blow himself up disabling landmines. If the guy wants a meal and a smoke before doing that, I think he's entitled to it.

He eventually disappeared down the trail, and about an hour later he came back to report that it was all clear and we could proceed. We linked up with another group and then, like before, quietly and quickly snuck across the Burma Army-controlled road. By supper time, we had hiked the final few hours back to where we had started the mission a month earlier. Trucks were waiting to take us the last stretch of the way back to camp. I was thankful for the ride and looking forward to being back at our training camp and to having a few rest days before we crossed out of Burma.

Resting at camp was beautiful. We had no responsibilities other than to rest and relax and wait for our exfil. We had some minor projects we could help with, but it was nice to lie in a hammock and reflect on the mission. In the evenings we would all gather for dinner and late into the night we would laugh as we recounted or reenacted stories from the past month, helping us all process all we had seen and done, drawing us closer to each other. Two of the HQ staff, Barry and Eli were at camp and provided us with meals unlike anything we'd eaten over the past month on mission.

The big talk around camp at the time was about a young patient at the Jungle School of Medicine. A mother had walked in a week earlier with her two daughters. The eldest was there to help, and the younger, only six years old, was having heart problems. Our team of medics were trying to figure out what was wrong with her heart and were in the process of deciding if she should be sent out to a hospital in Thailand to get better treatment. The team had the little girl on oxygen and were monitoring her closely. If she didn't improve overnight, they were going to decide the next morning to send her out or not. That night, the little girl's heart failed, and she died in her sleep.

I woke up to the news early the next morning. A heavy weight settled over the camp. The medics were taking it hard, and I wasn't sure what to do. I felt sad. We were supposed to cross out later that afternoon, and it was sad to leave this situation. I didn't know my place, and I didn't know what I should do, if anything. All morning I felt restless and paced around trying to think if there was some Bible verse or prayer that I could share with the mother to help her feel better. Or maybe to help me feel better. Nothing came to mind. I again felt out of place and inadequate.

I was pacing around wondering what I should do or say when one of my friends and lead medics walked past my house. I called down to him. "Hey Silverhorn, are you going to the clinic to see the mother?" He replied he was. "Are you going to pray with her or something?" I asked. He paused for a moment and thought about my question, then he said slowly and thoughtfully, "No... I'm just going to sit with her." I realized that was the right answer. We don't need to have all the right words or the perfect scripture verse; we just need to show up.

I walked down to the clinic with Silverhorn, and I sat on the floor near the mother. The little girl's body was still lying on a bamboo mat, and her older sister was combing her hair. The mother was busying herself and fiddling with things so she wouldn't break down sobbing. Her six-year-old daughter's body lay there; I couldn't even begin to imagine what she was feeling. I didn't speak her language, and I didn't know what to say even if I did, so I just sat there. For over an hour I sat there, every so often when we'd make eye contact I'd give her a sympathetic smile, but otherwise I stayed with her. I felt a bit like an idiot sitting there, but I felt like it was my place. I tried to avoid looking at the corpse, but when I did, and allowed the image to linger in my mind, a wave of nausea washed over me.

Eventually, they wrapped the little girl's body in the bamboo mat she was lying on and tied it with strips of bamboo. They tied her body to a long bamboo pole, and we carried her body across the river into the jungle. We found a small spot among the trees and dug a hole. We lowered her body in, said a prayer, and then buried her. We cut a cross out of bamboo and hammered it into the ground, and then it was all over. We walked soberly back to camp.

Later that day we packed all our stuff and started the walk out of camp back towards home. The mother and her eldest daughter walked with us. I walked right behind them, and I couldn't help but think that they were forgetting something. They had come into camp, three of them, and now left, only two. My heart was broken for this mother, and I still couldn't imagine how she must be feeling. We walked for an hour until we could arrange a motorcycle to drive the mother and daughter back to their village. They got on the back of the bike, and before they drove off, the mother reached out to me and grabbed my hand. I was surprised and looked up at her. She had big tear-filled eyes, and then she said, "Thank you, teacher." She held my hand and looked deep into my eyes for a minute, then slowly let go and told the driver of the motorcycle he could go.

I hadn't said or done anything for this woman other than sit there like a bump on a log. But at the moment that she held my hand and looked into my eyes, she told me it had meant something to her. I had wanted to say or do something that would help her, but I had nothing; there were no words that could help in that moment. But I had realized that if I wanted to show her I loved her, then I needed to show up. Love shows up. It doesn't need fancy words, speeches, Bible verses, gifts, or prayers. It needs to show up.

I realized that I sometimes feel like I don't know what to say or do when one of my friends is struggling, so I tend to hide or not involve myself instead of showing up. I also realized that when I want to show my friends that I love them, I don't need to bring or do anything other than show up. Being present in their lives, showing up when it's hard, or even when it's not—that's what love does. That's what Jesus did. The Bible says that Jesus was Immanuel, God with us. The Bible also says that God is love. When Jesus invaded our story and walked on the earth, love literally showed up.

My heart was full from the mission I had finished, and heavy with sadness for this woman who had lost her child. Sometimes loving people means you're willing to walk a long way and help bury their dead. The next day I was home; it felt surreal and strange to be back in a modern city. I missed my friends from the mission and quickly worked to make plans to visit them in their refugee camp. I knew I wasn't legally allowed to enter their camp, and I wasn't sure of the logistics around getting into and out of their camp, but at FBR we believe that love has no borders, and even though refugee camps and countries do, we want to serve in love.

Because love shows up.

Chapter 6

Trust

It had been nearly a month since I had come back from my first trip to Bangladesh. I immersed myself in work, but I never forgot the things I saw on that first trip. The stories and images played over and over in my mind, but I couldn't figure out what we should do there. I had resigned myself to the fact that if God didn't want me to work with the Rohingya, then I wouldn't, and whatever he had for me would be enough. It was right around that time that Hosie came back from another mission and asked me about my trip into the camps.

Hosie has been an FBR volunteer longer than anyone else. She has been working with Dave and FBR for over a decade and is a wealth of knowledge and experience. Hosie has more experience in war zones and on front lines than most soldiers in the army—and yet she is one of the most humble people I know. Hosie was interested in the Rohingya situation and wanted to hear about my experience over there and read our interview notes. After talking with her for a few days, she said something that surprised me. "I think we should go back over there." I asked her why and what we'd do and she said, "I'm not sure, but maybe we can conduct some more interviews and report on the situation a bit more and see if we can figure out a plan to work with the Rohingya." She didn't have to convince me much more than that. We got our permissions, and a few days later I was back on a plane to Dhaka.

I contacted Aman and told him I would be returning, and he was thrilled. On our last trip, Brad had told us which hotel to stay at and arranged all our drivers and translators, but now we were on our own. Aman told me not to worry and that he would set it up. We landed at the airport in Cox's Bazar and made our way out to find a tuktuk to bring us to our hotel. The driver, clearly inexperienced with foreigners, asked where we wanted to go, and I told him the name of our hotel and asked him how much. I knew that last time we came we had paid 400 taka to get to the hotel, and I didn't want to get ripped off. He didn't answer my question about how much but asked me how much I wanted to pay. "400," I said quickly and firmly. Without missing a beat, like he was a bartering expert, he shot back, "No! 200!" and I quickly said, "OK!" and climbed into the back of his tuktuk. It wasn't until we got halfway to our hotel that I could see him slowly understanding that he had just reverse-bargained me. We got out at the hotel, and I gave him 300 taka for his troubles.

A year earlier, Hosie had attended a conference in Thailand with a presenter named Razia, who had done research on the oppression of the Rohingya, and who was Rohingya herself. Hosie had taken her business card at the end of the presentation and somehow kept it. On the off chance that Razia might meet up with us, Hosie sent her an email. She wrote back quickly and said that she was in fact in Cox's Bazar and was helping the UN as a translator and that we could meet her. We were excited to be making some of our own contacts. We hired a van and driver through another contact I had made on the first trip, and made a plan for him to take us down to the camps and arrange some interviews for us. But first we were going to walk down to Razia's hotel and meet her.

The restaurant was empty when we arrived for our mid-morning meeting, and after a few minutes of waiting, Razia came in and met us. She was hesitant at first, unsure of who we were and what we were all about. Hosie did most of the talking, sharing what the Free Burma Rangers does and what we stand for. She quoted our FBR motto to Razia: "Love each other, unite and work for freedom, justice and peace, forgive and don't hate each other, pray with faith, act with courage, never surrender." Slowly we saw a spark form in Razia that eventually fanned into a flame. By the end of our meeting she was ranting and raving about the UN, she was so passionate about the work we were trying to do, and loved our idea that maybe we could train a team of Rohingya men to go back to Arakan State and help others still stuck there. We mentioned we were heading down into the camps to conduct interviews after we were done meeting with her and asked if she wanted to tag along. She immediately said "yes!" We loved our new friend and were thrilled she wanted to join us.

A few hours later we pulled up in our van in front of her hotel, and she came out dressed beautifully, her outfit complete with high-heeled shoes. Razia is a fireball and a princess, very strong-willed but very beautiful and well taken care of. We piled into the van and headed for the camps. Along the way it began to rain, and I knew from my last trip to the camps that it would make things muddy and slippery. I was right, and once we arrived at the camp to meet our translator, there was a small muddy lake forming. Razia didn't even hesitate; she hiked up her skirt and marched right through. We laughed and were all impressed with the gumption of our new friend.

We met our translator, and he told us that he had arranged a house for us to conduct some interviews in. We walked for about twenty minutes through the camp and eventually came to a small hut. It was newly built, a tarp and some bamboo with a dirt floor. Because we had Razia with us, Hosie asked if she and Razia could interview some women, while I interviewed the men. Everyone agreed and thought it was a great idea. Hosie went to one half of the hut with Razia, and they hung some blankets up to add some privacy. I sat on the floor with a few men on the other side. I wasn't sure what

I should do or say, so I started by sharing our FBR motto with the men in the room.

It was stifling hot in the tent as I conducted the interviews. The sun was blazing, and the tarp seemed to trap the heat. I was dripping sweat down onto my notebook as I scribbled notes, listening to the man tell me his story. Slowly the room filled up as passersby would poke their heads in and curiously come in and listen. All the bodies crammed into the little tent only raised the temperature. At one point, one of the older men gestured to a teenager and said something I didn't understand. The teenager got up and came and sat near me and fanned me with a makeshift fan. I smiled politely and told him he didn't need to do that; I wasn't anyone special that someone should sit and fan me. The boy stopped momentarily, and immediately the sweat dripped down onto my notebook again. The boy looked at me, looked at the sweat, then looked at the old man, who again nodded his head, and the boy continued fanning me again. I let it go and was thankful for the little moving air in the room.

My discomfort from the heat was only surpassed by the gravity of the stories the men shared with me. The first man wept as he told me about his farm and his lost lands, how he had no freedom and when the army came and burned his home and killed his family, he had to run away. Another man shared with me how he had been running from the Burma Army and saw them line up all the imams and execute them. He kept running until he reached Bangladesh. Slowly all the men in the room chimed in with their own stories and things that had happened to them.

One man told me some of his family had died, and when I asked how they died, the translator said, "Elephant." I was confused and thought the translator must be getting the word wrong, so I asked him to clarify. "You know, big, gray, animal, very big, elephant? You know elephant?" He asked me as if I were crazy for not knowing what an elephant was.

"Yes, I know what an elephant is, but an elephant killed his family member?" I asked back, still unclear we were both talking about the same thing.

"Yes, when he arrived at the refugee camp and built his shelter, there was a wild elephant that came through and trampled down his shelter and smashed his family member who was inside. You know, wild elephants are everywhere around the camps." I was shocked. It wasn't just the Burma Army killing people; now elephants were killing people. These poor people couldn't seem to catch a break. How could things get any worse, I wondered?

The next man who took the attention of the room was soft-spoken and told me he was a former Muslim school teacher. He told me that in the middle of the night, in the refugee camp, "bad men" came and reached under the tarp wall of the shelter, grabbed his sleeping child and took him away. He described how he had searched everywhere for his child and eventually they found him almost a week later. He had been dumped into a ditch, all his usable internal organs had been harvested out of him, and he was left to die. He cried slow and steady tears and then he looked at me and said, "You come here and ask us to forgive and not hate each other like your motto says, but how should I forgive the one who did that to my son?" I was fighting back tears and had absolutely nothing to say to him. Hatred seemed like the only reasonable response to that kind of inhumane evil. How could I ask this man to forgive and not hate?

I stopped taking notes and closed my notebook. I couldn't handle any more of their stories. I wiped a tear from my eye, and I reached out and squeezed his hand. I told him I didn't know the answer to his question. Then I looked at all of them and thanked them for sharing their stories with me. I told them that the Free Burma Rangers wasn't a big organization, but we believed in a big God, and they should call out to God. I told them that Canada, America, FBR, and God hadn't forgotten about them. I told them I would take their stories and turn them into a report and tell the world what was happening. They all listened intently and seemed appreciative of the words, but I felt like that's all they were—words. And I wasn't even sure if I was saying them to make these people feel better or to make myself feel better. I had nothing to give them, no way to help them, and it made me feel slightly better to leave them with a hopeful message—but it all seemed shallow.

I walked out of the tent into the fresh air and stood shaking their hands. The teacher came over to me and asked if I wanted to see where they were building a new mosque and school. I agreed, and he proudly took me around the corner and showed me the makeshift mosque. I told him I was thankful he was still teaching. He took my hand and through the translator he said, "Brother, thank you for coming to listen to our stories. No one has asked to hear our stories, and we have been sitting here rotting. We have these emotions inside of us, and to have someone ask us questions and care about our stories helps us. So thank you for coming."

I was again fighting back tears. I was not trained as a counselor, especially a counselor for this kind of trauma or grief. I didn't know what I was doing or how to conduct a good interview, but I remembered something that Dan Allender once said, "When you enter someone else's story, take off your shoes; it's holy ground." I wanted to respect their stories, and listening and caring was all I could offer. It moved me, what this man had said, and I couldn't help but think about the other 800,000 refugees sitting in their huts, each with their own story that needed listening to and a loving hand to hold. Sitting in the dirt with someone, holding their hand while they cry, crying with them, and telling them you're with them, you will not leave them, even if you die because of it, changes someone's life—and it's what I love about FBR.

Hosie and Razia came out of the other side of the tent, and Hosie looked as emotionally floored as I was. Their interviews with the women had proved as difficult to listen to as mine had. Hosie had held a three-day-old baby from one woman who had fled and then gone into labor almost immediately after arriving in the camps. This young infant was born in the middle of mass chaos, death, and a massive refugee crisis. I wondered what life would be like for that little guy. We walked back to our van in stunned silence, similar to the silence I had experienced on my first trip. The mind and heart need time to process things like this, and we all seemed to get lost in our thoughts and emotions.

As we drove back towards Cox's Bazar, we brought up the idea of doing a food distribution. We were not a legal organization in Bangladesh, and the government was already cracking down on illegal food distributions. There were stories of the police coming in in the middle of the distribution and arresting everyone involved. But we wanted to do something. Razia wasn't sure of the best way to do it and feared we would end up in jail if we were caught doing an illegal food distribution. We asked Akram, our driver, if he knew anyone who could help us with a food distribution. He understood the word distribution, but his English was not good enough to offer any help. But then he called someone on his phone and handed the phone to me. I talked for a minute to his friend, who introduced himself as Najim. His English was very good, and he said he could help us with a distribution if we wanted. I said sure and invited him over to our hotel later that evening to discuss his ideas.

When we got back to our hotel, we made a list of things we'd like to have in our food bags: rice, potatoes, oil, salt, garlic, and onions. We counted our money and had around $3,000 we could use for the distribution. A while later, Akram arrived and introduced us to his friend Najim. I could tell right away that Najim was a great guy and a wheeler-dealer. He reminded me of the typical Indian seller who wanted to drive a hard bargain and be your best friend in the process. We explained to Najim what we wanted to do and told him how much money we had. He did some calculations and then said that if we include transportation to the camp, then we could get around 200 bags of food, and it would feed a family for about two weeks. We thought that sounded good and handed the money over to him. He asked us what logos we wanted printed on the bags for the food, and we told him we didn't care about logos; we wanted to get as much food to the people as we could. He said he would go to the market the next morning, order all the food and have it delivered to his friend's apartment. I asked if I should go with him, partly because I did not know who this young guy was and if I could trust him, but he told me that if I went with him, the prices would nearly triple because I was a white guy. In the end, we told him we'd like to meet him in the afternoon the next day and we'd pack all the food together.

Hosie and I went back up to our hotel rooms and looked at each other and said, "I hope this guy is trustworthy. I hope he doesn't just disappear with all our money." I love trusting people like that. Believing in the good in people. We had only known Najim for about five minutes, and we gave him more money than he earns in a year working at a mobile phone shop. We put our faith in the fact that people are good and can be trusted until they give us a reason not to. Life seems to be better and more fun that way.

The next morning, Najim called me, saying he had purchased everything and we could meet him at the apartment around 2:00 in the afternoon. We called up Razia and asked her if she wanted to join us in packing the food. She quickly said, "I'd love to! The UN usually finishes its workday around 2:00 anyway!" We laughed at her continuous jabs about working for the UN. We found the only coffee shop in Cox's Bazar, ordered our first good coffee, connected to Wi-Fi and spent a few hours getting HQ work done while we waited for our packing party.

Around 2:00 p.m., Najim came over to the hotel to pick us up and bring us to the apartment. I was shocked when we pulled into the parking garage and he pointed to the mountains of bags and boxes sitting in one of the parking spots. "That's all your food," he said proudly. It was a lot! We got busy packing. Weighing out the rice, and potatoes, and lentils. We recruited a bunch of Najim's friends and family members, and Ivo, one of our HQ team members, ran out and got everyone snacks and cold drinks. We all laughed and joked and got to know each other as we spent the next few hours packing food bags. Razia eventually showed up, dressed as beautifully as ever, but jumped right in, getting her hands dirty with packing. I was eventually told that I wasn't allowed to pack the rice anymore because I was sweating too much and sweating into the rice. We definitely aren't perfect at FBR. We make a lot of mistakes and don't do things the right way a lot of times, but we pray and try our best. My boss once joked, "It's not easy, you know, to be as screwed up as we are and still function."

Once we had all the bags packed, and had taken some group pictures with all our new friends, we discussed the next hurdle, which was how we would actually distribute these food bags. Other organizations were setting up food distributions deep in the jungle, but these risked getting shut down and everyone getting arrested. While we aren't averse to those kinds of risks, we had a better idea. We decided we would load all our food into the back of a big truck and drive it straight into the middle of a military compound at one of the refugee camps. This was a bit of a risk. We were unregistered, illegally operating in the country, and we were going to drive right into the middle of the people whose job it was to stop illegal distributions from happening. That night I went to bed excited about our new friends we were making there, and about our distribution we were going to do the next day.

We woke up early and met Akram and Najim. They seemed equally excited about the distribution as we were, although a bit more nervous about our plan to drive directly into the middle of the army compound. Regardless, we got in the van and started driving down to the camps. We met up with our big truck; the back was loaded with all 200 of our food bags. It was slowly chugging along the highway towards the camps. We passed through two checkpoints and then entered the camp we wanted to do the distribution in. We drove straight up to the army compound that was at the center of the camp and pulled up to the barricade with our big truck full of food.

The guard looked confused and came over and asked what we were doing. We had given everyone Free Burma Rangers T-shirts so that we all felt like we were part of the team, and there was no denying that we were an organization. I shouted out of the window,

"We're the Free Burma Rangers and we're here to do a food distribution." The soldier seemed totally confused, looking at his clipboard, but opened the barricade for us and we drove right in.

Before we even shut off our engines, a soldier came over. I recognized his rank as lieutenant. The Bangladesh Army uses the same rank structure as the Brits, and so did Canada, and because of my years in the Canadian Army I could quickly identify all of his insignia. He came over and demanded to know who we were and what we were doing there. "We're the Free Burma Rangers and we're here to do a food distribution," I repeated. "Can I talk to your commanding officer?" The lieutenant seemed slightly confused and taken aback by the truck full of foreigners and Bengalis and the big load of food. He pointed to the command tent and said, "Come with me."

A few minutes later we were sitting in front of the colonel who was in charge of the camp. In his command tent were many whiteboards with a breakdown of all the people in the camp, the sectors, its leaders, and then on another big whiteboard was a list of NGOs, ones I assumed were approved. Our names were not on the list. Again I was asked, "Who are you guys and what are you doing here?" and again I told him, "We're the Free Burma Rangers and we've got 200 bags of food that we want to distribute to new arrivals." I could see the colonel reading the logo of my shirt, and then scanning the whiteboard with NGO names on it, trying to see if we were somewhere on the list. Hosie pulled out some literature about FBR and an FBR T-shirt and explained about the twenty years we've been working in Burma and trying to help the people in Burma.

When we were done with our speech the colonel looked up and said, "You want to help us?" and we all nodded eagerly, then he continued in an exasperated tone, "Then go back to Burma and tell them to stop killing each other!" We nodded in agreement and told him we'd been trying that for a while now, and we'll keep trying it, but in the meantime would he like an FBR T-shirt? He politely declined the T-shirt, but gave us his blessing to continue with our food distribution. He handed us back over to his lieutenant to handle all the details and thanked us for wanting to help.

We walked back out of the command tent, and the lieutenant came back over to us. "We have a slight problem," he said. "You said you have 200 bags of food, but we've already admitted 300 people to receive food today. Is it okay if we take your bags of food to our holding compound and you distribute the 300 bags of food from another NGO?" I looked at Hosie and then we both smiled and said, "Sure, no problem." The lieutenant continued, "The problem is the food bags have another NGO's logo on them, not your logo, so your photoshoot won't be very good."

I replied to him quickly, "We don't care about the photoshoot; we want to spend time with the people and want to make sure they're fed and loved."

"You don't care about the photos?" He asked back, confused.

"Not really," Hosie affirmed. The lieutenant smiled as he processed that. He led us over to where they did distributions and showed us the bags of food we'd be distributing. We went to work unloading our bags of food in their warehouse and then mingled with the people who were in line for food. They had them all set up in a queue that funneled them into the receiving area, and then out again, so no mobs of people could form. We immediately went to work handing out bags of food, talking to people, and making friends— that's one thing FBR does best. We can't always afford translators and fixers and drivers like other big NGOs, instead we want to make friends with everyone, and welcome everyone to be part of our team, and once they catch the vision of love we try to share, they're happy to help us for free. Najim and Akram were right in there with us, mingling with the soldiers, and handing out bags of food.

As we finished the distribution, Ivo shared the gospel story with some soldiers through our bead bracelets that we give out. The bracelet has five different colors, and as Ivo explained what each color stood for, the soldiers seemed to like the story. Then Ivo gave the bracelet to the lieutenant and told him, "Did you know David is a captain in the Canadian Army?" Suddenly the lieutenant snapped to attention and his demeanor changed. He had new respect and trust for me. He came to me and said, "You guys aren't like any NGO I've ever seen. Most of the NGOs that come in here are worried about photos, and you guys came in here worried about the people. Please take my phone number. Anytime you want to do a distribution in any of the camps, or anytime you want to work in any of the camps, please call me and I will arrange it all for you." I was floored. Suddenly we had full permission and a contact within the army to go anywhere we wanted in the camps. I couldn't believe how God was opening the doors for us—even though we were unregistered and totally illegal. We were trying to pray, follow God, and love people as best we could.

We were thrilled with how our distribution went and jubilantly drove back to Cox's Bazar. We called Razia once we got back to the hotel and told her all about it. She was so excited and then praised the Bangladesh Army for the fair and good job they've been doing to help the Rohingya people. She was shocked when we told her that we had been given permission to go anywhere in the camps, even though we were unregistered. She then went on to tell us that she had heard about a wing of the Cox's Bazar hospital that had been cordoned off specifically for Rohingya, and she asked if we wanted to go and try to sneak into that wing and meet some people. We said yes right away.

After dinner we went to the hospital, and Razia went to work befriending security guards and janitors to find a way we could sneak into that wing. It was past visiting hours, and they didn't allow visitors to the Rohingya wing anyway, but eventually we snuck our way onto the wing of the hospital. It was one big room packed with beds and people. There were people sleeping on the floor, under beds, and on beds. There was one nurse who seemed exhausted, and although she looked up when we walked in, she seemed too busy and tired to care that we were there. We wandered around a bit, smiling at people and shaking their hands. We sat on a bed beside an old man, and

Razia asked him what had happened; he told her that the Burma Army had come into his village shooting. "They killed my wife right in front of me and then told me to run," he said. "We had been married for over twenty years. And I ran, and then they shot at me as I ran, and they hit me twice in the back." He tried to point to the wounds on his back that he was getting treatment for. Then he broke down and wept. Razia wept with him and held his hand.

We found a small room in the back of the wing that contained two young boys. Both were around the same age, maybe twelve years old, and both boys had full-sized casts on their legs. We came in and did what we do best—goofed around with the kids, making them howl with laughter, and let them play with our cameras and phones. Ivo interviewed one boy, and while we played with him, we listened to their stories.

One boy had been out playing when the Burma Army came shooting into their village. He ran home as quickly as he could, and when he ran into his house, he ran right into a Burma Army soldier. The soldier turned around, pushed him to the ground and shot him. The bullet went into his leg, and the boy passed out. His mother carried him for days through the jungle until they got to Bangladesh and eventually were transported to the hospital. The other boy shared his story as well, from a separate village, but a similar account. The Burma Army came into his village at night. They came to his house, locked the door, and then lit the house on fire. The burning roof of the thatched house collapsed on the boy before he could crawl out through one of the bamboo walls. The burning wall burned all the skin off his leg that was pinned under the weight of the roof. He crawled out and was carried to Bangladesh.

We spent almost an hour playing with the kids and making them laugh. We gave them all Good Life Club bracelets and told them what all the colors of the beads mean. Then we prayed with them. Eventually, the nurse came in to give them their medicine and gave us a look like maybe it was time to go. We silently agreed and made our way out of the hospital. I finally had a feeling like we were doing something helpful there. Instead of listening to horror stories, we were doing something different from most NGOs; we were giving out love. We had little money; we couldn't do many food distributions, but we could give love to everyone we met, from a Bangladeshi soldier, to kids in the hospital, to Najim, Akram and Razia, our new friends.

Throughout our time on that trip, Hosie kept asking people about the idea of training a Rohingya team and sending them back to Burma. Most of the people we talked to, from UN workers to Rohingya activists to Bangladeshi soldiers, thought it was a nice idea, but totally impossible. Most people thought we should forget the idea. At one point, Hosie was showing a video of what our FBR training is like to a young Rohingya teacher as we drove back from the camps. Halfway through the video, he needed to stop so he could throw up. I don't think it was from the idea of Ranger training, but his sentiments weren't much less enthusiastic.

As we boarded the plane to head back to Chiang Mai, we felt like we had had a successful mission there, but it seemed like training a relief team was impossible. If we couldn't train a relief team, I wasn't sure if there would be a sustainable way for us to stay involved with the Rohingya. I chewed on this puzzle as we flew back towards our HQ. I felt like God had something for us, for me, with the Rohingya, but I still couldn't figure out what it was.

I had to trust.

Chapter 7

Training

Over the next three months, I would make two more trips back to Bangladesh to meet with Aman and our new Rohingya friends. Hosie accompanied me on all the trips, and together we kept making new friends and asking people about conducting a Ranger training, but everyone we talked to thought it was impossible. We did a few more small distributions—blankets and jackets as the Rohingya entered cold season in the camps, GLC school packs at a small orphanage where Aman lived and worked— and kept trying to make friends with the Bangladesh Army.

One soldier put it this way: "Have you ever had your friend come to visit unexpectedly? Of course you welcome him in and give him a meal and a place to stay. But what if that friend stays for a month or three months? Now there needs to be a new conversation." The patience of the Bangladesh Army was being strained, and five months into the crisis, people were still arriving almost daily.

The landscape had been totally decimated. Rice crops were destroyed and overrun, eventually turned into more space for shelters. Everyone was cooking over open fires, harvesting firewood. With over 800,000 people in the camps, it didn't take long for the forests and trees to totally disappear. Wells dug in September were already running dry, and toilets were already full and needing to be moved. Several medical centers had opened, but provided only basic painkillers and immediate first aid. The World Food Program, a branch of the UN, was there and slowly feeding people, but they estimated it would cost around $900 million per year to feed all these people. The refugee camps eventually swelled until they swallowed up Bengali houses and farms that were in the way, adding nearly 50,000 displaced Bengalis to the list of people needing food and support. The situation was dire.

We were having a difficult time getting some of our other ethnic partners on board with supporting our work with the Rohingya. The Burmese government is excellent at spreading propaganda and fake news. In Burma, Facebook was offered for free; all you need is a SIM card and phone, and you're able to access Facebook. You don't need a data plan or credit on your phone. For many in Burma, the word Facebook is synonymous with the Internet. The Burmese government quickly took advantage of this and spread many fake news stories about the Rohingya. At the time of the Rohingya exile, Facebook had two Burmese-speaking employees who could monitor the site for hate speech and invocations of violence. If someone flagged a message as abusive or hateful, it could take Facebook's two employees up to six months to review the post and delete it. In a country of nearly 55 million people and a government fueled by corruption, Facebook's free services became one of the prime ways to spread hatred about the Rohingya. Many people, some of our other ethnic team leaders themselves, didn't trust the Rohingya and warned us that if we worked too closely with them, we could jeopardize other relationships with other ethnic groups. At one point, a report showed that most central Burman people supported the government's efforts to rid their country of the Rohingya people.

Meanwhile, in what had now become the largest refugee camp in the world, the Rohingya continued to survive each day by finding food, firewood and water. Every chance I would get to talk about the

Rohingya with our other ethnic team members in Burma, I would tell them what was happening. That year, FBR celebrated its twenty-year anniversary, and I got to share a report on the Rohingya to the students and guests, but still no one seemed interested in helping.

One thing I love most about the FBR model is that we train people from all over Burma and give them skills so they can help their own people. Instead of the white guy going to save the day, handing out food or helping people who are oppressed, we train and empower the people to help themselves. I wanted some of our ethnic team leaders to step up and help the Rohingya people. I gave a rousing speech to all of our ethnic leaders at one of our annual meetings, saying, "On the back of our T-shirts, our FBR motto says 'love each other.' But I'd like to propose a vote to add an asterisk to the shirt and a footnote that says 'unless you're Rohingya.' Can we take a vote?" I chided them sarcastically.

We have one Karen staff member in Chiang Mai named Kaw Say. He is the head of our patient care department and deeply loves his Karen people. Kaw Say came to me one day and said, "Brother, will you take me to Bangladesh with you on your next mission?" I was thrilled that he wanted to go, and if I could get him on my side, then maybe he could help to convince some of our other ethnic leaders. On our next trip over, Kaw Say joined Hosie and me.

Kaw Say grew up towards the end of some major fighting in Karen State; he lived in a refugee camp for several years, and he knew what it was like to be oppressed. He came with us to the camps and would find people who could speak Burmese, and he'd disappear with them. Later we'd find him sitting in a house somewhere, chewing betelnut with them, laughing and crying with them, and telling stories. Kaw Say loved Aman, and one evening as we were walking back to our hotel in Cox's Bazar, Kaw Say and Aman walked ahead of me. He had his arm around Aman's shoulder, and Aman had his arm around Kaw Say. I thought it was so amazing seeing a Karen and a Rohingya walking together. It is amazing what a little bit of love can do to change people's lives.

Bangladesh was now becoming familiar to me. I had made half a dozen trips, and the chaos of the Dhaka airport and the circus of Cox's Bazar seemed normal. The long drive along the beach down to the refugee camps, and even the smells and sights, had all become normal. Aman would greet me at the airport each time with a giant hug and smile. He even knew to bring the hot water pot we had bought so we could make coffee right away! Aman loved us, and we loved him. He often remarked how different we were from other organizations that worked with the Rohingya. He said we were more focused on loving the people instead of taking pictures and writing stories. Aman felt deeply loved by me and Hosie and whichever other HQ staff came over on trips with us. Love nourished his heart and his soul, and it was on our third or fourth visit that Aman sat me down and told me he wanted to coordinate an FBR training for Rohingya.

My heart leaped at Aman's offer, but I had my doubts. Coordinating a training took a lot of work and planning. We had been looking for some sort of ethnic or cultural leader who would get behind our training, but no one was buying into it. At FBR, when we train a new Ranger, we don't "own" that Ranger. Instead, after they're trained, they go back to their own ethnic group, where an area coordinator will organize missions and future trainings for them. The problem was the Rohingya didn't have any organized groups to go back to. There was ARSA, and we had heard a lot about them, but couldn't put our finger on if they existed or not.

Everyone I interviewed, I would ask if they had heard of ARSA or if they knew anyone in ARSA or had ever seen ARSA. People would think for a minute, say they had heard of ARSA but had never seen them or knew anyone who was part of them. I was beginning to think that ARSA didn't even exist. Since there was no Rohingya political or military group for them to belong to, and for us to partner with, it meant that the burden of organizing a training and missions would fall on me and Hosie and whichever other HQ team member we enlisted to help us. But if Aman wanted to do it, I was willing to try.

Aman sent photos from his phone of a house he thought would work. The house was in the mountains on the western side of the peninsula. It was at the very back of a small village, and the house's backyard opened up directly into the mountains. There was lots of room to practice land navigation and do PT. It was only 500 meters off the beach, and the owner was willing to have us come and do the training there. It had two large rooms we could use for sleeping and classrooms, and he even arranged for a neighbor to cook meals for us and the team while we trained. Looking at the photos in my office back at HQ, I began to get excited about the possibility of doing a training. The house looked perfect; I couldn't believe it. I showed the pictures to Hosie, and she was also excited about the idea of the training actually happening. Everyone had told us that it wouldn't be possible, that we'd be risking too much, that it's not the right thing for the Rohingya. No one had believed in us except Aman. I was willing to trust this young man with our security and the coordination of an FBR training.

In January 2018, I assembled a HQ team. We put together a training plan and all the gear we would need for a new team, and we flew over to Bangladesh. The team consisted of me and Hosie, Adam and his wife Aimee, and their four-month-old daughter Eden. Adam is a former US Army soldier and works as our training officer at FBR. He does an amazing job running trainings and teaching Rangers the skills they need to become effective relief team members. He and his wife had just had their first baby a few months earlier, and when I asked them to think and pray about coming along, they were unsure about bringing Eden with them. They prayed about it a lot and sent out an email to some of their prayer warriors back Stateside. One of them, a longtime doctor who had worked in humanitarian crises before, wrote Aimee back an email that said, "DO NOT BRING YOUR BABY TO BANGLADESH!" It freaked her out a bit because they trusted this doctor and knew he was experienced in the diseases that surround these types of places. Adam and Aimee prayed over the decision for a while and eventually both felt like they should go, and that they should bring Eden with them. They had peace about it, and so did I.

Having kids tag along on missions is not anything new at FBR. Dave Eubank and his wife decided right when they started FBR that if they were going to do this mission God had called them to, working in war zones, they would do it as a family. Eventually they had three kids of their own, and Sahale, Suu and Peter grew up in the jungles of Burma. They had countless "uncles and aunts" in all the rangers and ethnic people we would go on missions with, and grew up loving and being loved by all sorts of different people. Dave was in Kurdistan with his son Pete, meeting with a top Kurdish general to get permission for their team to go and help people being killed by ISIS. When the meeting finished, the general looked at Dave and then gestured to Pete and asked who he was, and Dave replied, "He's my son." Then the general looked at Dave and said, "You're willing to bring your most precious possession into our war-torn country. I can see that you love him and love us. You can go anywhere you want in my country." Having kids joining the mission opens up doors that normally wouldn't open. The people we go to serve have kids who are in the conflict zone too. They can't hop on a plane and fly away—why shouldn't we bring our kids there too?

Our team flew over to Bangladesh; it was six months to the day that the Burma Army had started attacking the Rohingya, and a little more than six months since my first visit to the refugee camps. We picked up some last-minute supplies in Cox's Bazar—clothing to outfit our new team and food and snacks for them. Then, loaded with all our gear into two vans, we headed south towards our training house. When we arrived at the house, Adam immediately started to explore the area, and I could see him imagining how training would unfold. I met with the house owner and Aman and thanked him for letting us use his house. Soon after we began to unpack all of our gear into the house—computers, projectors, medical gear, GPS units, maps, compasses, hammocks, t-shirts, and on and on it went. The house owner watched us unpacking with a surprised look on his face.

We busied ourselves getting organized waiting for our new rangers to arrive later that evening.

Suddenly, Aman came in with a concerned look on his face and asked to speak to me. My heart sank as I thought maybe the rangers had backed out. I had a rush of thoughts that maybe we had spent all this money to fly over there and purchased all this gear, and the training wasn't even going to happen. He assured me that the rangers were fine and still ready to come when he told them to, but the house owner was now afraid and no longer wanted us to conduct the training there. We were being kicked out. I asked him why and Aman couldn't make sense of it, other than he thought all of our gear spooked the house owner, and he decided it was too risky. Hosie and I went and met with the house owner to see if we could change his mind, but he wouldn't; he didn't want any of the Rohingya to come to his house. I was shattered. We all were. Now what were we going to do?

We met together as a team and prayed together. We were all disappointed, and we asked God what he wanted us to do. Aman suggested that we still bring the rangers to the house, but they can go and sleep in the jungle behind the house. The house owner was fine with our HQ team staying at his house, but he didn't want any training to happen or any Rohingya on his property. We talked about it for a while, and it was Hosie who eventually said, "Aman, if we're going to do this training, we need to do it the right way. We don't want to sneak around and lie to the house owner." I agreed with Hosie, but I was sad at the truth she was speaking because I desperately wanted the training to happen. I was glad she was there; if she wasn't I may have continued with Aman's idea, and I think it would have led to big problems. But we had no alternative plans.

We did what we do best at FBR; we decided to go for a walk in the jungle mountains behind the house. We thought maybe we could hike far enough back into the jungle and find a place to make a base camp and conduct the entire training in the jungle. Everyone had hammocks, and we could hike over a few mountain ranges and disappear into the jungle. We hiked for an hour into the jungle but couldn't find any trees that were suitable for hanging hammocks on, or offered the shelter we would want from both the sun and outside observation. Any large trees had been cut down and burned as firewood; only small shrubs remained. There was no water, and it was smoking hot when we were exposed to the sun. The whole time we walked and talked about other options, Aman was furiously making phone calls trying to sort out another place. At one point, Aman had two phones, one held up to each ear, yelling into both. He had called the mosque where the orphanage was and asked if we could do it there, but they said it wouldn't work and would be too risky. He called his cousin and enlisted him to try to find another house we could use. They had an idea of a house at the southern end of the peninsula, but after talking to the owner, he also refused to let any Rohingya training happen there. Only one suggestion seemed half plausible—going into the town of Teknaf and staying at one of the two hotels and conducting the training in the hotel rooms.

Teknaf is the southernmost city on the peninsula and is south of all the refugee camps on the eastern side. It is also home to five different Bangladesh police or military groups working with the Rohingya, including the very police group that was out looking for illegal training. It would be suicide for us to walk right into the heart of their headquarters area and conduct an illegal training. We kept searching. We called Razia and asked if she knew anyone that could help us, but she wasn't able to. I even called my lieutenant friend in the Bangladesh army and posed a hypothetical question to him about the possibility of conducting a training for the Rohingya in one of their army compounds—it was a risky thing to ask him, but I trusted him. He laughed and quickly said it would be totally impossible. Adam and I looked at each other and then circled around to the idea of going to Teknaf. We both knew the risks of going there; even walking around Teknaf is not very safe, let alone conducting a train-ing. Adam thought about his wife, who was back at the house feeding their newborn. We both were wondering the same thing: "God, is this what you have for us? Where do you want us to go?"

All doors seemed to close, except one, Teknaf. We prayed together as a group and decided that early the next morning we would go and check out the hotel and see if it was possible. That evening we went for a walk on the beach. The beauty of the beach and the setting sun ministered to my heart, which was full of dread and disappointment. I was afraid of going into the heart of the beast, and I was also afraid of failing and screwing the whole thing up. I asked God to show me the way and what he had for us. He painted a beautiful sunset for me to remind me I can trust him. I slept soundly that night.

Teknaf is a trade hub and is indescribably packed with people and noisy. It's not a very big town, it has the main road running through the center, and maybe one or two other crossroads. There is a lot of wood that is floated into the city to be sold, and also a lot of illegal drugs that pass through Teknaf. Everything about it indicates that you are now in one of the roughest slums in Bangladesh. Surrounding the city are large military and police compounds, and police are everywhere in the city. Every fourth or fifth vehicle is some sort of police or military vehicle. Teknaf has two main hotels; one is called the Milky Hotel, which seems to be the nicer of the two, and is constantly full of NGO workers. The second of the two is called the Green Garden and is constantly empty.

I use the word hotel, but that is a stretch to describe the Green Garden. It was filthy, and even when someone would come and clean the room or floors, the mop they used would only spread dirt and grease over the tiled floor. A lot of the bedsheets were covered in a layer of filth, and it wasn't uncommon to find blood on them. The electricity wouldn't work for most of the day, and in the evening they would turn on a loud generator to power the lights. There was a small bathroom and shower, and when you would bathe, the water would leave you with a layer of grease on your skin. At one point our door— the only bit of security and secrecy we had—completely fell out of the wall. I went to open the door, and the entire thing, frame and hinges and all, fell inwards, dragging me along with it (much to the amusement of our team). The hotel manager looked at our door and the door frame as it lay on the floor of our room and then advised us, "You should probably use the deadbolt to keep it in place when you leave."

Not only was the hotel short on amenities, it was expensive, about $30 a night, and we'd need at least two rooms, one for us, and one for the team. I tried to explain to Aman that we prefer to sleep in the jungle, at least when we do that we don't need to pay to sleep in the dirt. He seemed to understand but said it wasn't possible for us to stay overnight in the jungle. We talked with the owner and, after arranging two "family rooms," we told him we'd take it. The Green Garden was about to host the first ever FBR Rohingya training. It was down the street from the police, who were strategizing how they could find us and arrest us.

Into the heart of the beast we go.

Chapter 8

Joy

As we unpacked our bags in the hotel, there were many curious onlookers watching the hotel's new guests. A young man dressed smartly in a collared shirt came into our room and asked if he could help. I thought he was one of the hotel staff, and I dismissed him quickly, saying that it was okay. A few minutes later, Aman came into the room and said, "Brother, I want to introduce you to one of your new rangers!" and then promptly pointed to the young man I had dismissed as the hotel staff a few minutes earlier. I shook his hand and apologized for having sent him away. He had a big smile on his face and seemed curious and eager about what he was getting himself into. His name was Elias.

It wasn't long before the rest of the rangers showed up at the hotel. We had originally planned to have eight to ten rangers at the house training, but now that we had to move locations, we decided we would cut down the size of the group to just six rangers. One by one they came in and introduced themselves: Amin, Rahman, Ibrahim, Akram, Abdul, and Elias. We had Aman, who would help me coordinate all the logistics of the training, and Aman's cousin, who would translate the classes.

We put the new rangers in a family room right across the hall from our room. Their room would serve as a classroom, gym, and their sleeping area. I was excited and shocked that it was actually happening.

Normally in Ranger training, the teams learn about thirty different skills. At our large training camp in Burma, we have lots of space and time with the rangers to make sure they understand and are competent with the skills. We have mountains and rivers surrounding camp for us to practice skills like making and crossing a rope bridge, swimming, land navigation, and lots of physical training. Since we were now confined to limited time and space with the rangers, we had to choose which were the most important skills we wanted them to learn and that we could deliver in the small hotel room.

Aman and I kept working on different ideas for the training, and we found a small wildlife preserve not far from Teknaf. Aman's cousin knew one of the wardens in the park, and he called to ask if we could use the park for our training and practice. The warden agreed but said that we need to arrive early in the morning, take one of their park workers with us for protection and guidance, and we'd need to leave the park before dark. This was great news because it meant that we would be able to practice the things we were going to teach in the "classroom". I was relieved we'd be able to get into nature, and I could sense a personal shift in myself—I now preferred the jungle to the city.

FBR is a very active organization. We walk long distances and carry heavy loads to the remote places we want to go. We thrive in the mountains, and we were thankful for the opportunity to use the park. We decided that we would teach for one full day in the classroom, then go to the park the next day and practice everything we had learned. We would cover six topics: Good Life Club, Medical and First Aid, GPS and Land Navigation, Interview and Reporting, Camera and Video, and Human Rights. Also mixed into the classes were lots of lessons on the "FBR way, motto, and beliefs." We also always teach servant leadership throughout all the classes and try to model this for our teams.

Since it was getting late in the day, we decided we would send the team for dinner and then to bed early because we would get up around 3:00 a.m. to head to the national forest. We wanted to start the training there in the jungle so they can get familiar with where we love to operate. I went to bed that night excited for what the next day held, and with a sense that God's got us.

The next morning we woke up early, wanting only a hot cup of coffee, but couldn't because there was no electricity in the hotel. We headed to the park, where we were going to meet up with our Rangers who were traveling separately from us for security. We carried supplies and big jugs of water and had decided to have the park ranger lead us a few kilometers into the jungle, away from any normal foot traffic and out of sight. As the sun began to rise through the hazy smoke of the refugee camps, we snuck quietly into the mountains and jungle. Just like coming to Bangladesh and the chaos of it all had now become normal to me, I had a strange feeling of being "at home" as we entered the jungle.

We hiked up a big mountain and eventually came to a small clearing at the top. We decided this would be a good place to stop and conduct our first class. We showed some videos about FBR on a laptop and then I welcomed them and led the team in a morning devotional. It was quite amazing to be a small group of Christians, sitting together with a small group of Muslims, hoping to change the world together through love. The team knew and respected that we were Christians and asked that we know and respect their Muslim faith. Whenever class would get hard or boring for them, they would suddenly hear the call to prayer in the distance (even when sometimes we couldn't hear it) and then would tell us they must go to perform their prayers. In the jungle, they would walk down the trail a bit, use some of the drinking water we had brought with us to perform their ablutions, find the direction of Mecca, and then in the dirt, perform their prayers. It was kind of beautiful to watch the dedication and reverence they had for Allah, their God.

Adam introduced the team to push-ups early on the first day. Most of them had never done a push-up before in their lives. Aman, who was enthusiastic about our training, wanted to lead by example. He was in the push-up position, his arms extended, holding his body weight up. Then Adam instructed, "Now, you release your arms and lower yourself to the ground." Aman misunderstood these instructions as to just completely remove his arms, causing him to faceplant into the dirt and smack his chin hard. He looked a bit shocked and stunned at this horrible exercise called a push-up. We laughed at him as he rubbed his chin and brushed the dirt off his face. Anytime the Rangers would start to look restless or bored, Adam would quickly put them through their paces in a PT session. They moaned and groaned and laughed along with us as we had them performing these funny movements. The PT sessions confirmed in their minds that we were not a normal NGO and this would not be a normal job or training for them.

We spent most of the first day explaining who FBR was and what we believed in. We hammered home our Ranger motto to them and explained what a relief team does on mission. They loved the ending of the motto that said, 'never surrender' and took it to heart. At the end of the day in the jungle, we had begun the process of them understanding FBR, but also the starting point of learning to love and trust each other. As the sun began to set, we decided we would make our way back to the hotel for more evening PT and an evening class after dinner. Taking separate cars, we met back at the hotel and broke for dinner. After dinner, we came in prepared to teach an evening class only to find the team already falling asleep, exhausted from their first day as Rangers. We gave them the night and let them sleep.

The next day we started early with the classes. Hosie taught them first aid and CPR all day. They were quick learners and wanted to understand the material. They constantly brought it back to the idea that they wanted to "help their people." This concept of their people needing help was all still relatively fresh in their minds and hearts. The days went on, and we grew closer to the team and loved their personalities and desire to be Rangers. We were going back and forth from the jungle to the hotel on alternating days and so far seemed to be evading any problems with the police.

One afternoon in the jungle, we were practicing setting up a secure area and practicing some GPS navigating when we were spotted by a police officer. Aman quickly ran over to talk to the police and ended up paying him something to leave before we had even seen him. We were shaken by the report of the police and reminded how fragile and dangerous our training was.

The next day we were back in the hotel teaching in the classroom and later learned that the policeman, along with some of his colleagues, had shown back up at the park looking for us and asking the park rangers questions. Not finding us in the jungle, they left to keep searching. The next day we headed back to the jungle and later found out the police had stopped by our hotel and were asking questions about any foreigners staying at the hotel. Not finding us at the hotel either, the police left again, wondering where the foreigners were who were conducting the illegal training. For a few days we seemed to play cat and mouse with the police, and I was in awe of the way that God, not me, was coordinating our security and schedule.

The things I wanted to do always seemed to not be possible, and instead we'd be forced onto a different schedule. But this new schedule and plan always turned out to keep us one step ahead of the police that were looking for us. I thought about what a bad plan it would have been for us to stay in one location, like at the original training house that we had planned to use. The police would have been able to watch us and predict our movements and plans easily. With all the back and forth to the park on different days, our movement seemed to keep the police guessing. I was amazed that God would take care of our security, design a better security plan than I could, and could be counted on to be our Protector.

Hosie had to leave us early to head to the Middle East and join up with another FBR mission happening there. She said her good-byes in the jungle to our team and then hiked out of the jungle to meet our driver, who would then take her to the airport in Cox's Bazar. Our plan was for the driver to drop her off at the airport and then come back and pick the rest of us up and bring us back to the hotel in Teknaf at the end of the day. We didn't know, however, that the President of Indonesia was flying in that day and driving down to see the Rohingya camps. This would cause total traffic gridlock and chaos. Hosie barely made her flight, having to walk/run the last mile to the airport because her driver couldn't get any closer. It also meant that our driver wasn't able to get back to pick us up in time.

We finished our training for the day and moved to the meeting place where we normally would jump straight into the waiting vehicles and quickly get out of there, only to find that our driver wasn't there. The entrance to the national park is on the edge of one of the refugee camps, and the longer we stood out in the open, the more attention we'd gather. We waited a while and then made some phone calls to the driver, who told us he was still a long way away. Unsure of what to do, we decided the best thing would be to flag down a passing taxi-truck and get moving back towards Teknaf. These pickup trucks put benches in the back of the truck and will pick up passengers like a bus as they drive back and forth along the road. We flagged one down, told him where we wanted to go and joined the other passengers in the back of the truck. I was happy that we were moving and not standing out in the open anymore and was looking forward to getting back to our hotel. After a few kilometers of driving, we pulled over to pick up some more passengers, not paying much attention as they told the driver where they wanted to go, but my heart almost stopped as they walked around the back of the truck to get in: two police officers from the department looking for foreign trainers.

We all sat in wide-eyed silence as the police got in directly across from us and sat down. I was sitting next to Aimee, who was holding baby Eden on her lap, and Adam was on the other side of her. We were all sitting still, as if we could avoid the police noticing us if we didn't move. The police looked at us, slightly confused as to why foreigners were in the back of one of these trucks, and then shifted their gaze to baby Eden. Eden then stole the show. She smiled at the police and gave them a look that would melt your heart. The police instantly forgot about us, sitting paralyzed in fear, rubbing knees with them, and focused only on Eden. For the next ten kilometers, the police laughed and poked Eden, who played along brilliantly, smiling, giggling and being adorable. The police took pictures of her and selfies with her, all the while ignoring the rest of us. When the driver finally pulled over at our hotel and we got out, Aimee held up Eden's hand and waved bye to the police, who laughed and waved back, then drove away down the street. We quickly moved into our hotel in total disbelief at what had just happened. Eden, this little four-month-old baby, had saved us! I thought for sure the police would start asking us questions and ask us to come to the station with them, but instead, they hardly even glanced up at us as they were smitten with baby Eden. That night we thanked God for the amazing way he works and leads us—even when we don't understand.

Adam set up a GPS course in the jungle for the team to put into practice their new navigation skills on one of the training days. We gave them a series of coordinates that they had to navigate to in pairs, and then take a picture of what was at that location using the photography skills they had learned. We sent the team out from our perch on the top of the mountain and then strung up some hammocks while we waited for them to return. Aimee played with Eden, trying to point out some monkeys playing in nearby trees while Adam and I sat in our hammocks listening to hear if we could detect our Rangers.

We reflected on how amazing and surreal it was to be nearing the end of our training. Something that had seemed so impossible, we were now almost finished with. As we laughed and joked about the training and our team, Adam looked over at me and said, "You know, none of this would have happened if you had accepted that other job offer." It sent shivers down my spine as he said it, suddenly realizing the impact of his words. He was right. Had I taken the money and job offer from the other organization, it's unlikely we'd be sitting there together as our Rangers bushwhacked through the jungle practicing their GPS skills. People had told me that the other job wasn't bad, but was a diversion from what God had for me. I had no idea what it was that God had planned for me, and at the time FBR had no further plans to keep working with the Rohingya. But here we were, half a year later, finishing up our first ever Rohingya training.

I thought back over all the trips that Hosie and I had made to the refugee camps. We had no idea what we were doing, me more so than Hosie, as we tried to figure out our place there. We tried our best on each trip to love everyone that we met. Sometimes we loved someone and they couldn't help us very much, but became our friend. Other times we would love someone, and they would want to help us however they could. Slowly and organically, our team on the ground there grew, out of love, fertilized with laughter and joy. In the early days, we had no idea who we could trust and if we were getting ripped off or not, so we decided we'd trust everyone and pay what we could for things. We slowly learned the ropes of operating in Bangladesh, passing illegally through multiple checkpoints every day, and learning about operating in a Muslim country as a Christian. We learned more and more about Islam, and we shared more and more boldly about "Isa." As our relationships and trust grew with our Rangers, team and friends, we were able to be more open and bold about the things we believed in and the person of Jesus we believed in. We respected our Muslim friends; they called us brother and sister, and we called them the same. We loved them and they loved us, and love is a powerful thing that can change hearts, nations, and wars.

When we would pray together as a team, we would hold out our hands in the way of a traditional Muslim prayer, and we would end our prayers in Isa's name, and our Muslim brothers would say "amen" with us. It was beautiful to watch our team coming together in a bond of love and service for oppressed people. I shared an audio Bible with Aman that was in the Rohingya dialect that he understood. He was curious about the audio player, and only vaguely curious about the Bible. I was okay with that. My job isn't to convert or change Aman; my job is to love Aman and introduce him to Jesus. Jesus and the Holy Spirit will do the converting part. If I can trust Jesus with all of our security plans and the wellbeing of baby Eden, then surely I can trust Jesus with the precious souls of Aman and our team.

Several months later Aman pulled me aside and told me, "Brother, you gave me that audio Bible, every time I listen to it my heart burns with fire." Aman shared with me how he had often had dreams about our FBR team and when we would return to see him. He told me that one recurring dream he had was to play soccer on the beach with us.

While this may sound simple enough, it's actually a huge security risk. Not only is there a very good possibility that a group of foreigners and Rohingya playing soccer together would quickly draw a large crowd, which would inevitably draw the police, but the Rohingya are held captive within the confines of the camps. The camps run along the eastern side of the peninsula over a span of approximately 30 miles. The beach on the western side of the peninsula has at least a half dozen checkpoints between it and the camps. The checkpoints are in place to control the movement of the NGOs working in the area and to stop any Rohingya from trying to get further into Bangladesh. Any Rohingya who were caught outside of the camps were quickly punished, sometimes beaten, sometimes imprisoned without trial. Aman's dream of playing soccer on the beach, while beautiful, had a number of very serious security concerns associated with it. But during our training, I had learned that our security is in God's hands, and I should try my best to follow him. I started to get the feeling that we needed an afternoon of joy and fun with our new team, something like soccer on the beach.

I shared the plan with the rest of our HQ team and asked what they thought. Everyone thought it was a great idea, but the security concerns quickly dawned on everyone. Transporting vehicles full of Rohingya through that many checkpoints would surely cause problems, if not get everyone arrested. We prayed about it, and these words came into my mind: "Fight for joy." It's so easy to get bogged down in the problems and hassles of life and not fight for things that bring us joy. We all felt peace about the idea and brought it to our team that evening. We told them our plan, and they erupted in cheers and excitement. They jumped around the room at the thought of the ocean and beach and playing soccer together with us. The excitement died down quickly when one of them asked what my clever plan would be to get them all through the checkpoints. I told them we would pray and go. They looked at me, expecting me to continue with more of the plan, but that was it. They looked at each other and said a few things to each other in their own language. Not only was I asking them to risk their security, I was also asking them to have faith that Jesus could protect them. My security plans to date all reminded me of Mr. Bean; they were unusual and harebrained, but somehow managed to work out in the end. This plan was no exception. They agreed, but looked apprehensive about it.

The next morning we arranged for two vehicles to come and get us all and drive us to the beach. We decided to split the team in half and sit them in the back of the vans, with the foreigners in the front. If one van seemed to be getting searched or in trouble, the other could turn around and avoid the checkpoint. At least half the team could stay out of jail, and potentially help the other half. We said a prayer. I asked Jesus to help us fight for joy and protect us as we traveled. We all said amen and got into the vehicles. A feeling of trepidation hung in the air.

The vans were quiet as we departed towards the beach. I was sitting in the front passenger seat of the lead vehicle. If we were going to get in trouble, I thought it best if I were in the middle of it all. As we approached our first checkpoint, the armed soldiers manning the checkpoint stepped out onto the road as our vehicle approached. I said another silent prayer, "Jesus, please help us to pass through this checkpoint." We approached slowly and then, suddenly, the soldier waved us through and looked the other way as we drove past. We let out a collective sigh of relief in our van. I watched in the mirror as the follow-on van had the same thing happen, passing through the checkpoint without any problems. Still watching in my mirror, I could see the soldier stop the next vehicle to come along.

The next checkpoint came soon after, and again, I prayed a silent prayer, and again we were waved through without any problems. At one checkpoint the guard was sitting looking at his phone, waving vehicles through mindlessly. At another, the guard walked out to the road to stop our vehicle, then was suddenly called back to their guard hut, our vehicle passing smoothly through. At each of the six checkpoints, we passed through without any problems until we turned onto the western highway that ran alongside the beautiful beach. We stopped at a small market to buy some snacks and a soccer ball, and then drove further until we found a relatively private and remote area of the world's longest beach.

I signaled for our driver to stop. When he pulled over, I turned around to the rest of the team in my van and smiled. I jumped out and opened their side door. They slowly and hesitantly stepped out of the van, staying close to the open door as if ready to jump back in, and stared at the ocean. In one of the most incredible things I've ever seen, the team stood silently for a minute, and then on some sort of unspoken cue, they let out the most amazing whoops and hollers and yells of laughter and began running as fast as they could towards the ocean breakers. They leaped into the water, clothes all still on, and splashed around in the waves. They laughed and flipped each other and got knocked around by the waves. I got tears in my eyes as I watched Ibrahim stand and stretch his arms wide open and stare out into the vast ocean, as if he was receiving it all, all the beauty and power and freedom of the ocean, into his heart and soul. These young men, who were forced to flee from their homes, who were prisoners rotting in refugee camps, were, for a moment, free.

We played in the water for a while, laughing and shouting. We had arm wrestling competitions on the shore, and then we set up two goals to play our soccer game. I was overcome with the emotions of it all as I watched Aman running after the soccer ball and trying to kick a goal, Hosie and Ivo trying to stop him. It was a look of pure and total joy on his face. A dream come true.

I called my friend Khan, who managed our favorite restaurant in Cox's Bazar. I said, "Khan, I want to bring some of my friends to your restaurant for dinner tonight. They're all illegal. I don't want to cause any problems for you, but what do you think?" Without even hesitating, he said, "Brother David, bring them. I will prepare it all."

When we finished our soccer game, wet and sandy, we piled back into the vans, with only one more major checkpoint to cross to get the team into Cox's Bazar. We prayed our way through the checkpoint and an hour later arrived at Khan's restaurant. He had a table all set up for us, menus out and fresh-cut flowers in the center of the table. He welcomed each of my friends as if they were his own family, and sat them at the table. I looked at the team and told them, "Boys, order whatever you want!" and they did. Fruit shakes and cokes, and fish and rice and nan and all sorts of delicious curries and meat dishes kept coming out of the kitchen. The boys ate and ate and ate until they flopped back in their seats totally stuffed. "This is the kind of food distribution I like to do," I thought. We talked and laughed and recounted funny moments from our training. It was a time of thanksgiving for us, and our family was circled up around a mighty feast, hearts full of joy, rescued from the clutches of the beast by Jesus. It was an amazing picture of heaven.

As the evening came to a close, my thoughts shifted to what was coming next for this team. We had one last thing to do with them. We had to plan their mission. We were going to ask them to cross the Naf River, back into Burma, the place they had fled from, where murders, rapes, and killing were still happening. We were going to ask them to go and try to help the people and shine a light on what was happening.

We were going to ask them to risk their lives for love.

Chapter 9

Rangers

I left Cox's Bazar with a heavy heart. I was still in shock at how the training had come together. Not by my doing at all, totally by God. I was sad to be saying goodbye to my new friends, our first Rohingya team, but there was something else that started to weigh on me almost as soon as I boarded the plane. I started to wonder about their mission.

We spent a full day in the hotel planning out what their mission would look like and what we wanted them to accomplish out of it. It was risky, to say the least. We were getting news every day that the Burma Army was planting landmines all along the border. There were Burma Army boat patrols that were regularly stopping boats on the river, and they were in the process of building a huge barbed wire fence where people were crossing by land. They clearly did not want any Rohingya back.

I wondered if we had done a good enough job training the team. It was a fast training, and we didn't get a ton of time to practice the skills we'd taught. We had barely touched on landmines, let alone how to disable them if they came across them. We had hardly done any security training, and the one day we did talk briefly about it was the one day we were seen by the Bangladesh police, hiding in our makeshift patrol base.

For days after I returned home, my brain was in a fog. I kept having these thoughts of the team crossing the border and then getting blown up by a landmine. How would I react if that happened? This whole thing was because of me, and I had encouraged the team to walk into certain death. I wrestled with dread for several days.

At FBR, we often talk about how we're more of a movement than an organization. Up to this point, I never understood this line of thinking. We seemed quite like an organization to me. But, it finally clicked in my head and heart what my boss was talking about when we started to discuss the mission plan with the new Rohingya team. As we talked about what a realistic mission might look like, and the threats that could come up with that mission, I started to realize that these guys believed in us and the FBR motto. They believed in the movement of love that we were encouraging; they believed in the FBR way of doing things, and they believed that helping and loving their people was worth risking their lives for. We weren't going to pay them anything to do this mission. They weren't employees of FBR, but rather they were Rangers who believed in the movement and wanted to go.

I started to remember the ways that God had provided for my finances over the years of volunteering with FBR. I remember that when I made my budget; I surrendered it to God, and then whenever I was worried about not having enough money, I reminded myself to trust God. I had to do the same thing with our Rohingya team. I prayed for each one of them, surrendering them to God, surrendering their safety, their hearts, and their mission to God. I asked him to protect them and love them and save them. I immediately felt the dread lifting. I knew that God had them and had a plan for them. He wasn't done with them yet.

Our team in Bangladesh began the process of preparing for the mission. They first went into the national park one last time to practice all their skills again. They sent pictures to me daily of all the different things they were doing to practice and prepare—they were even continuing to do push-ups. They began to research different ways to cross the border back into Burma. I had encouraged them first to try to find a walking way. At FBR we love to walk, and even if we have to walk for a week to get around landmines or the Burma Army, we'll do it. The team didn't seem that keen on walking for a week, but said they would try to find the way.

They went out and found the new fence the Burma Army had built. The Bangladesh soldiers weren't letting anyone near the fence, but Ibrahim, our youngest Ranger, went up to the Bangladesh soldier and said to him, "Hi, I work for the Bangladesh border guard, it's my day off, and I wanted to come see this big fence being built. Is it okay to walk along it for a while?" The soldiers looked him up and down, shrugged, and waved him past. Ibrahim walked for nearly a mile along the fence, taking pictures, looking for places the team could sneak through, but it was solid. There was no way to get around the fence, and it seemed to go on for miles and miles.

Next, they started researching boats to take them across the river. Fishermen had been banned from using the Naf River shortly after the crisis had erupted, so the only people on the river were commercial shipping boats, tourist shuttles to a nearby island, and smugglers. They eventually got a hold of a smuggler who agreed to take them across the river for a high smuggler's price. The team wanted to practice more of their skills and also rehearse the boat crossing before they went live with it. They headed into the jungle near the border for another day of training and practice. They were in the middle of nowhere when suddenly they heard people coming through the bush. Before they had any time to react, they were surrounded at gunpoint by a group of soldiers.

The team first thought they were Burma Army soldiers, but quickly realized they weren't wearing any uniforms, and weren't talking in Burmese. Our team leader started to talk in Bengali but eventually overheard some of the men speaking in their Rohingya dialect. He asked them, "Are you Rohingya?" and they said, "Yes." Then he continued, "We are Rohingya too. We are the Rohingya Free Burma Rangers team." The leader of the militia patrol looked at them suspiciously. He asked them some questions about the Free Burma Rangers, as he had never heard of them before. They explained everything they knew. They showed them the GPSs, medical equipment, and binoculars we had left with them. They showed them their video camera and photo cameras and explained about their mission they were trying to do. After an hour of talking about FBR to the leader of the patrol, he told them, "We are ARSA." Then he asked them, "Who is your leader?" and our team leader quickly said, "David Small!" The patrol leader said back, "I would like him to meet your leader."

I was anxiously awaiting messages each day from our team, waiting for the green light from them saying they were going to cross the river. Aman was sending me daily updates about what was happening with them. I saw a message come in from him and was dumbfounded when I read, "ARSA leader wants to meet with you." I didn't believe it was true, so casually replied, "Sure, whenever he wants, I'll come over." Then Aman went on to describe the events of the day and then sent me photos with the ARSA patrol group. I started to realize that maybe this was true. I asked Aman if he could go and meet the leader to set up the meeting. He agreed.

At this point, I had basically made up my mind that ARSA didn't exist. In fact, a Rohingya journalist friend of ours had shared a long, thorough report with us outlining how it didn't exist. Over the course of a half dozen trips to the camps, anytime I would do an interview, I would ask about ARSA, the Arakan Rohingya Salvation Army. The answers were always the same: "I've heard of them, but never seen them." I was beginning to think that ARSA was made up by the Burma government to give them cause for their massacre. But now I wasn't so sure. I was glad that our team was alright, and even more I was shocked that they had stumbled upon the group that hundreds of people had been searching for for months.

Aman is an amazing young man. He loves his people passionately, and he gives of himself so much to help them. When Aman isn't helping us or other NGOs, he is working in an orphanage and trying to finish high school. I sometimes need to remind myself that Aman is young and has lived his whole life in the camps. Now I was asking him to go and meet with a potential terrorist. He didn't even hesitate when he agreed to go.

Later I would learn that when he attempted to meet the leader, they had taken his phone away from him and searched him. They blindfolded him and led him deep into the jungle. He told me that he was so afraid he almost peed his pants. But he didn't quit. He kept reminding himself of the Ranger motto, "Never surrender". He was led deep into the jungle and eventually brought to a tent. When they took the blindfold off him, there were a lot of people and a lot of guns. Everyone was looking at him suspiciously. He was led into the tent, and he met the leader. He shared all about FBR and how we wanted to help the Rohingya people. He shared with them how we had defied security concerns and everyone telling us it was impossible, that we never surrendered, and that we loved him and the Rohingya people very much. He told them that we risked our own security and lives, even baby Eden's safety, to come and help them. He asked if their leader would meet me. After some discussion with his aides, he agreed.

So this is how I found myself standing in front of the ARSA leader, while he waved a gun around and yelled in his Rohingya language. Aman calmed him down, and eventually we sat down at a table. We sat in silence. We sat there staring at each other. I waited and waited, and after a few minutes I leaned over to Aman and whispered, "What are we waiting for?" and then Aman whispered back to me, "Brother David, we're waiting for you to start talking." I embarrassedly motioned to Dave, my boss, that he could begin. Dave is an expert in these kinds of situations. He is so full of passion and love, and it comes across in everything he says. We shared about FBR for a few hours. Dave showed videos of what our teams were doing in

Burma and around the world. He showed pictures of his family and told him that he brings them with him everywhere; his daughter Sahale was there with us. We told him all about the training that we conducted and about our new Rohingya team. We introduced Elias, whom we had brought along as our security guy. We talked with ARSA for over four hours.

As we were ending our conversation with him, we gave him copies of the Jesus film in the Arabic language, and we then we prayed together with him. We told him that it's okay to fight for your people and defend them, but do it out of love, not out of hate. He had answered candidly and honestly the questions we had asked. He had told us that they weren't a terror organization and that they had no ties to ISIS or Al Qaeda. They had no outside funding. He said, "We have about forty guns. If we had outside funding, don't you think I would have more than forty guns?"

He told us that his plan was that he wanted to get all forty guns together in the same place, attack a Burma Army patrol of six or seven soldiers, kill them all, and then take all their weapons. Then they'd have forty-six guns. Then they would disappear into the jungle again and not resurface for a few months. Then they'd repeat this type of attack over and over again until they had enough guns to be a real army. He told us they have a few thousand foot soldiers, and they train them in the jungle, but they have only machetes and clubs. He told us that they weren't a religious army, but rather an ethnic army. He said, "You don't need to be a Muslim to join ARSA. You need to be willing to fight for the Rohingya. You can be a Christian, a Hindu, or a Buddhist." He showed us fresh bullet wounds in his chest and back and told us that a Burma army spy had snuck into the refugee camp and started shooting at him. They had hit him in the chest, and the bullet went straight through and out his back. He was lucky to still be alive.

We continued to talk with him as people started coming out of the back room and setting up a table for lunch. They brought out more food than I could imagine. There wasn't enough room for it all at the table we were sitting at. I wondered where all this food had come from as we were in the middle of a refugee camp. There was chicken and beef and fish and all sorts of different curries. It was a feast. Before we started eating, he looked at us and said, "Brothers, the way I see it, we have three options as young Rohingya men. We can stay in Burma, where the Burma Army will kill us like they killed our families. We can sit and rot in the refugee camps. Or we can fight back. Tell me, brothers, what would you do if you were in my situation?" My heart went out to him. I could see in his eyes that he was sad about the atrocities that had been committed against his people. He showed us pictures of his wife and kids. He told us about relatives who had been killed by the Burma Army. I didn't know how to answer him, but I knew that he wasn't an evil man like some of the media and the Burma government were making him out to be.

We ate a feast together and sat together talking about life. I was starting to like this man, and I asked him if I could meet him again when I came to Bangladesh. He said he would like it very much. We were soon interrupted by one of his foot soldiers, who came in and whispered something in his ear. He looked at us and said, "The police are looking for you guys. They are coming. We must end this now." We prayed with him again, and then he said, "Follow me," and he led us out through the camp. We thought maybe he would send us with his soldiers, but he stayed with us, guiding us back through the maze of the camp until we were safe with our driver. He shook our hands again and then disappeared into the crowd of refugees.

That would be the last time I would see my friend. On my next visit to Bangladesh, I called him and asked to meet. He said he couldn't meet me. He said the Burma government had been putting lots of pressure on the Bangladesh government to find him. He said they had a "shoot on sight" order issued for him in Burma and Bangladesh. He didn't want to come out of hiding, and he didn't want me to be caught up in the middle of something dangerous. I prayed with him over the phone and wished him well. A few months later they found him, and he was shot and killed as he tried to run away. Aman convinced a local policeman to share the photos of his body with him, and he sent them to me. His body lay in the dirt, contorted in an unnatural position. It didn't even look like him, but it was. Blood was everywhere. I mourned the loss of my friend.

Our Rohingya team went back to trying to find a way across into Burma for their mission. There had been a number of delays while we sorted the ARSA stuff out, but now they were ready to go, and had the blessing of ARSA behind them. Bolstered by this support, they started to plan their crossing. But then the Bangladesh border police caught a boat smuggling drugs, and they shut the river down. No boat traffic was allowed on the river at all. Aman texted me, "Brother, pray to Allah that we can find a way to do the mission and cross the river." They waited for several weeks and soon the ban on the river was lifted. But then the monsoons blew in. Day after day, storms battered the refugee camps. Aman would text me almost every day, "Brother, pray to Allah that we can cross the river." I would always respond to him and tell him I was praying and try to encourage him to push the team. Weeks turned into months, and I was starting to get frustrated. I thought maybe the team was afraid, and that they didn't want to go on mission. I thought maybe they were making up excuses to not go. It had now been almost three months since we had approved their mission and given them the green light to go. But still they waited on the shores of Bangladesh.

Aman could sense my frustration. He tried to tell me the team was doing its best, and he continued to ask me to pray. The team wanted to go, he kept telling me, and if I would ask Allah for his favor, then we could go. I texted Aman back, and I said, "Aman, I will pray, but I will pray to Jesus. I think you and the team should ask Jesus to make a way for you to go." He wrote me back and said, "Okay, we will pray to Jesus." I couldn't believe it. For a Muslim to say they would pray to Jesus was unbelievable. Later, Aman would tell me that he got the team together, and he asked Jesus to make a way for them to get across the river and into Burma.

Two days later, they were in Burma.

They crossed in the middle of the night during a storm. Rains pounded down on the smugglers' boat as they tried to quickly cross the river to Burma, being smuggled back into their own country. As the team jumped out of the boat on the Burma shore, they saw spotlights and flashlights scanning the shore trying to find them. The boat driver quickly turned around and started to head back to Bangladesh. The team started to run. They heard gunfire and shouting coming behind them, but in the dark and the rain, they didn't stop running to find out what was happening. They ran and ran and ran. For four hours they ran through the jungle, motivated by a mix of love and terror and adrenaline. They eventually found a small house with a Rohingya owner who said they could hide there. They collapsed into the house and quickly fell asleep. They felt lucky to be alive and safe.

The boat driver didn't end up so well, however. On his way back across the river, the Burma border guard came alongside him and demanded that he report to a checkpoint. When he came to the checkpoint, they accused him of smuggling and asked him why he hadn't checked in on his way across the river. Within the next twenty-four hours, he would have his boat confiscated. He'd be accused, tried, convicted and sentenced to seven years in prison. By the time we mobilized an Arakan team to go to the local jail to ask about him, he had already been transferred to a central jail in Sittwe. I didn't know how to feel about this situation, but it also showed the risk the team was willing to take to do their mission.

Once our team got to Burma, we lost all communication with them. Aman stayed in Bangladesh waiting to hear from the team and coordinate all the logistics from that side. He sent me a message telling me about their crossing and about the boat driver's situation. He told me he would update me as soon as he heard from the team. Days went by with no word. I was anxiously waiting to hear something, anything, from the team. Days turned into weeks. I started to wonder how they were doing, and every day I would surrender them again before God, asking him to guide them and protect them and reveal himself to them even more. I was relieved when I finally got a message from Aman just over two weeks later, saying, "The team will be back in Bangladesh tonight. Please come and meet them."

I was thrilled they were alive and well. I couldn't wait to hear all about their mission. I was also amazed at their bravery. This team constantly seemed to surprise me. Normally, an FBR team gets three months of training followed by a month-long training mission where they practice a real mission with the staff. Our team got two weeks of hotel training and then was sent on a mission, alone, far more dangerous than most missions our other teams were going on. I couldn't believe it. As quickly as I could make the arrangements, I booked myself back over to Cox's Bazar. I wasn't going to be able to be there when they arrived, but I wanted to be there as soon as I could to debrief them.

Aman told me the team would meet me in Cox's Bazar at a hotel. I asked about the checkpoints and security risk of going to Cox's Bazar and with a new confidence told me they would deal with it. He said he would arrange the hotels for us and that he would be there at the airport when we arrived. Hosie, Adam and I, flew back as quickly as we could; we were all so proud of our team. True to his word, Aman greeted us outside the airport, hot water pot under his arm for our coffee, and with a big smile across his face. We exchanged hugs, and he waved us over to a vehicle he had arranged for us. He took us to a hotel to get settled, and a few minutes later our team started to arrive. Each one of them looked me in the eye, and I looked deep into their eyes, hoping to be able to convey with my eyes how proud I was of them, and then gave each of them a long hug.

Before we began our debrief, the team asked if we could go eat at Khan's restaurant again. I made some calls, and he was thrilled to welcome us back. We ate a celebratory feast together again. Several times throughout the night, I caught myself staring at this ragtag team in disbelief. Disbelief at the mission they had done, the training we did together, the way that God has been in and through this entire process. I found myself slowly weaving bits of the story together, like it was a great tapestry, coming together into this beautiful image, this beautiful celebratory feast. And that's kind of what our lives are like when we follow God. They are small moments that, when we pause for a minute and look back on, we can see God weaving a most beautiful tapestry of our lives.

Back at the hotel, we got down to business. I wanted to hear everything from start to finish. We talked for a long time about their crossing and the situation with the boat driver. We all agreed that we would find his family and give his wife some money to support herself and on a future mission try to see if we could find the boat driver. Then we got down to the mission.

After their long run in the night, the team hunkered down in the house they had found for two or three days. They were afraid and thought maybe they were being followed or chased. So they waited. Finally, after three days, they decided that they wanted to collect evidence of the Burma Army burning down villages. They met with some local guides and got pointed towards the villages. What they came across stunned them. Entire villages torched, nothing remaining except the black charred ashes. Houses destroyed, schools burned, and mosques trashed. One local guide took them to where he used to live, and he stood silently as he showed them his destroyed house, a smashed-up bicycle lay in the mud, a memory of lost freedom. He took them to the local mosque, which was nothing more than a pile of rubble.

Using their new skills in interviewing, photo and video, the team documented everything. Then they took GPS coordinates for all the locations they visited. Elias passed me his notebook with all the coordinates. Adam quickly went on Google Earth and punched in the coordinates. I connected my computer to a projector and projected the satellite images onto the wall of the hotel. Google Earth has a feature where you can scan back over the same satellite images year by year. We went back a few years and could see a thriving village. The team could point out different things they saw and showed us where the mosque was. Then we slid the year to the current date, and in place of the village was a black, burned circle in the jungle.

Looking through the images from ground level taken by the team brought it all to life. It was amazing. We were looking at some of the first real, hard evidence of the Rohingya genocide. I was again speechless as I looked at the images our team had gathered and listened to their stories.

They had originally planned to only stay for a week or ten days and then cross back into Burma. They hadn't found out about the boat driver until they went to meet him at the predetermined location and he didn't show up. They eventually were able to borrow someone's phone and call the boat driver's wife. She told them what had happened to him. They then started making calls and eventually arranged another boat to take them back to Bangladesh. When they arrived back in Bangladesh, they were changed. They were now warriors for their people. They were stronger and more confident. They were Rangers.

We took all of their notes, interviews and media and put them together into reports. We passed on all the information to the UN, which was very thankful for it. The UN rep, who I gave it to, asked if I'd be willing to testify at an International Criminal Court case if it ever came to it, and I told her I would. We sent our report and photos of the burned villages to our newsletter list all over the world. News agencies responded by wanting to know more, wanting to interview our Rangers, and wanting to republish the evidence they had gathered. Our team was shining a light on what was happening inside Burma. They were getting the news out.

I was so proud of them.

Chapter 10

Beh

Over the course of two years, I made thirteen different trips back to Bangladesh to work with the Rohingya. My time there was always hard, humbling and holy, like the best of adventures. Each year that I followed God on adventures with the Free Burma Rangers, I thought there was no way to top what he had done and who he had been the previous year, but God is eternally creative and eternally generous of himself. It's no wonder that the angels that stand before the throne of God fall down and cry, "Holy Holy Holy!" Then they get back up and take another look at God and he is even more amazing than he was before, causing them again to drop and cry out how holy he is. If these brief glimpses of heaven on earth, and adventures with God, are any sign of what heaven will be like, I am excited and confident that it won't be boring.

In the fall of 2018, a series of events took place in my life that shook me and left me emotionally drained and vulnerable. It started in the summer when I was back in Canada. I was doing some work with the Canadian army and stationed at a base. My contract was supposed to have ended, but I had prayed and felt the nudge that I should extend my contract by ten days. On the first day of my extended contract, I walked in on a colleague of mine shortly after she had attempted suicide. I sat with her for a few hours as we talked through the suicide attempt and then got her over to mental health for follow-up. As I sat with her and was silently praying, I felt Jesus was sitting with us, and I felt him whisper to me, "This is why I wanted you to stay." It was a holy and humble moment.

Another event weighed on my heart that summer as one of the new recruits that I was responsible for came forward in tears and confessed to his staff that he had been raped before coming onto the course. Every night he would wake up silently screaming as he had nightmares of the assault. He was afraid to shower and was afraid of being alone with his fellow course mates. I brought him over to the clinic to be tested and then over to the military police where he could give an official statement. The Military Police could put a case together and then forward all the statements onto the city police in the boy's home city where the event took place. I sat with him for several hours as he tearfully recounted the events of the night that his innocence was stolen from him. Even one of the MPs who were helping with the interview wiped a tear away as she listened. I was so proud of this boy, for having more courage than I had when a similar thing had happened to me. I had told no one. I had never reported it, and who knows if that neighborhood boy did the same thing to others. As I sat listening to the young soldier tell his story, I couldn't help but think that he was like that young boy in the Bible, up against a giant, with nothing but a few smooth stones in his pocket and a slingshot.

My work in the army that summer was great, and I knew I was there for a reason—but it left me emotionally exhausted. I moved straight from that contract into a marathon speaking engagement that I had committed to; fourteen messages on a wilderness canoe trip. I had spoken several times before on this trip, and it is one of the high-lights of my year—it's an amazing trip out into the wilderness of Northwestern Ontario, canoeing across some of the most beautiful lakes. But it's also exhausting. Two messages a day for a week. It's heavy on the heart. And to add to the weight of the trip, as we came back into cell reception on the last night of the trip and some leaders started checking their messages, we got word that my grandmother had passed away. The next morning I gave a tearful last message and then hurried home to figure out what the plans were. I was scheduled to fly back overseas in a few days, and if I needed to change my flights for a funeral, then I wanted to know.

My family discussed things for a couple of days and in the end decided I should go back overseas as they would not have any funeral. So I left back to the FBR headquarters. I arrived at HQ, spent the weekend there getting settled and trying to get over a twelve-hour time change, and then on Monday flew to Bangladesh to meet with the Rohingya team. While I was there, I got word from back home that my family had decided that they were going to get together in Toronto for an informal funeral, but no pressure on me to go. I prayed and felt "Go." So I booked a ticket. I wrapped up the week in Bangladesh, got back on a plane and flew all the way back around the world to Canada. My body had gotten over the jet lag, and now I was turning around and flying back, this time over thirteen hours of time change. I had such a great time over the course of a few days with my family, celebrating my grandma, and also celebrating family. It was fantastic, and I was glad that I had gone. Since I was back in the country, I decided I'd pop up to my good friend Cam's wedding, and then the next morning got back on a plane and flew all the way back around the world back to the HQ.

I felt like my body was saying, "What the heck, dude?" as I crammed into another airplane seat. Breathing in the recycled cabin air and the lack of sleep for several weeks led me to come down with a bad illness. I was scheduled to hike into the jungle to help with our training camp in a few days, but I had a fever and was utterly exhausted. The hike inside is never easy, especially the first hike of the year as you get your legs back under you and try to get used to the sweltering heat and humidity again. I knew it would be a horrible hike, and I wondered if I should delay my crossing until I got stronger. I prayed and again felt, "Go." So I went. I inched my way into the jungle and barely made it to camp. By the end of the two-day hike, only about one kilometer from camp, I collapsed on the side of the mountain. I was delirious, and my heart was beating so fast. I was seeing spots and couldn't walk over ten meters before I had to stop and sit down. One of the Rangers came down and grabbed my pack from me and helped me get to the top of the hill where I could get some water and shade. I limped myself into camp, holding down the vomit, and then went and collapsed into my hammock.

Physically, I was tired and worn out. But I think what was holding me down more was how emotionally tired I was. The summer work rolled into times of joy and grief that left my heart feeling as tired as my body. I am a pretty big wimp when I get sick. Emotionally, I want someone to care for me, and when there is no one, I feel alone. For two days I lay depressed in my hammock trying to recover physically. Finally, after two days I decided I should limp down to the river for a swim. The cold water of the river would be refreshing for my sore muscles, and my achy body from the fever could use a cool down. As I walked slowly towards our swimming hole, I could see a bunch of the new Rangers playing and swimming. They looked at me curiously as I slowly eased my way into the water and stood waist-deep on the sandy bottom. One boy was laughing and climbing the rock cliffs and vines that hung down.

There is a bit of white water current that runs along one edge of our swimming hole, alongside a small cliff face. If you swim hard through the rapids, you can reach out and grab a rock underwater and pull yourself up onto the cliff face. The boys were playing a game where one person would hold out their hand into the middle of the rapid water and try to catch the others as they floated by. I signaled to the boy, who had been climbing the vines, that I was going to swim over. I gestured with my hands that I would reach out, and he should grab my hand and pull me up onto the rock ledge. He seemed to understand my charades and nodded his head and smiled. I swam upstream a bit, then dove into the current and swam hard towards him. He reached out his hand, grabbed mine, and pulled me up laughing. I climbed out of the water and smiled and sat next to him.

They all were laughing and curious about this big white guy who had invaded their game. I tried to speak to him in English, but he understood nothing. I then tried a little Karen, but he still didn't understand. I tried to figure out where he was from and what his name was. In the end, I started gesturing like I was a monkey, and eventually they got it and shouted the word in their language for monkey: "Yo! Yo!" they shouted in laughter. I pointed at my little buddy and said, "Yo!" and he howled with laughter. He pointed at me and said, "Deshet," and all his friends died laughing. Then he scampered up the cliff face and dove off into the rapids. We spent the next hour playing this game of catch in the rapids and jumping off the cliffs. I felt a small spark of life in my heart as I laughed alongside these young Rangers.

That year we had the biggest Ranger class in our history; over 160 Rangers that we were training. Once they get into their uniforms, and shave their heads, they all kind of look the same. It always takes me a few weeks before I recognize different people and faces when I look into the crowd of Rangers. But now I had one face that I could recognize, my little friend the monkey. I later found out that his name was Beh Reh and he was Karenni. At first, our relationship consisted of us walking by each other throughout the day, and I would whisper "Yo" as I passed, and he would whisper back, "Deshet," and then we'd both walk away laughing. Whenever I would wander by a classroom, I would scan the faces until I found his. He was always looking back at me, waiting until I found him in the crowd, and then he would laugh. I found out that Beh Reh lived in a refugee camp along the Burma/Thai border, and between him and his teammates they spoke a little bit of Thai. With our limited knowledge of Thai, we could communicate a little, enough for me to invite them to hike to a nearby waterfall with me on the weekend. They weren't sure what I was trying to say to them, but they agreed.

On Sunday, when the Rangers have a free day, I got Beh and

some of his friends and we hiked out of camp. I knew there was a waterfall somewhere out there. I had been before a few years earlier, and I knew the general direction of it. We walked and walked for nearly an hour. We hiked and bushwhacked in the tropical sun until I had to admit to them I was lost. They laughed at me, and we headed back to camp to swim in the swimming hole again. The next Sunday we repeated the adventure to find the waterfall, and again I got us lost. On the third Sunday, after having asked for some better directions from some locals, I felt confident I would find the waterfall. Again, we hiked for nearly an hour. Again, I got us lost in the jungle. Again, they laughed at me. Along the way, Beh found a small stream, and they all pointed and laughed, "Waterfall! Waterfall!" they said as they howled with laughter. We stopped to take a selfie next to the waterfall.

My friendship with Beh grew over the weeks that I was at camp. We would constantly play hide and seek in the crowd or make faces at each other. He was shy and wasn't sure what to make of having a friend who was a big white guy. We couldn't speak the same language and couldn't talk to each other. One afternoon I had gone for a run over the mountain during afternoon PT. When I came back, I looked around at the other groups doing PT, playing our game of trying to find Beh in the crowd. I couldn't see him. I went over to where they were doing hand to hand fighting, but he wasn't there either. I wondered where he was. Finally, one of his teammates could see that I was looking for Beh, and pointed over to a small platform on the hill. I could see two people laying on the platform sleeping. "Lazy teenager!" I thought as I walked over to him. I gave him a little kick and said, "Beh, what are you doing?" He moaned and rolled over. Just then they blew the whistle, signaling the end of PT and that everyone needed to line up for roll call. I kicked Beh again, "It's time to get up." I said. He slowly got to his feet, and I helped him down off the platform. He walked slowly towards roll call and was leaning into me more than normal as I walked beside him. About halfway across the PT field, he suddenly collapsed.

I wasn't sure what to do, but my body reacted quicker than I could think things through. I scooped him up into my arms and started to walk quickly towards our medic hut. He writhed in pain and was yelling as we hurried across the field. A few of his teammates saw what had happened and were quickly at my side, talking to him, trying to figure out what was going on. We got to the medics. I threw a bunch of stuff off a table and flopped Beh onto the wooden table. He tossed and turned in pain, holding his stomach. The medics tried to figure out what was wrong with him, but the pain level was too high for them to get any answers out of him. They decided he needed to go across to the Jungle School of Medicine.

This time his teammates helped me pick him up and carry him across the river to where we had our main clinic. The medics went to work treating him right away. The sun was setting as we arrived at the clinic, and the solar hadn't charged enough that day for lights. Without hesitating, the medics all flipped on their headlamps and started to put an IV into Beh's arm. At this point, Beh had thrown up from the pain and was moaning and crying. They gave him fluids and pain medication and started him on some antibiotics. After about half an hour, the pain medicine seemed to kick in, the pain eased off, and Beh went into a daze. I had been sitting next to him the whole time. When they had put the needle in his arm for the IV, he had turned his face to look away. He saw me sitting next to him and reached out and grabbed my hand. He hadn't let go the whole time they were treating him.

Now that he was stable and the pain was under control, I wondered what I should do. Do I sit there and hold his hand for a while? I was still in my PT clothes, wet with sweat and dirt. Beh seemed to be asleep, so I let go of his hand and ran back across to my house where I could have a quick shower and change clothes. I hurried back to him, where he was still sleeping. I brought some food and drinks for him, and he woke up as I set them down beside him. I sat with him for a few hours, the medics coming in to check on him occasionally. He was lying on the hard wooden floor of the clinic and had a blanket rolled up under his head as a pillow. The IV was still dripping fluids into him, and if he moved too much, I could tell by the wincing on his face that he was still in pain. It was getting late, and I wondered if I should head back to my house to sleep soon. I wasn't sure what was appropriate in the situation. I wasn't sure where I should be or what I should do. I prayed with him and then stood up to go. I gestured that I would go back to sleep, and then come back tomorrow.

He didn't say anything but looked up at me. Then slowly he lifted his head, slid the rolled-up blanket out from under his head and then pointed at me, and then pointed at the blanket. He was gesturing for me to stay with him. My heart broke. I looked down at the hard wooden floor I'd be sleeping on, and nodded to him. I lay back down next to him. Eventually, the medics came in and gave us another blanket to lie on and one for warmth. I stayed all night with Beh, helping him with his IV bag a few times as he needed to go to the toilet during the night. The medics would come in every few hours to record his vitals. They weren't sure if he had a twisted bowel, appendicitis, or a stone. They were giving him medicine that they were hoping would work, and each time they took his vitals, the medic would close their eyes and say a short, silent prayer for him. It was beautiful to watch.

I spent most of the next day at the clinic with him and then a second night beside him. On the third day, the medics released him. They still weren't sure what had caused his pain, but he seemed to be better. I gathered up his stuff, and we slowly walked back to the other side of camp together. I helped him settle back into his dorm and said another prayer for him. He smiled at me and nodded. I told him to rest while I went to PT and that I would check on him later. He silently nodded again.

I headed down to the PT field, and it didn't take long to sense that something had changed. All of his Karenni teammates that he had come to training with were all staring at me. I didn't know what to make of it, except that it made me slightly uncomfortable at first. I wondered if I had done something wrong or made a cultural error. But as I would catch their eyes throughout the PT session, they would hold my gaze and then nod their heads. Slowly I realized they were saying thank you. There was a strange shift in the group that I can't understand or put words to, but it was as if they had silently accepted me as one of their own, as part of their tribe. I had taken care of one of their own and showed a level of love and care that had resonated with them. I did not know that this was the beginning of a long series of adventures with Beh and this Karenni team.

Beh eventually returned to full strength, and we would go back to laughing and joking with each other. Our bond seemed stronger than before. The time came when I had to return to HQ and say goodbye to Beh. I was sad to be leaving. Beh seemed sad too. He came up to me one day and handed me a folded-up piece of paper. I unfolded it, and there was a letter he had written to me. He had found someone who could speak English, and he told them what to write. He said, "I want to say to my brother, thank you so much. Because of my brother, he makes me happy and gives me a smooth smile, and takes care of me every time. And then, I was so happy when stay with me dear brother. I think after my dear brother leave from here I will miss you. But I will pray for to meet with you my brother again." I had tears in my eyes as I read the letter. We had never been able to communicate with each other using actual words up until now. These words that he had written to me, his thoughts translated into words on paper, his feelings as a teenager towards his new "brother," were amazing to read.

I suddenly felt like the words weren't only from Beh, but also from God. Coming into camp this year, I was feeling lonely and burned out. I needed a friend and someone to care for and to care for me. After the hospital, Beh would find me at some point almost every day, and come up and give me a big hug. These hugs from him slowly cared for my own heart and soul. Being loved. Being cared for. Not being alone. I hadn't realized how much I needed a hug, but Jesus knew, so he sent me a little brother. After the hospital, it seemed that

Beh had adopted me as his big brother. It felt like it had been a long time since I had felt cared for in my life. And I had never thought that Jesus could care for me. He seemed too busy with widows and orphans and bigger problems than to care for me. But he helped me see this new category to experience him in, in being loved. Being accepted into the tribe of Beh's team, into their group, was unlike any team I had been on before. They were now always watching me, making sure I was safe, comfortable and cared for. And because I was so emotionally tired, I didn't have enough strength to act like I humbly didn't need to be cared for. So, I received it. I received Beh's little hugs each day, and I would smile and squeeze him tight. I could feel the love of Jesus in each hug, caring for my heart. Beh would smile, whisper "Deshet" and then run off.

On the day I was leaving camp, I was saying my goodbyes to everyone before I started the hike back to HQ. My heart was full; it felt restored, and I felt sad to be leaving. There were many people coming up to say goodbye, but I kept scanning the faces, looking for my little Monkey friend. Eventually I saw him, standing shyly at the back of the crowd, trying to avoid making eye contact with me. I walked through the crowd over to him and held his shoulder and looked him in the eye. "I have to go now, brother. But I will do whatever I can to see you again." He didn't understand my words, but he understood my glassy eyes. I could see that he didn't want to say goodbye and that if this lasted too long, he'd probably shed a tear, which would be embarrassing in front of all these people. I pulled him in for a long goodbye hug. He squeezed me tight. I whispered in his ear, "Yo," and he whispered back, "Deshet!" I smiled and turned to go. I walked up next to one of our guides, and we started to make our way out of camp. I asked him, "Hey, do you know what the word, Deshet, means?" He grinned, knowing that was the name Beh had given me after I had called him monkey. "Yes brother, I know what it means." He said back to me, "It means elephant!"

I laughed and wiped a tear from my eye before it had time to slip out into public. "The Monkey and the Elephant," I thought. Perfect.

As I thought back on the story of Beh, as I walked, I realized it wasn't a story about a young Karenni boy becoming my brother, it was about a God who became my Father. Opening myself up to receiving love allowed me to experience the fathering that God had for my tired heart. This young Karenni boy was just the conduit of that love and the lessons were just getting started.

Chapter 11

Language

The year was 1999. I was fifteen years old, and my family had been living in Chiang Mai, Thailand, for just over a year. Dave Eubank had made frequent trips to the border region and into neighboring Burma to help people being displaced by heavy fighting. Tens of thousands of people had fled across the border into Thailand the year before—Karen, Karenni, and Shan—all seeking refuge in makeshift camps inside Thailand. The Free Burma Rangers didn't technically exist at this point. It was just Dave with his vision to go and help people. The name and structure would come soon, but for now it was just Dave trying to help as many people as he could. His wife, Karen, also wanted to help and was inspired by the second half of the verse in John 10:10. The first half of the verse seemed evident to people in Burma: "The thief comes to steal, kill and destroy." But she wanted to do something to remind people of the second part of the verse where Jesus contrasts the evil in the world with His purpose: "...but I have come that they may have abundant life." She wanted to remind the kids especially, who were caught in this war zone, that there is a good life available to them, so she started the Good Life Club. Her first project was to record some stories of good life, stories that demonstrated human rights, and fun dramas onto cassette tapes, and then distribute them along with cassette players into all the refugee camps. She wanted the voice of a young teenager in one of her dramas, and somehow I volunteered to do it.

We spent two days in a recording studio recording the stories and dramas. It was fun, but I didn't know the bigger picture I was involved in, or the bigger picture God had for my future with FBR. A few months after we finished recording, the tapes had been edited, produced, and finally delivered. Dave was planning a trip into the refugee camps to deliver the tapes, and he invited me to come along. Knowing what I know now about the situation, I have no idea why my parents let me go, but they did. The Karenni had fled by the thousands into Thailand and had settled into five main refugee camps. We were going to visit Karenni Camp 5, somewhere in the jungle outside Mae Hong Son, Thailand.

I remember clearly the drive up in the back of Dave's truck. The fearful and timid youth I was was immediately intimidated and afraid of Dave. To put it lightly, he is intense. We would drive along the road, making small talk and telling stories, and suddenly he would pull the truck over, get out of the driver's seat, and start running. Without saying anything, he would disappear into the fog of the mountain roads, leaving those of us in his truck wondering what he was doing. Ten or twenty minutes later he would reappear, get back into the truck, and keep driving as if nothing had happened, carrying on the conversation or story right where he had left off. A few hours more and he would again pull over, jog to the front of the truck, do fifty or a hundred push-ups, and then get back in and carry on. I had never seen anyone with this level of intensity before—and maybe since. When Dave wasn't running off into the fog, he would tell us stories of his work along the border. At one point he said, "I was with a guy and we were running from the Burma Army. He stepped on a landmine and blew his legs off. I put him into a garbage bag and put him right on my back seat where you're sitting now and drove him to a nearby clinic." For a young guy who was afraid of everything, these stories blew my mind. I was nearly paralyzed with fear before we even got to the refugee camp, and from there things only got worse.

We walked through the camp when we finally arrived after several hours of off-roading. Dave walked me to the edge of the refugee camp and pointed to a trail leading into the jungle and said, "If the Burma Army is going to come and attack the camp, they will come down this trail." He wasn't trying to create fear; he was matter-of-factly explaining the situation, but I gulped as I looked down the dark narrow trail, picturing every war scene I'd ever seen in movies. Later, they brought us to a big log at the edge of the camp. It was soaked red with blood. "They found a Burmese spy in the camp a few days ago and executed him here," Dave said to me.

There comes a point when your mind stops participating in the reality you're in and instead goes into a fog. At this point, my brain went into that fog and stopped taking anything new in. That night when we slept in the bamboo hut, I lay awake listening for the Burma Army coming through the jungle. Every time a camp dog would bark, my eyes would open wide, and my imagination could see the Burma Army slowly sneaking into the camp with their guns and machetes drawn.

We spent a couple of days at the camp. We handed out lots of rice and food and Bibles and supplies, as well as the cassettes I had been a part of making. The Burma Army never came while we were there, and after a few sleepless nights in the camp, we returned to Mae Hong Son. I had never been more relieved to be going home. A few weeks later I saw Dave at church, and he came over to say hi to me. He slapped me on the back and said, "Good job on that trip, man," and then as he started to walk away he casually added, "I just got word the Burma Army burned that camp down. Too bad, but I'll head back up there soon." This time I could picture the faces of the people I had met, people I had photos with, having to flee into the jungle as the Burma Army burned the camp down behind them. My brain didn't know how to process it, but it also didn't know how to forget.

Fast forward twenty years. I had been working with the Free Burma Rangers for five years, and I was driving a truck up to Mae Hong Son to sneak into a Karenni refugee camp. I had finished an incredible few months at camp, where I had met Beh Reh, and then gone on a mission with him and the Karenni team, leading my first real FBR jungle mission. When we all said our goodbyes, I had promised him I would try to come and see him at his home in the refugee camp. I was now making good on that promise.

It had been years since I had driven the road to Mae Hong Son, the same road as twenty years ago. As I drove, I remembered the young fifteen-year-old in the back of Dave's truck, remembered Dave disappearing into the mist on a run. Since then, I had befriended the Karenni, and they had adopted me into their group. It wasn't until that drive up to the camp that it clicked in my mind that all those years ago the first and only ethnic group I met was Karenni. The refugee camp I was going to, now called Camp 1, was outside Mae Hong Son, maybe not far from the very place I went twenty years earlier. It all seemed too surreal and ordained for my brain to fully comprehend, but I knew I was where God wanted me to be.

We had organized with Beh Reh and Htwar Reh to meet in a small Thai town called Nai Soi, about thirty minutes outside of Mae Hong Son. Nai Soi is the last town before the refugee camp. I had never been there before, and when I asked Htwar where we should meet him, he replied, "Don't worry, we'll find you." So I drove into the town slowly, all the way down the main road until I got to a dead end. I turned my big truck around on the narrow lane and slowly made my way back down the road, wondering what I should do. Suddenly a gang of motorcycles, maybe a dozen strong, came buzzing by me, two, three, or four people crammed onto the little scooters, all smiling and waving and laughing—all our Karenni ranger team, Beh leading the charge.

Beh and Htwar took me to meet the Karenni General in charge of the camps. I shared a bit about FBR, and then he wrote me a letter giving me permission to be in the camp. As the sun started to set, we got on motorcycles and made our way to the camp through bumpy jungle trails. I was on the back of Beh's motorcycle, taking in the adventure of it all, and I said a simple prayer, "Lord, let this become familiar. Let this one day feel normal." In my heart, I was referencing my feelings towards Bangladesh and the Rohingya refugee camps. A place that had seemed so crazy and foreign to me on my first visit now felt normal after over a dozen visits. So as we bumped and weaved our way along the dirt trail in the jungle to avoid the checkpoints, I prayed, "Lord, let this become normal." And He was faithful to answer my prayer.

A few months later, and after nearly ten trips into the Karenni camp, I couldn't help but feel at home as I made regular trips up to Mae Hong Son. I would land at the airport, and Beh and a couple of others were there waiting. After quick hugs, we'd jump onto the motorcycles, me driving one, and they on the others, and then what followed was like a dance. I knew exactly when I needed to lead them, and then I knew exactly when they needed to lead me. They are refugees and not allowed in the main town, not allowed at the airport, and had snuck through or around a few checkpoints to meet me. So as we drove the now familiar roads back towards camp, it was my turn to lead. Here I was legal, so I would cautiously approach the checkpoints and they followed at a distance. If the checkpoint was manned or I got stopped, they would go another way. But if I gave them the predetermined signal, they'd know it's all good, and we'd all proceed. Then as we entered Nai Soi, I would know, "Now it's their turn to lead." No words needed. Now we were entering the area where they were legal and I was not. We'd turn off the main road onto a dirt trail, and I'd smile, because adventures happen on dirt trails. We'd weave our way to a random house, stop while we waited for the sun to dip behind the mountain, and then we'd get back onto the motorcycles, this time I'd be a passenger on the back, and we'd start to make our way towards the camp, sneaking me in. The road familiar. My heart smiling and full.

We'd cut through a jungle trail, yelling to passing motorists, "Is the checkpoint manned?" and then, like before, my bike would slowly let the others cautiously approach the checkpoint—then a hand in the air, meaning it's all good to go, and we'd zoom into the camp. Like a dance, we could anticipate each other's moves, following and leading as needed, no need for words, and it was all beautiful.

I've lived more of my life outside of Canada than in Canada, and that means for most of my life I have lived in a place where I don't speak the main language. Our motorcycle dance with the Karenni was beautiful, and as our friendship grew, we were able to interpret each other without the need for language. The only one on the entire Karenni team who could speak any English was Htwar, but it never stopped us from being able to communicate. On this trip we were preparing for a mission. I spent a few days in the camp as we gathered supplies, before we moved to the border area to a Karenni army base, to wait for our security team to meet us, and then I was going to step off onto a mission with this new Karenni team. The thing about this mission was I was going alone. No other foreigners. No other English speakers. And we didn't know how long the mission would take—a month, maybe more. I was afraid for a lot of reasons. I doubted my ability to lead a jungle mission on my own. The last time I had KLLS with me, a seasoned expert. This time I only had Htwar, who had only finished his ranger training a few months before. He had no idea what he was doing, and neither did I. Combine that with having no one to talk to, no one who understands your culture, no one to bounce ideas off of or vent to, and I was worried I had made a big mistake.

Before I left for the mission, I was talking to Jesse at the HQ. Jesse has done many missions, and I assumed he had done them at some point on his own. "Other than a few short ones, a couple of days here and there, I've always been with other foreigners," he told me. I was surprised, thinking it was normal to at some point go on your own, but was starting to realize it was going to be much harder than I thought. And then we began the hardest mission I had ever done to that point.

Our first move on the mission was a four-day walk. Long days. Hot days. We would get up around 3:00 a.m. to cook rice, tear down camp, and then start walking before the sun had even come up. And then we'd walk and walk and walk. Sometimes up to fourteen hours a day. And we were bushwhacking for a lot of it. Bushwhacking in the jungle is maybe one of the worst things to do. The jungle is so thick and entangled, it's like a wall of vines and plants and trees. As you hack your way through with your machete, you're constantly scraped and cut by the sharp vines webbed all around you. The Karenni, who are at least a foot shorter than I am, would often lead the way, hacking a trail, but this meant I would have to crouch, duck, or even crawl a lot of the time. And my pack was heavy. For four days we would not pass any villages; we would not get any resupply of food; we had to carry it all with us, along with our own gear and our team gear. Each time I would drop onto my hands and knees and squeeze my way under a fallen tree and then get back up, my body would ache.

We had to pass below a Burma Army camp at one point. They were up on top of the mountain, and we were wading in the river far below. We walked for hours in the river. At first, the cool water seemed refreshing as we crossed the river once or twice. But then, as we got closer to where the Burma Army camp was, we had to wade in the river, about knee deep, for hours. The bottom of the river was football-sized rocks, and my feet were constantly searching for a solid place to plant themselves. Blisters had long since formed and popped on the back of my feet, and as we waded in the river, silt from the river bottom was stirred up in the water, eventually settling into my socks and shoes, creating a fine sandpaper between my blister and the back of my shoe. Each step was excruciating. Sweat poured off of me as we inched our way along the map in the scorching heat of the April sun. It was hot season, with the temperature going up to 100 degrees, and that also meant burning season, when farmers would burn their crops and the air quality would be unbreathable. Yet, we trudged on.

That night as we set up camp, tying our hammocks to bamboo near the river, I sat defeated on a rock, soaking my feet in the river. Beh wandered over, seeing the look on my face, and then looked at the sad state of my feet, noticing the oozing red blisters on the back of each foot. He motioned with his hand to "wait" and then ran off to his backpack. A few seconds later he returned with a small unlabeled jar. He squatted down in the water, taking my feet in his hands. He splashed some water over my feet, cleaning any bits of sand off of them, and then drying them with his dirty t-shirt. He then opened the small jar. Inside was some sort of homemade balm, which he scooped out onto his finger. In my mind, the only balm I had ever seen the ethnics use was like Tiger Balm, or some version of an icy-hot muscle relaxant. Before my mind could process the idea of Beh rubbing Tiger Balm into my open bleeding blisters, he jabbed his finger right into the blister, confirming what I had feared. The icy-hot balm scorched unbelievable pain through my foot. I yelled and tried to pull my foot away. Beh held on tightly, and kept rubbing and massaging the balm into the open wound. Then repeated the process on the other foot. I thought he was crazy, but at the same time I knew he was trying his best to take care of me. When his torture ended, I limped off to my hammock and didn't move until I was woken the next morning.

It was still dark except for the orange glow of fires and head-lamps. The team had already been up for at least an hour, cooking breakfast, but like the sun, I hadn't fully woken up to any of it. In the dark, I fumbled for my headlamp and rolled out of my hammock. Every inch of my body felt sore and tired as my mind scanned my aching body until it got to my feet. The pain from my blisters was gone. I shone my light down on my heels, and much to my surprise, the blister was nearly completely healed. I poked at the new skin. It was firm and hard, and not painful. I couldn't believe it.

That next day brought more of the same. Bushwhacking, fording rivers, up and down mountains, and crawling through the jungle. My legs were scraped and bleeding, and my sweat would sting as it poured down into the open cuts. I started to wonder, "Why am I doing this?" It wasn't the sort of slightly sarcastic question I would ask out of displeasure, but rather it seemed to be a genuine curiosity as to my purpose there. I knew what lay ahead on this mission: village programs, medical programs, kids' programs, maybe a small food distribution or service project, a recon of the Burma Army, interviews of human rights violations. I wondered, "Is that worth all this? Is that worth risking my life for?" I walked along in silence, having no one to talk to anyway, thinking about the mission. It's nice to be able to do a medical program and treat sick people, but I felt it wasn't enough. It's nice to be able to make the kids laugh and do a Good Life Club program in the village, helping them forget for a moment they're in the war zone, but it also didn't feel like it was enough. It's also good to shine a light on what the Burma Army is doing and get the news out about the situation there, but it too seemed to fall short. "So what is enough? What is worth all this effort and risk?" I wondered.

I chewed on that thought for the next two days as we made our way closer to our mission area. The thought bothered me, and I was sad not to have another English speaker there to bounce my thoughts off of. So I decided I'd bounce my thoughts off Jesus. As I walked through the jungle, I quietly prayed and asked Jesus what is enough to risk my life for. As I walked along, taking in the beauty of the river and the jungle, one word popped into my head, and as soon as the word came, I knew it was the reason. I knew it was enough. That word was "gospel."

If I walked all that way but didn't share the gospel, it wouldn't be enough. If I treated sick people and healed their bodies, but didn't share the gospel of Jesus, it wouldn't be enough. If I spent this entire month, day and night, with this team of young Karenni men, but didn't share the gospel with them, it would be a waste. If we shone a light on the Burma Army, but didn't share the gospel, it wouldn't be enough. The only thing worth risking my life for, that was worth walking all that way, all that pain and suffering, was the gospel of Jesus.

It seemed in that moment my legs and feet were strengthened, my heart rate slowed and dropped out of my ears, and my mind cleared. A new mission was unfolding in front of me; a new purpose for being there was being presented. I sensed Jesus walking with us on that mission, and I sensed the entire plan: that first visit to the Karenni over twenty years ago, the meeting with Beh, our brother-hood, the connection with this team, all of it had a purpose—the gospel of Jesus. I felt buoyed by this new purpose for my place on that team, and knowing Jesus was there, the loneliness I was feeling started to leave. "Ok Jesus," I said in my heart, "I will share the gospel." But then in my mind I tried to think how I would clearly describe the gospel to the Karenni, especially without language.

One thing I've learned from all the years living in a place where I don't speak the language, and making friends, sometimes amazing friendships, with people I can't even speak with, is that love comes before language. Just look at a newborn baby. They can't talk, but they know who Mom and Dad are. They know the people who love them, and then they eventually learn the language that comes from that love. It happens as we make new friends, often bonding over an experience or adventure together, a common goal or place where hearts are bound and beating for the same purpose. Before the words, love comes. And think of God and his relationship to us. The Creator, who made the whole heaven and earth and all that is in it, who is pure and perfect and righteous, and who created us, loves us before we even have the words to describe or respond to that love.

Mankind chose a path of sin; we chose a path apart from the Creator, a path to make ourselves into gods. But at the end of the day, we are each accountable to God, whether you believe in God or not, whether you are an atheist, or a Karenni Buddhist or animist, it makes no difference to the truth, that when we die, the story and actions of our hearts and lives will be held to account by the Creator God. And if our lives don't measure up to his righteous and perfect standard, which I can assure you, and the Bible would confirm, that they won't, and mine surely doesn't, then there will be hell to pay, quite literally.

But the Creator loved us first, before we had the words to describe that love. He loved us before we were formed from the dirt; he loved us when we lived a life separated from him, and he loved us so much that he formulated a plan to bring us back into perfect relationship with him. The cross of Jesus. He sent his son to be a once and final sacrifice for sin, for our separation. And when Jesus conquered death and rose from the dead, confirming he was the Christ, he offered a path back to the Creator. It's only through Jesus. And it's our job to respond to that good news. As love covers a multitude of sin, as love restores us to God, slowly the language of our response comes next, "Forgive me, Jesus. I give you my life."

Love always comes before language. When you can't speak the same language, you learn to read each other's faces, bodies, moods, eyes, and actions to interpret how things are going. While on mission, I would often walk behind Beh. I've often noticed that when you can't speak the same language as someone else, but you can sense their loving acceptance of you, the first thing you do is start to mimic each other. Beh and I would walk along in silence for a long time, but eventually I would tire of the silence and whistle a short tune, and then Beh would repeat it back to me, mimicking my song. We would walk, whistling a tune back and forth to each other, creating a song, creating a language, a connection. Then come simple sounds, grunts and noises that tell a story: my groan as I would stand up under the weight of my pack after crawling under a fallen tree, or a sigh as we peak a mountain and the indescribable beauty takes our breath away. The way Beh would laugh, or mimic my laugh, was creating a language to communicate with each other.

The last thing that came to us were words, only a few words, that we would begin to recognize in each other's language. The root of all the communication was love. Sometimes we would speak full sentences and thoughts to each other, knowing the other person didn't understand. Sometimes we'd be walking along and Beh would start talking to me, as if I understood everything he was saying. And other times I would have something on my heart that I wanted so badly to be able to say to Beh, so I would say it. He would look at me, wishing he understood the words, but understanding the intention of my heart as I spoke. As Beh and my friendship grew, and along with it our vocabulary, it became a reassuring place of comfort, being able to pick out Beh's sounds, his voice, his laugh, from a crowd or in the dark. Hearing everyone laughing and, right away, without sight, being able to pick out his laugh from the roar of the group, I could pinpoint exactly where he was.

I wonder if we learn God like this too.

Sometimes it might feel like God is speaking full, complete sentences and thoughts to us in a language we haven't learned yet, and we don't understand a single thing he's saying, but we sense his heart towards us. We slowly start to be able to point him out, pick out his voice from a crowded and noisy world. Hearing his laughter and knowing he's not far, we can be oriented as we get to know him. And slowly we start to learn the words of his heart, the language of his love, and we can pick out a word or two in the sentences and songs he's singing to us. The apostle Paul urged the church in Corinth to "imitate him" as he imitated Jesus (1 Cor. 4:16). And we mimic God with the responses of our lives as we learn how to communicate with him. In the Bible, it is said he sings a song over us. I wonder if the sweet song of our lives is us whistling the song back to him, answering his call with a love song.

Chapter 12

Death

I've been seeing a counselor lately. For the past couple years. There is a lot to work through in my heart and life, and a lot to process in the mission field. In the past year there have been seven deaths in my life. It seems like a lot. We know that death happens and is inevitable, and we sometimes aren't surprised by a death or two, but seven? Seven felt like too many. Seven in a year felt like "what the heck, God?"

I wasn't super close to all of them, like that little girl at JSMK that died of heart failure. I didn't know her, but I was there, and helped bury her, and I carried her loss in my heart. Others, like my grandmother, I was closer with. They were family. One of my best friends from childhood died in a skiing accident, leaving his wife and three boys behind. I spoke at his funeral when I got home to Canada, and realized that no amount of public speaking or speech writing prepares you for that. And then Zau died.

Zau Seng was one of our Kachin rangers and had been with FBR for a long time. Zau had made many trips to help people in the Middle East. After years working in Burma, the FBR mission expanded to other countries. We first were invited to Kurdistan in northern Iraq, to help the people there under oppression from ISIS. We put the invitation before God and our ethnic leaders, asking if we should go. The ethnic leaders prayed together and said, "We have lived under oppression for a long time. We know what it's like. We can help them." So we went. We would help our ethnic leaders get passports and visas, and then, those that wanted to go, we could slot them in and book them tickets to Iraq. It seems so strange when you think about it. These ethnic guys from the small villages in the hills of Burma, who are still being attacked by their own government, going to help people halfway around the world. Only God can orchestrate something like that.

Soon the mission expanded from Kurdistan to helping be part of the liberation of Mosul. My boss wrote a great book called *Do This For Love* about FBR in the battle of Mosul. Then the mission expanded again into neighboring Syria. It was on one of these missions where Zau was killed. Turkey had invaded with tanks and heavy weapons, although they were denying it to the international community. Zau, being a videographer for FBR and knowing how important it is to shine a light on what's really happening, captured video footage of Turkish tanks inside Syria.

We were able to send this footage out to news agencies all over the world. But this upset Turkey, and from what we can gather, the Turks started targeting our team with drones. In one drone strike, Zau was sitting on the ground, leaning against the tire of their vehicle when the projectile came in. Zau tried to duck and protect one of our local team members but was hit by shrapnel, probably killing him instantly. Back in his home in Kachin State, Burma, his wife was starting the celebration for their daughter's first birthday party. As Joseph, one of our Karen medics, worked on Zau, trying to bring him back to life, his phone was buzzing in his pocket, his wife sending pictures and videos of the joyous celebration of their daughter.

In another time zone, I was in the jungle of Burma, at our training camp. We were preparing for our nightly staff meeting when I got a voice message from Dave: "Zau's been hit. Pray for us. It's bad. Please pray." I went up to the home of one of our ethnic leaders. Several of our ethnic leaders were gathered there. I played the message for them. They all stopped what they were doing and we took turns praying for Zau. About an hour later we got a message that Zau was dead. We were all in shock, wiping away tears. The next day we cancelled training and held a small memorial service for Zau. Our Kachin team shared heartfelt and tearful tributes to Zau. We gave time and space for our staff and students to grieve his loss.

I had first met Zau on a mission into Kachin State. I stayed in his house, and we kidnapped his wife and took her on mission with us. I brought Zau his video camera which had been in Thailand for repairs. He was happy to get it, and after a few jokes he got on a motorcycle and zoomed off to try to find the front line with the Kachin Army.

Kachin State, which is in northern Burma, borders China to the east and north. The leaders in Kachin State had signed a ceasefire with the Burma Army that lasted for 17 years but crumbled in 2011 when the Burma Army began attacking Kachin positions to gain control of lucrative energy projects and valuable natural resources. Since then there has been heavy fighting, and consistent clashes between the Kachin Independence Army (KIA) and the Burma Army. Thousands have been forced to flee and have run all the way to the China border. The Chinese do not allow the Kachin to enter into China and build refugee camps. In times of heavy fighting or shelling from artillery, the Chinese have let some Kachin cross into China, but as soon as the shelling stops they send them back. A Kachin general once told me, "I spend fifty percent of my time worrying about Burma Army, and fifty percent worrying about China."

The Burmese control a lot of central Kachin State, and many Internally Displaced Person (IDP) camps have sprung up hugging the Chinese border. To conduct a mission to these areas is extremely dangerous. The region is caught between multiple conflicts—the Burma Army on one side, complex border dynamics on the other.

The political situation, the active fighting, and the challenges of operating in such a contested region all create layers of risk that require careful planning, constant prayer, and complete trust that God will protect us. Each mission into Kachin State means threading between threats we can see and threats we can't, bringing help, hope, and love to displaced families who have nowhere else to turn.

The Kachin people live in extremely difficult conditions. We often go in the middle of winter and Kachin State can be very cold. One IDP camp school had their roofs collapse after a heavy, wet, snowfall. We try to bring winter coats and hats for the kids in these camps, and often their only source of warmth is a fire they build in the center of their shelter, everyone sleeping around it at night. Cold baths are one thing in Karen State, but a totally new level of pain in Kachin State when you sometimes have a small layer of ice on the top of the water.

We move village to village, camp to camp, treating medical patients, holding kids programs with sometimes 600 kids in attendance, trying to encourage and love the Kachin people. We face threats from multiple directions, but we don't let fear stop us. We have a motto at FBR that we don't want to be led by comfort, fear, or pride. This is never more true than when you know the risks but go anyway, trusting God's protection with every step.

There is a rhythm to life and to death in the jungle. Death isn't something we're surprised by, but that doesn't make it any easier when it comes. When you live in an area where there is a war going on, you know that death is always a possibility, a reality, but it still doesn't make it any less painful when someone you care about dies. I had to make peace with the fact that I could die, or end up in a Chinese prison, when I go on missions in Kachin State.

I've learned that you can't plan for every eventuality. You can't plan for every possible scenario. You have to trust God. You have to trust that he will protect you, and if he doesn't, then you trust that he has a plan. I've learned that you can't live in fear. You have to live in faith. You have to believe that God is in control, and that he has a plan, even when you can't see it.

Dave's father says he always prays, "Lord, I want to be in the right place, at the right time, doing the will of God." And as much as I don't understand it, I believe that's what Zau was doing when he was killed in Syria. I don't know or understand God's timing, or the way he lets things happen, but I do know that Zau was walking with God when he chose to go to Syria.

So we pray, and if we all feel in our hearts God is saying "go", then we go and leave fear and comfort and our pride behind.

On my first mission to Kachin State I met Naw Kham, one of our Kachin Rangers. Naw Kham wasn't the most amazing Ranger, he wasn't the most handsome, and wasn't the most talented. He didn't stand in the spotlight leading the programs like other rangers. Sometimes he would rather be in the kitchen preparing our next meal. But for some reason, maybe stronger than I've ever felt it before, I sensed God urging me to support Naw Kham financially. I had never done that before, and I didn't have much money to support myself, but I kept having this urge that I was supposed to be involved in his life.

He and I never talked much on the mission and never spent much time together, so I was confused about this feeling God had put in my heart. I asked God to confirm it, and the feeling to support him remained steady. I asked God how much I should support him, and right away felt like I should send him $50 every month for the next year. It may not seem like much but on my meager income, it felt like a generous offering to him—but I remembered something my boss always said: "If its God's idea, then he'll pay for it. If it's your idea, then you get to pay for it."

Toward the end of the mission I called Naw Kham aside, and with one of our translators, asked him about his story. Naw Kham's father was a soldier with the KIA, and had been killed when Naw Kham was twelve years old – died in battle with the Burma Army. His older brother was also a soldier in the KIA, serving on the front lines. Naw Kham stayed home to take care of his aging mother and his younger sister. I asked him how much money he earns each month to support them. He said (the equivalent of) $50 a month.

Then I told him that God had put it on my heart that I should support him, and for the next twelve months, I was going to send him $50 a month, doubling his monthly income. He could use it for whatever he wanted. There were no strings attached. He seemed shocked and confused as the translator explained this to him, but then his face turned to a look of shame. He lowered his gaze and said through the translator, "Teacher, thank you, but you have the wrong person. You cannot give a gift like this to me. I am not perfect." His words broke my heart. "I am not perfect." It was a sentiment I could strongly relate to. Naw Kham went on and explained that he smokes, and drinks, and sometimes even sleeps with his girlfriend, and he reiterated to me that he is not perfect.

I lifted his gaze so his eyes met mine and I said, "My brother, I am not perfect either, but Jesus gives me this undeserving gift of grace every single day. Nothing I do deserves God's generous mercy towards me, and many times my actions seem only to slap his face, but he still gives of his love and mercy to me so generously. And it's with that, and in that, and because of that, that you are absolutely the right not-perfect person for this." His eyes filled with tears as the translator explained this to him. The downcast look of shame slowly lost its grip and hope glimmered in his eyes and smile. He shook my hand and said thank you.

So each month, for the next twelve months, I sent Naw Kham a money transfer through Western Union, and each month I would remind him that God's love and grace is undeserving, and pray a blessing over him. And each month I would learn more about him, and more about his family. He would send me pictures of his mother and sister and his home in the IDP camp. And after the twelve months finished, I prayed and asked God, "Should I continue or stop?" and sensed God saying, "Another twelve months." And after that twelve months came and went, I asked again, "What should I do, God?" and sensed his response, "Until I tell you to stop." And so, each month, I check in with my Kachin brother. I get to be a part of his life, and each month as I deposit money into his account, God deposits joy into my heart for this relationship.

Naw Kham and I have done several missions together in Karen State, and in Kachin State. I helped Naw Kham get a passport and then he was anxious to use it, so I flew him to Thailand and arranged English lessons for him for a few weeks. Naw Kham never became perfect, and neither did I, but each month, we're both reminded of our generous God.

When Naw Kham asked me to help support his little sister's wedding, it felt like an honor to do it, and I shared so much in his joy as he watched his sister get married. And then when his mother got sick, he again reached out to me. The hospital bills were piling up and he had no money to pay them. He was thinking he would have to sell his family farm, and I could sense he was worried sick about his mother. I told him not to worry about the hospital bills. The first round of bills was nearly $1,000, but I paid it for him. They released her back to her home, but she didn't get better. After a week at home he brought her back to the hospital, and again the bills started to pile up. I didn't want him to have to worry about money. I only wanted him to focus on his mother's health. I told him I would take care of it.

Our FBR HQ staff boldly jumped in to help him when I was out of money. Within a few hours of telling his situation to our staff we had more than enough money to cover her next round of treatment. Each time I would transfer him money, I could sense he was overwhelmed by the generosity of it all. Just as I am overwhelmed when I think of the generosity of grace that God gives me. It makes no sense, and I'm totally undeserving of such lavish generosity, and yet, like sunlight, I get more and more each day.

The last round of treatment for Naw Kham's mother was inconclusive, so they sent her home again to see what would happen. A few days later, she died. Naw Kham was crushed and I could sense his feeling of being suddenly alone. His father was gone, his brother was away with the army, his sister was married and now belonged with her husband, and Naw Kham, whose mission in life had been to care for his mom, was now alone. As I shared his joy when his sister was married, I also shared his sorrow when his mom died. I had never met her, but for the past three years I have felt adopted into their family as each month we experienced life together.

Dave told me once, "Sometimes we carry hard things and God will wash us out with tears." It feels like there have been more tears in the past year than there should be. But maybe that's part of God's way of washing us out with our tears. Dave also says often, "A person can live well with sorrow, but we can't live well with shame." I hope that's true, and I hope that each visit to my counselor, after a death or risky mission, that I am working towards living well with sorrow. To carry the lives of those I love and lost in my heart. A Ranger who died of appendicitis while on mission last year, too far from anywhere to help him. Or a young boy in the refugee camp who died from alcohol poisoning, and his cousin, a friend of mine and Ranger, asking if I can pay a few hundred dollars so they can have a funeral for him. Little bits of sorrow, reminders of the decay of the world, but hoping that through the decay, light will shine through the holes. That we can stay focused on the mission at hand, and keep moving forward, risking in the greatest way possible, risking loving other people.

Naw Kham experienced more death in his life than he should. His father and mother both died. Later he would get married himself and have a beautiful baby boy - who would later die from an unknown disease at one-year-old. Death is inevitable, but never easy. Maybe it helps to have a friend at your side when you're grieving.

Chapter 13

Broken

This morning I am hesitant to write because I have an eye problem and looking at my computer screen causes it to dilate and water. It's an injury I should get looked at, but I think fear that it's something major is stopping me. About a year ago I was hiking through the jungle out of the Karenni refugee camp when a sharp vine swung back and sliced my eyeball. It was as sharp as a razor blade and it lined up perfectly to slice a cut directly on my eye. Now every month or two it seems to get infected or irritated and acts up. It is painful when it's acting up, which in turn causes my whole head to hurt, and the constant watering and sensitivity to light makes it awkward. And thus, makes me not want to do any writing but makes me want to lie in my hammock all day feeling sorry for myself.

I am a wimp when it comes to most things, but especially when it comes to pain. It's as if my false self has a strong warning light that comes on as soon as there is the slightest sense of discomfort or pain in my life. I try to avoid pain at all costs. But pain has a way of finding us all, no matter how hard we try to avoid it. On a short mission last year I was staying on a small base next to a big river. I was overseeing our Arakan team as they were helping with some building projects.

We were putting in clean drinking water filters for an army base and a small Karen Bible college. We were also building a brand new toilet at a river checkpoint. All three projects were happening simultaneously, so I was bouncing back and forth from one project to another to help them solve problems. Our teams worked hard and we had a lot of fun as well. Within ten days we had all three projects finished. In the evenings I slept at the checkpoint with some other members of our team. We all slept on bamboo mats on the floor with no mosquito nets. I don't know if it was arrogance or forgetfulness, but I didn't take my anti-malaria medicine while I was on that short mission. None of us did. If I was going to get bit by a malaria mosquito, so would they, and they didn't seem at all concerned about it, so neither did I.

When I got back home I went out to celebrate a friend's birthday. We enjoyed some beers and great food and lots of good laughs. It was nice to be home and nice to drink a cold beer after a physical mission like that. The next morning I woke up and felt terrible. My body ached, my head hurt, everything was tired. I thought to myself, "I only had a couple beers with Mike last night, I can't have a hangover..." but it sure felt like that. So I pressed on and went to work. All day I felt like I was in a fog but it wasn't too bad. That night I went to bed exhausted but had a fitful sleep. I woke up the next morning feeling worse. "Am I getting old?" I wondered. Or, "Did I eat something bad the other night?" I struggled through the day feeling weak and unfocused. That night around the time the sun set the first fit of malaria hit me hard. I started to shake uncontrollably on my living room floor. My body convulsed and ached. All I could do was try to lie still and not vomit. I didn't know what I was ill with, but I knew it was the worst sickness I had ever had. I lay on the floor shaking for a few hours before hauling myself up to my bedroom where I shivered and sweated all night. I had to lay a towel down on my bed to sleep on. In the morning I wrung the sweat out of it.

I thought I must have a flu or picked up a bug somewhere, and that if I gave it a couple days it would pass. So for a week I fought this virus off, while still going to work every day and trying to get something done. Finally, on the seventh day of being beaten up by the virus, I was on Skype with my parents and my mother told me I needed to go to the hospital as soon as we finished the call. So, like a good son, I obeyed her orders and went to the hospital.

The nurses screened me at the door and then separated me to wait for the doctor. When the doctor eventually saw me he said he was going to run a full battery of tests for the most common illnesses in the area and hopefully we'd figure it out. After being poked and prodded a number of times I was eventually left to wait for the results. After about an hour the doctor called me back in and said to me, "You have malaria! But don't worry, you have the good kind." Up until this point I hadn't known much about malaria, nor had I known that there was a "good kind" of malaria. I thought they were all bad. And they are, and they are all potentially deadly if left untreated, but my kind of malaria is very responsive to medicine and rarely requires being admitted to the hospital. They loaded me up with pills to take throughout the day and told me to return if things got worse or in two weeks so they could test my blood again to make sure the malaria in my blood was gone.

The pills for malaria are strong and I could feel them starting to work after the first dose. I was able to play a soccer game that evening at our annual meeting. I nearly vomited a few times, and it may not have been the smartest thing to do, but I didn't want to be seen as weak. When my boss found out I had malaria he laughed and said, "Welcome to the malaria club!" I had a few more nights of convulsing on the floor that leaves your muscles aching, but then the malaria passed. On day fourteen I got my blood re-tested. Negative for malaria in the blood. The doctor warned me, "It could still be hiding out in your organs or fat cells, and might come back one day, but it's definitely not in your blood anymore." The next day I left on a mission into Karen State.

A few months after the malaria was forgotten about I ended up having an accident up in Karenni State that left me broken and stuck. I had been fighting for another mission with Beh Reh and the

Karenni team but a number of factors had delayed us. I had kept pushing and trying to find a new way. Before I get into the accident, I think it's important to be honest about my heart and my doubts about following God.

I wanted this mission badly, and I was willing to argue for it. But it seemed that no matter what I was trying to do, the doors kept closing. Selfishly, I was not paying attention to God. I wasn't putting my desire for the mission before him, and I wasn't giving myself time to sit quietly before him and listen to his idea about it. I think deep down I was afraid that if I put it before God, he would tell me not to go. And then I'd have a real dilemma on my hands, because I wanted to go. Have you ever had that conflict in your heart? Where you want something and are afraid to put it before God because what if he says no? I remember reading a book about prayer by John Eldredge and he said of listening prayer, "You're unlikely to hear a 'yes' unless you're willing to hear a 'no.'" I was unable to hear a no, and so I was pushing and trying to find every way I could to get this mission going.

Part of the delay was crossing through a provincial border checkpoint that had recently been tightened. I probed the checkpoint on my own before I went with a truck full of mission supplies. I wanted to see if there was a way to get through. As I was nearing the checkpoint, I thought, "These soldiers manning the checkpoint are out in the middle of nowhere. Maybe I should bring them some drinks and food." This is an old checkpoint trick I have learned along the way. If you start to have issues at a checkpoint, your mission changes from trying to get through the checkpoint to trying to make friends with the checkpoint soldiers. If they wave me through I would have brought the food and drinks to the refugee camp, but if they stop me and start to question me, which they did, then my mission suddenly wasn't about getting through the checkpoint, but rather it was that I drove all the way to the provincial border to bless them and give them food and drinks and tell them good job. So when they told me to park my truck and come into the office, they were surprised and confused when I started to unload cases of soda and water from the back of my truck and bring them over. Cases of noodles and cookies came next. We piled them up on the table and the leader told two of the young soldiers to go and help me unload. I made friends. We laughed, and then we posed for photos beside the donation and I prayed with them. When I got back into my truck the commander said, "You're free to go," and pointed his hand back the way I came, and then onwards to where I was hoping to go, and then shrugged and smiled.

I had made friends with this border checkpoint and I thought I was now able to make the next step to plan my mission. After a few days talking with leaders at the border about the mission plan, I returned home and kept making plans. We bought medicine and all the supplies we would need to do village programs. I loaded them into my truck and headed towards the border. I got to the provincial border checkpoint. They stopped me. I picked out one of the soldiers that was there when I stopped a week earlier and I waved at him. He recognized me, smiled, and said something to the guard at my window, who then waved me through. I thought I had outsmarted them and that I was finding a way to make this mission happen. I drove about twenty kilometers and suddenly came across another checkpoint. This was new. It wasn't here when I passed through a week ago. They stopped me. They were certain I was not going to be crossing that checkpoint. I parked my truck and went to talk to the commander. I explained that I had been given permission from the other checkpoint to come here, and that I had a truck full of medicine and supplies for people on the border. I explained that I had all the proper documents and paperwork. He refused. He said I needed permission from the Governor of the province in order to enter. He genuinely wanted to help me, but he also wasn't going to break any rules for me. We made some phone calls, and eventually I was on the phone with the aide of the Governor explaining my situation. It was a Sunday night. The aide assured me that he was not going to call the Governor at home on a Sunday night about this, but that if I wanted to go home and send him all my paperwork then he would be sure it would get on the Governor's desk for his decision within a few weeks.

A few weeks! I couldn't believe it. I felt heartbroken and angry. But after an hour of trying to talk my way across the checkpoint, it seemed it was a dead end. I had to turn around and drive home.

As I started my drive back home a mixture of feelings swirled around inside me. I was mad. I felt sorry for myself. And I was disappointed that the mission was going to be delayed again. I thought I should call Dave, my boss, to let him know what had happened. I dialed his number. He picked up. I started to explain with my sad voice what had happened and before I could even finish the story he interrupted me: "Praise God!" I was surprised by this, and then he continued, "Praise God that you were blocked at the checkpoint! God has a different and better plan!" and then he hung up.

I held the phone to my ear for a few more seconds, shocked and confused. I was not in a mood to be praising God, nor was I in the mood for some nice Christian words that didn't seem applicable to this situation. I drove onwards, towards home, his words stirring in my mind, bugging me. I remembered he and I had talked recently about trying to "praise God in all situations, good or bad." It seemed crazy and I didn't want to do it. But I aimed my heart towards God and prayed, "Father, Jesus, Spirit, I don't understand this situation and I don't know why we were blocked, and I don't feel much like praising you, but I will. I praise you, God. I know you are good. I trust you. I praise you, God. I worship you, God." And slowly, the words started to melt my heart. My heart softened towards God. I noticed I was blaming God for not being the magic genie I hoped he would be when I was praying to him at the checkpoint. Praising God in the middle of chaos and confusion disarmed my anger and selfishness. I had been driving home with my tail between my legs, that my genius plan had failed, but as I started to praise God, I didn't need to feel the shame of failure. I could rest in the hope that he has another way.

The next day I met with our team and regrouped. I wasn't ready to give up on this mission and I kept pushing for it. I knew of a secondary road I could try to use to get to our staging area. It also had checkpoints, but it was hit or miss if they were ever manned. So we decided we would put my motorcycle into the back of a truck with all the mission supplies, then a coworker would drive me and my bike. If we got stopped at the checkpoint, we would unload my motorbike and I would drive it home and he would continue because he had a resident's card for that province, so he was allowed to go. He would then continue and deliver the mission supplies and medicine and the Karenni team would go without me. That day we drove and passed seven checkpoints and not a single one was manned. I laughed that we were able to drive so freely and easily this way, but the other way was so clearly blocked. It made no sense to me.

We arrived at the staging area and unloaded all the supplies and my bike. We would leave my bike in the refugee camp until the mission finished a month from now, and then I would drive it home. I was excited that things seemed to finally be going my way and that this mission might actually happen. The Karenni team and I hiked through the camp until we were on the top of a mountain that straddled the border. We were told to make camp here for a few days or a week until we got news that the way we planned to go was open and our security team arrived to escort us. Our team came and went from the staging area but we hung out for a few days waiting. The days were hot and the nearest water source was at the bottom of the mountain. We took turns carrying water up to the top, each person doing one load per day so we had water for cooking and cleaning. Taking a bath was done down at the spring at the bottom, but I was soaked with sweat by the time I walked back up to the top. I was getting antsy to go, and I could tell that our team didn't like sitting up on top of that mountain with nothing to do.

I tried to keep the team active with jobs and mission practice and some workouts each day. One afternoon I got a group of them together and we were going to go jog along the ridge for some exercise. I ran in the front. Beh was right behind me. We were jogging down a slight hill when I looked over my shoulder to say something to Beh. At that moment my right foot went under a root that was sticking up. The root was strong and tripped me, but because of the decline of the ridge, my body weight took me flying downwards, with my knee and ankle stuck in the root. I tumbled about ten meters down the side of the hill and I instantly felt pain like I had never felt before. My shoulder was dislocated, and when Beh got to me and tried to help, thankfully it popped itself back in. But my knee and ankle were already starting to swell up, and I had scrapes all over me from the mountainside. My two fingers on my right hand were dislocated and pointing out at a strange angle. I was most concerned about my leg though. I thought my ankle could be broken.

We were about an hour by motorcycle to the refugee camp, and then at least another hour walking from there before I could get to a proper hospital. But I was on the top of the mountain and couldn't walk. Beh and the guys helped me up and carried me back to the hut I was sleeping in. I collapsed on the floor, writhing in pain. I closed the door to the hut and wept. I was afraid. What if it's broken? What if I am stuck here? I am totally illegal here. What am I going to do? And then I started to realize that this injury meant that the mission was now lost for me. I grieved the mission and felt sorry for myself.

Htwar Reh had come to check on me and after seeing the state of my knee and ankle and fingers sent someone running to find some help. A few hours later they came back and they brought over a man who looked like he had come straight out of the jungle. He was dressed in dirty, ripped, soccer shorts and flip-flops with a t-shirt that most people would have long since turned into a rag. He started to look at my ankle and knee and I asked Htwar who he was. "He's a massage therapist," was his response. I somehow doubted that. It almost seemed comical, the thought that this guy, who looked rather homeless, had undertaken any sort of professional training in massage therapy. I was wary of him. I didn't want some crazy jungle man who didn't know what he was doing to make things worse. Htwar looked at me and said, "It's going to hurt a lot, but you have to trust him and let him do it." I didn't trust him, but I trusted Htwar.

Prey Reh, one of our other team members, was there beside me and seemed concerned about my fall. Prey has a big heart and is always concerned that I am okay and comfortable. The massage therapist, whose name I never learned, started to focus his attention on my two crooked fingers. He held my hand in his, and gently held the two dislocated fingers with his other hand. His touch on the fingers was more painful than I wanted, and then he looked up into my eyes and with a quick motion popped my fingers back into place. Intense pain shot up my hand and arm. I quickly pulled my hand back from him and lay down howling in pain. Prey nervously laughed at me but then got up and ran off. A few seconds later he came back with a cup and said, "Drink this." As I put the cup to my mouth I could tell it was homemade whiskey. I could sense Prey's heart, that we had no pain medicine, but maybe the whiskey could dull the pain. I didn't argue.

After my fingers were back in place the massage therapist disappeared into the jungle. He didn't say anything, and no one questioned what he was doing. They trusted him. About half an hour later he came back with a bag full of roots and leaves and plants that he had gathered in the jungle. He boiled them in water, and then pounded them into a balm. He came back first with the boiling water, soaked a cloth in it, a t-shirt that had less holes than the filthy one he was wearing, and pressed it against my hand. I'm not sure if it was more painful him pressing against my fingers, or if the scalding from the water burning my hand hurt more. He soaked my hand thoroughly with his soup, and then repeated the process on my ankle and knee. Then he took his balm and started his massaging, first on my fingers. For half an hour he massaged them, pulled them, twisted them, slowly bent them, and massaged a finger more than I knew a finger could be massaged. Then he moved onto my ankle.

At this point my ankle was swollen. While he was gone on his jungle shopping trip I had tried to stand up. It was hard to even get to standing. My shoulder that had been dislocated couldn't bear any weight, and neither could my leg. When I finally got to standing I tried to stand on my ankle and I immediately fell over with a thud that brought Prey Reh over to check on me. I lay in a heap of self pity and pain on the floor of the hut as Prey stood in the door unsure what he should do. The pain when I had tried to stand was so instant and so strong that it buckled my other leg. That wasn't good.

The massage therapist took my ankle and began to massage it. He seemed unconcerned with me as a person, but it felt like his strong fingers were only listening to the tendons and ligaments and muscles in and around my ankle. He massaged his balm into my ankle and paid little attention to my moaning and groaning as I lay on the floor. At one point the pain was so bad that I had to sit up and grab his hands and say, "You have to stop." He looked at me without any expression on his face, took my hands off of his hands, and motioned for me to lay back down, which I slowly did, and then he went right back to torturing me.

After thirty minutes on my ankle, he repeated the process for thirty minutes on my knee. When he finished with my knee, he moved to my shoulder and tested my range of motion. I couldn't lift my arm above my shoulder, but he didn't spend time massaging it. He left it and told me not to move it. Then he said to Htwar that he would repeat the process every six hours and asked where he should sleep. Htwar pointed to the hut next to mine and he went in and lay down on the floor, no pillow, no blanket, and went to sleep. My body felt broken and beaten up. I was exhausted from his torture session and it didn't take long for me to fall asleep.

Six hours later I was woken up by Htwar. "It's time again," he said as he shone his headlamp on me. I could see through the shadow the massage therapist standing behind Htwar with a container of steaming liquid. He repeated the process: scalding hot soup, followed by an hour and a half of massaging his jungle balm into my body. He never spoke to me. He never seemed surprised or worried or fazed by my injuries. I wondered what we had interrupted him from to come and help me. He never complained or asked for anything. He focused on my injuries. He repeated his massage torture four more times, giving me six hours of reprieve between each session. After his last session he looked at Htwar and said, "He'll be fine," in Karenni, and then got up, packed his small bag, and walked off into the jungle. I never saw him again.

The next morning I woke up and, much to my surprise, the pain and swelling had gone down a lot. The guys cut me a piece of bamboo to use as a walking stick and I was able to hobble around our camp. I couldn't believe it. A few days ago I had been unable to put even the smallest bit of weight on my ankle and now I was walking, albeit with a lot of support from the bamboo pole. We stayed in place at the camp for a few more days. Htwar and the guys took turns making a jungle soup and soaking my injuries in it a few times a day. Then we made an extraction plan. I would need to walk down the mountain to get to the motorcycle trail. Then I'd need to get on the back of a motorcycle and ride back to the refugee camp. From there I would use my bamboo pole and walk over one mountain back to a small town. It usually takes an hour of hiking. And then I'd need to somehow get myself upright onto my motorcycle that I had left there, and drive myself five hours back home.

The walk down the mountainside was slow, but okay. The boys carried my pack while I hobbled along behind them. I got on the back of Htwar's motorcycle and we started our drive back towards the refugee camp. The trail was bumpy and full of ruts. At one point Htwar was trying to keep his tire from falling into a rut as we hugged the side of the mountain we were going down. Suddenly his tire slipped into the rut. He lost control of the front wheel and next thing I knew we had crashed, right onto my ankle and leg. I rolled from under the bike and rolled a few times down the side of the mountain hill. I couldn't help but laugh. The pain seemed irrelevant at that point. After a few apologies, Htwar got us back upright and we continued on our way.

From there Htwar and I walked the mountain back to the small town where we would sleep for the night. The next morning my leg was stiff but I loaded my things onto my bike and then climbed on. I took a few painkillers, and then needed to use both hands to bend my knee enough to get it into place on the foot peg. It hurt a lot to shift gears with my ankle and hurt to squeeze the clutch with my fingers, so I did most of the five-hour drive in second or third gear.

When I finally got back home I went to the hospital. The doctor seemed to think I looked like quite a mess and ordered x-rays on everything and an MRI on my shoulder. Thankfully nothing was broken, but the MRI revealed a fifty percent tear of my rotator cuff. In the end he said I had a level-four sprain in my ankle, a dislocated knee that had been put back in place almost perfectly, two dislocated fingers with a volar plate fracture in my middle finger and said it will probably be painful and swollen for a year. When my shoulder dislocated it tore my rotator cuff, which is why I had lost mobility in it. He put me in braces and bandages and told me I needed to rest for a few months. I limped outside to my motorcycle. Standing beside it I surveyed my body: my shoulder in a sling, my fingers in splints, my knees and ankles in braces. I wondered how I was going to drive my motorcycle. So I unbandaged everything there in the parking lot, shoved it all into my backpack, got on my motorcycle and drove back to the office.

It took months before I was fully recovered. I was useless in the field so I took the time to return to Canada to see family. In Alberta I went and saw an incredible physiotherapist who gave me a two-hour session for free. She created a recovery program for me and followed up with me over the next few months. It was amazing. She was so gifted as a physio, and she was also impressed when I told her about my massage therapist and his treatment in the jungle.

I don't have the theology to fully understand if God would hurt me like this on purpose in order to stop me from doing this mission. But I know he is good and loves me and if he did it's for a better reason. Months later, on the eve of my next mission, I sat before God and prayed, "Jesus, I give you permission to throw me down any mountains when I am going my way instead of your way. I don't know if this is a very good prayer or not, but I give you my yes. I give you permission. I want to walk with you. Help me walk with you." And I meant it. I'd rather tumble down a mountainside and spend months of painful rehab than charge ahead in my own selfish plans. I don't know how to reconcile all the theology of this in my head, but I know that I am where God wants me, learning the things he wants me to learn, and that walking with him, through pain and injury, he won't leave. This morning I sit with my eye painful and watering, and I realize at some point as I think about his goodness and love for me, that the watering in my eye continues, but the pain has lessened and it's tears, not water.

Chapter 14

Receiving

After that night in the tent—when I was a young teen and my neighbor assaulted me—any thought of love turned negative. It became broken, dirty, something to be ashamed of. Prior to that night, I had no memory of sexuality. That night, two things happened: shame entered my story, and my innocence vanished—along with any capacity to receive love. I locked my heart up tight. Put it away. Who knew the key would be found deep in the jungle of Burma.

I'm hunkered down this morning under a tarp in my hammock watching the rain fall around me. I am outside a small village called Tha Dah Der in northern Karen State on a mission. Thankfully it's Sunday, so we can rest today and take shelter from the rain. We'll spend a week in this village, doing a kids program, New Year's, a medical program, a run-for-relief 5k race, and a recon of a nearby Burma Army base. Yesterday I said goodbye to training camp. I had spent nearly eleven weeks there this fall for Ranger training. It was sad to leave camp. I love it there. We had a seven-hour hike through the jungle mountains to get to this village. Beh Reh had gone ahead the day before in the advance party.

Yesterday morning I was praying and asked to experience God's love and receive his love in new ways. Lately this has become a prayer I pray often when leaving for a mission: "Jesus, let me love and be loved by our team." I was the last one to leave camp, making sure that everything we needed was gone, and making sure no one was left behind. As we slowly swept through the empty camp we would find things forgotten and most of them ended up in my pack. By the time we left camp the sun was already high in the sky and I was already sweating. As my seven-hour hike dragged on and my legs started to feel tired under the heavy load of my pack, which was easily over thirty kilograms, I wondered if Beh would think to hike back and meet me.

As I peaked my last big mountain I could see the rice fields of Tha Dah Der below. One final descent and then about an hour of walking through the rice paddies and we'd be there. I was beat and ready for this hike to be over. Suddenly I saw someone running across the rice paddy below. I recognized Beh's run and outline before I could make out the details of his face. He came running over, gave me a big hug and insisted on taking my pack.

When I got to our camping spot, Beh had my hammock all set up and a tarp over it. Htwar had a fire going and was putting the finishing touches on dinner. I couldn't help but feel that these young Rangers, barely more than teenagers, were expressing love as best they could. And then the Father nudged my conscience and I had this thought: "This is my love for you."

Beh had run to meet me. I thought about the prodigal son story. How tired he must have been from his walk towards home, his muscles aching and cramping, his feet and knees sore. Like the father in the story, as soon as he saw my silhouette come up over the mountain, Beh ran to greet me. To carry my load. To give me a hug. And then to lead me home where a feast was waiting for me! A celebration of love and food and friendship and sonship. These young Karenni refugees were conduits of the Father's expression and outpouring of love for me. So this morning as I lie in my hammock and the rain falls,

I am warm and dry and thankful: for glimpses of heaven on earth, for a good good Father who runs to me. My heart drifts to other moments like this over the past years where I have felt the Father loving me in the jungle.

Last year, as I hiked back into the jungle after a summer home in Canada, I was excited to see all my ethnic friends again. I had done a number of missions in the spring and made a lot of good friends on those trips, and now, after a relaxing summer at home in Canada, I was back and heading back to see them all again. My friend PaLu came all the way across the border, volunteering to hike out to meet me. It was so great to see him. We hugged and right away started laughing and making some of the same jokes from last year's mission. I felt loved and it was great to see my friend. We hiked for an hour and then got in our boat and headed upriver. As we approached one village I sat up and looked at the shore and could see two boys squatting by the riverside. As we passed, one casually waved at me. I looked closer and realized it was my old friend Wah Shee. Wah Shee had spent a long time getting medical treatment in Thailand and I had met him and become friends with him there. He was one of my first and oldest Karen friends.

Our boat pulled into the village and Wah Shee sauntered over to me as if this was all planned. I was so happy to see him. I gave him a big hug and asked him what he was doing there. "I heard there were some foreigners crossing today and thought it might be you, so I waited by the river and checked each boat until I saw you." Amazing. Before I even had time to process this story Beh Reh and Htwar Reh came running down to the shore to meet me. "What are you guys doing here!" I said, surprised to see them. "We came to walk with you back to camp." They had walked nearly forty kilometers, over a huge mountain, just to come and greet me and walk forty kilometers back to camp with me. In Canada we sometimes drive a few hours to the airport to pick up someone or drop someone off, and I wondered if walking forty kilometers to meet someone was their equivalent to an airport pickup.

I was overwhelmed by the love I felt. It was a new thing for me, to feel loved. I felt like these young guys, my friends, were making these extravagant gestures, to say in the best way they knew how, they loved me. And the thing that was different in my heart was that I just received it. Instead of trying to justify it, or earn it, or make up for it, I gave myself permission to be loved. It was a new and foreign experience for me. It felt like new frontier, but it also felt like it was from God. That each time I would allow myself to receive love from someone, to open up a bit more of my heart, that I would be receiving the love of God.

After saying goodbye to Wah Shee, I started my forty-kilometer hike with Beh and Htwar. We were like family, reunited after many months. The conversation was easy and light and fun. As we trudged along the trail we slowly separated ourselves from the rest of our group, but we didn't mind because we had walked that trail dozens of times before and we would find our way. We got deep into conversation to distract ourselves from the steep mountains that were wreaking havoc on my legs and lungs, and eventually when we stopped for a break, we looked around, and didn't know where we were. At some point, deep in conversation, we had taken a wrong trail and we were now a bit lost. Maybe not lost. We had a general sense of where we were and where we were going, but we also thought maybe we would be adding a few extra hours onto our hike. By nightfall we made it back to the familiar trail and a house that we would often stop at. I was dead tired and we decided we'd stop for the night. We stayed in the house for the night, eating some instant noodles for dinner and laughing at their valiant attempt to come and walk with me, only to get me lost! But isn't that the best kind of love? It's an imperfect expression, their best intention, to show they loved me as best they could, and it may not have worked out perfectly or the way they imagined, but it made it better. I felt like PaLu and Wah Shee, and Beh and Htwar were all part of God's welcoming committee, welcoming me home.

On mission in Karenni State one time, we were camped on top of a mountain trying to avoid the Burma Army that had moved a platoon into the village we were outside. We camped for a few days on the mountaintop in a small patch of trees. One of the Rangers, Kee Reh, had been assigned to me as my personal security. Kee is super switched on and I trust him with my life. Kee can't speak any English at all but he never let that stop him from doing his job. In the villages I would often be swarmed by villagers, a kind of spectacle, a foreigner who had never been in their village before, often the first foreigner they had ever met in person. I would often joke that all of the white people picked their most handsome and funniest person to come and visit these villages and I was it. My joke would often fall flat despite how amusing I found it. But eventually telling jokes and being in the center of the crowd of people gets tiring and Kee could sense that. After a while he would tell people to leave and give me some space to relax. He was never rude or forceful, always did it with a smile, but he was able to read my body language that some space would be nice. In the small grove of trees hiding from the Burma Army, Kee set up his hammock not too far from mine. He wasn't directly on top of me or beside me, but from where he put his hammock I was in clear view of him. He never crowded me and he would go about his business, but I sensed that he always had his eye on me, always watching and checking to make sure that I was okay. I knew that if things suddenly got bad, Kee would be beside me in an instant, and he wouldn't leave me, no matter what the cost.

The nights on that mission, and camped out at the top of the mountain, got very cold. I would wake up around 2:00 a.m. shivering in my hammock. I would pull my blanket up over my head and curl into a ball to try to get warm and fall back asleep. One night, I was drifting in and out of sleep when suddenly I felt a blanket drape over me and hands tuck it in around me. I could hear Beh's footsteps make their way back to where he had hung his hammock not far from mine and get back in. The warmth from the extra blanket was almost instantaneous, but I also knew that it meant that Beh had given me his blanket and now had no blanket. Normally, I object to these types of sacrifices. Normally I would refuse his gift and insist that I was okay and that *he* should take *my* blanket. But in that moment I sensed Jesus' whisper in my heart: "Receive it." It's not as easy as it might sound, to receive love, but we must practice. Receiving Beh's blanket wasn't done with a selfish heart. I wasn't going to die if I didn't have a blanket. I would survive, but it was done as a spiritual practice to learn to receive the Father's love. I couldn't help but think of Peter's objection to Jesus' request to wash his feet. But I wonder what was going on in his heart as he eventually received that love from his master?

As our mission went on and the nights remained cold, there was more than one occasion when I would wake up and feel the warmth of a small fire burning beside my hammock. Kee would get out of his hammock, and without making a noise, come over to where I was sleeping in my hammock and build a fire next to me to keep me warm. What do you do with such loving gestures? No matter how locked away my heart was it seemed impossible to not let bits of healing in with each act of love that I allowed myself to receive.

I took my friend Ivo up to visit the Karenni team in the refugee camp one time. I hadn't seen the guys for a few months and was looking forward to reconnecting with them. As soon as we saw each other, it felt like family coming home. We laughed and talked and spent the weekend having adventures and celebration together. After the weekend was finished I was talking to Ivo about it and asked him what he had thought about my Karenni friends. He thought for a moment and then he said, "You were one of them." I don't know why, but that brought tears to my eyes. It was one of the best compliments I could receive. These guys who had adopted me into their lives and families and hearts, whose language I couldn't even speak, loved me and I loved them.

I have this new friend named Meh Bwe. He is from Karen State and lives in a small village a few hours walk away from our training camp. He likes to make me french fries. I'm not quite sure how it started, but somewhere along the humble beginnings of our friendship he got it in his head that all foreigners love to eat french fries. He doesn't know many foreigners. I might be the only one actually, but he may not be wrong about the french fries. So every time I see him, he runs out and borrows potatoes from someone and makes me fries. I always insist that I can eat whatever is easiest and I don't need fries, but he smiles and makes them anyway. I've learned something watching Meh Bwe make me fries. He carefully cuts all the peel off the potatoes. He makes sure that not any blemishes or bits of the peel are left. He chops them finely and in the shape of fries he has probably seen in movies. They look like they've come straight from McDonald's. Then he uses fresh oil to cook them—usually oil is recycled over and over since they have to carry it a long way from a shop to their homes. He adds salt and other seasoning and makes sure they come out perfectly golden and tasty. He never serves me leftover rice, but always makes me a fresh pot of rice. He uses soap when he washes my plate and spoon, and knows I prefer to eat with a spoon than my hand. He will never let me wash my own dishes or contribute in any way, even when I try to insist. He wants to serve me and bless me and he wants everything to be perfect. I just need to sit back and receive.

I've noticed this when I make a new ethnic friend. It's not often in their lives they get to be friends with a white person. When I show them I am interested in their lives, that I want to spend time with them, meet their families, see their homes, eat with them, they want it to be perfect. They always serve me the best cuts of meat, the best bits of the chicken.

As I was watching Meh Bwe peel the potatoes it struck me, in an almost humorous way, how Beh Reh and Htwar Reh, my Karenni friends, don't do this for me anymore. They have gotten so used to me being around them, they've stopped trying to make everything perfect for me. They let me do my own dishes. If they're cooking fish, then I'll eat it. If I want something else then I should bring it and be prepared to cook it. They still love me as much, but they are slowly treating me more and more like family instead of a guest.

This goes for times when we spend weeks on end in the jungle. In the beginning they would do everything for me. They would pick the trees for me to put my hammock up. They'd make sure others were always beside me. They would make a fire, chop and collect all the wood. They'd hunt and cook everything. But after some time, they stopped pointing out where I should sleep and let me sort it out on my own. They stopped building me a fire, because they know if I'm cold then I will get out of my hammock and build one myself. This isn't unkind of them. In fact it's the opposite. They know that if I have any hope of ever surviving in the jungle, I'm going to need to be able to do some things on my own.

On a recent mission the boys were out hunting and came back with four or five squirrels they had killed. One of the guys wandered over to me, handed me a dead squirrel by its tail, blood still dripping out of its head, and said, "This one's for you." Then walked away. I sat there in my hammock, holding the squirrel upside down by the tail wondering how on earth I was supposed to clean, cook, and even eat a squirrel. Thankfully Beh wasn't far off, and after letting me bumble around with the squirrel and fire for a while, came over, took it from me and grilled it up nicely, serving me the best bits.

The thing I learned as I watched Meh Bwe prepare my fries was that I think our relationship with God goes a little bit like this too. In the early days of my walk with God it seemed he was so close. I could hear his voice. Sense his presence. Reading scripture seems alive and exciting. My prayers seemed powerful and I saw some results. I got some freebies when it came to being delivered from bad habits or addictions. But then something happens. The relationship goes on over time, but one day God doesn't feel as close as he was in the early days. Scripture seems to be a struggle to read. My prayers feel flat and like I'm talking to the walls. And addictions, habits, and wounds take a lot of work to heal and get free from. I think it's God's way of growing us up, and it's a shame that so many people don't make it through this hard time of maturing spiritually. God doesn't want to leave us how he found us. He has this great plan for us, and he has this man or woman he wants us to become. But he knows that if we have any hope of surviving this world, and the spiritual world, we're going to need to learn to do some things on our own. We're going to need to know how to have faith and trust his goodness even when we can't feel it. We're going to need to learn to hear his voice and sense his peace in new, deeper ways. He never stops loving us, and like Kee, he's always got his eye on us and is ready to be with us if we end up in a messy situation.

We just need to be open to receiving it.

Chapter 15

Water

The river water was icy cold, and the December air was not much warmer, even in the midday sun. Only a few moments in the water and your muscles start to ache with the pain of the cold. We had to keep moving, keep swimming. It was only a training exercise, but the risk was real, and it was painful. We call it Big Swim, a two-day swimming event that combines several different skills that our Rangers have learned with water: rope bridge over the river, rappelling down the cliffside into the water, jumping from the bridge into the water, rappelling from the bridge into the water, and of course swimming back and forth across the freezing river. The actual skills aren't the hard part of the exercise. It's the fear and discomfort of the water that makes this exercise hard. They perform all the exercises throughout the day, and then repeat them again in the middle of the night, the darkness adding to the fear. When you leap off of the bridge in the middle of the night, you have to trust that the water is down there somewhere, and without warning you break into it. Headlamps and flashlights shine all across the river as the staff watch carefully to make sure they don't lose a student. Two inflatable canoes float in the water ready to respond to an injury. It is quite the scene.

Earlier that day one of the students, a female student, was struggling on the bridge rappelling. It takes courage to get yourself over the edge of the bridge, with nothing between you and the water twenty meters below. When you rappel against a rock or wall you're able to jump backwards, let some slack out so you descend and then land back on the rock, almost walking yourself down. When you remove the wall and rappel from a bridge, you don't have that ability to stabilize yourself and your rope. Sometimes as you bounce down the rope, the rope will twist into a tight spiral, and, as in the case of this young female student, if you're light enough the spiral will eventually come undone and put you into a spin.

The student was already experiencing a high degree of anxiety about the rappel, and she didn't want to be in the freezing water below. To top it off, she was not a strong swimmer. Halfway down the rope she suddenly found herself in a spin, spinning round and round faster and faster as her rope unwound her. She started screaming and maybe from the fear, or maybe from the spinning, she eventually lost consciousness and dropped into the icy waters below. As soon as her body hit the water she began convulsing.

I was the closest to her and I dove into the water and swam towards her. I was wearing a lifejacket and when I reached her, I was able to lie on my back and hold her convulsing body on top of me, trying to stabilize her and keep her head above water. I waved to the life rafts to come over. Po NaNa was in the closest boat and was on his way towards me already. When he came alongside me, I lifted the girl into the boat and climbed in behind her. I lay her down on the floor of the boat and held her head and neck in my arms, trying to stabilize them as she was still convulsing, her eyes rolling around in her head.

I looked up at PoNaNa and shouted at him, "Paddle! Paddle! Paddle!" Po NaNa looked at me, his eyes wide, and then, much to my disbelief and shock, he didn't start paddling. Instead, he quickly got up and leapt out of the boat into the water, paddle still in his hand. I looked at him in shock as he floated beside the boat, and yelled, "What are you doing!? Get back in the boat!" and motioned for him to get back into his seat. He quickly climbed back into the boat, looking lost and confused. I pointed to the shore where our JSMK medics were already waiting for us to take over the scene and said, "Paddle." This time he seemed to get it and started to paddle with all his might. It only took a few strokes of the paddle before we were at the shore and the medics quickly took the girl out of the boat and carried her to a safer spot where they could treat her. She would eventually be fine. Po NaNa and I flopped backwards in the boat. I looked at him with confusion and said, "What was that?" and with an innocent look on his face, he lifted up his hands and shrugged his shoulders and said, "Teacher, I don't know what means paddle paddle." We both lay back laughing.

There are often funny moments of slapstick at FBR. It's one of the things I love about working here. As my good friend Kawsay puts it, our teams are "crazy, but the good kind of crazy." And sometimes it's these crazy moments that we laugh about afterwards that bind us together. When we go through crazy things together, hard things, long walks, or near-death experiences, those that come along with us often find a special place in our hearts. Dave always jokes, "Keep being a wild man! I need people to go to jail with." One step ahead of the police or army, one step removed from a landmine or major accident, one step around deadly insects or animals in the jungle, one step, together. My friend Adam always jokes, "You're one jungle parasite away from your ideal bodyweight."

One of my main jobs at our training camp is teaching swimming. I spend hours in the river for the first few weeks of Ranger training. We start by evaluating the students' swimming abilities: a one means they can swim, a two means they won't drown if a boat were to flip or they had to cross a river, and a three means no ability and will drown.

We teach swimming in an area of the river running through camp that has about fifteen meters of somewhat calm waters to get people comfortable with the water. There are white water rapids that flow into this fifteen-meter stretch, and white water rapids flowing out the bottom end. Along the far wall is a small rocky cliff where the current flows the fastest, this is where I first met Beh Reh. It's not the ideal spot to teach swimming to someone with no abilities and a lot of fear, but it's all we've got, and we've been doing it here for twenty years.

One swimmer I always remember was a young Karen student named Saw OK. He was a small guy, but solid muscle. Not an ounce of fat anywhere on him. He never talked and was determined to never do anything poorly. But he was a Three. He had no swimming ability at all. When he would get into the water, he would charge forward on the sandy bottom, thrashing his arms as hard as he could, and slowly as it got deeper and his feet lost their ability to touch bottom, he would thrash along for a few strokes and then like a big boulder, go right to the bottom. On the first day of the swim training I had to dive in and lift Saw OK off the bottom of the river. When I got under the water to where he was, he seemed so calm, like he was resigned to the fact that there was nothing he could do to get to the top of the water and he'd have to sit on the bottom and wait until someone came and got him. I had my eyes open under the water and so did he. We made eye contact and the look on his face was not of panic, but rather a look wondering what took me so long. I swam around behind him, put my arms around his torso and pushed off the bottom with my legs. We shot up out of the surface of the water like a rocket. He coughed and spit and now looked more like a drowned cat, but then, once he caught his breath, he started thrashing forward again, determined to get across the fifteen meters. I swam alongside him, my hand under his chest keeping him up as he thrashed his way down the river. When he finished the fifteen-meter length he was totally exhausted. He sat on a rock in the water panting and looking defeated.

The next day I was in my house, puttering around, and suddenly

Saw OK came walking up the steps. He didn't make eye contact with me, but he reached out his arm and handed me a pink Karen bag. These are hand-sewn shoulder bags that the Karen people wear everywhere. I took the bag from him, and he looked up, his eyes almost reaching mine, and he mumbled, "Dah-bloo," which means thank you in his language, and then he turned and walked away. He was thankful after all that I had pulled him from the bottom of the river.

Saw OK and I became friends after that. Each day we'd go down to the swimming hole and he would find me in the water and wait until I made eye contact with him and gave him a short nod, signaling to him, "I'm watching you. I won't let you drown." And then he'd leap in and start thrashing his way across. It's amazing the things you can say through your eyes. It's amazing how the language of the eyes is universal and doesn't require a vocabulary, only a heart behind the eyes. As Saw OK would swim, he would fix his eyes on mine, looking nowhere else, and through my eyes, I could tell him he was doing okay, that he's got this, that I'm proud of him.

I've seen amazing stories being told through someone's eyes. Rohingya women in Bangladesh refugee camps, whose entire faces were covered in their burka, but their eyes shining through, could say so much through their eyes. They could plead, they could smile, they could thank, without any words. It makes me think of these great benedictions in the Bible where God says his face will shine upon us. It reminds me of a loving parent who puts his hands over his face, and then much to the baby's delight, says "peekaboo" as they shine their smiling eyes and face upon their beloved child. God's face shines upon us. The veil that separated us from the holy of holies, the intimate face of God, was torn in half when Jesus died on the cross, giving us full access to the face of God. No words needed. And we can behold God, beholding us, and smiling, through his eyes.

The cold water of the rivers, which often are also the place where we take our daily baths, and do our laundry, become a second home for me. I spend a lot of time around the water, and I'm thankful that I grew up on a lake and swimming is second nature to me. I still gasp and whimper when I need to take a cold bath. That first dump of water over your head and down your back is so painful. And some days, even if it's hot out, I don't want to go swimming.

There is a Karen ranger named Kwar Kwar. He's a young guy, one of our junior instructors, from 2nd Brigade. He's kind of a funny guy, a class clown, but a bit lazy at times. He and I had problems once on a mission. He was being a real pain, to the point where I called him out on it in front of the whole team, and then we didn't speak after that. That lasted almost six months and it bugged me. I don't like leaving things undone. Then one day I was walking by myself over to a small village where the car road ends to carry a load of supplies back to our camp. I was hot and thirsty but thinking how I was hoping I wouldn't have to swim for the bamboo raft. There is a big river that you have to cross about an hour outside of our camp and we have a bamboo raft tied to a thick rope that runs the span of the river. This is the same river where we do our Big Swim event every December. The raft is tied to a clip that you slide along the rope as you pull yourself, the raft, and your load across the river. Sometimes you come down to the raft and it's on your side of the river and you can hop right on and go, and other times the raft is across the river, meaning you have to swim across the river to get the raft and bring it back across.

The water was high and fast moving that day. And cold as ever. I didn't feel like swimming for the raft. I came down to the riverside and noticed two things: the first thing I noticed was that the raft was across the river, not on my side. And second, Kwar Kwar was there. He had arrived from his village, a three-day walk, to help with our training that was about to start. When he saw me he jumped up and ran over and gave me a big hug and said, "Teacher, I am so happy to see you again." Then he pulled a beer out of his backpack and said, "Sit. Drink a beer. I will swim across and get the raft for you." I didn't argue about that; I sat and enjoyed a beer while he got the raft and it seemed for a moment all was well with the world. I was also happy to see Kwar Kwar there, I thought, as I watched him swim across the river. I wanted to make things right with him and I was happy for the opportunity to spend a few months together at camp.

Once he got the raft and pulled himself back over to my side of the river he said to me, "Teacher, sit in the middle so you don't get wet and I will pull you across." So I got on the raft and we started going across. Halfway across the river he stopped pulling us, let go of the rope for a minute and turned to me. He looked at me for a moment and then said, "I am so happy to see you..." and then I could see he was starting to get emotional. I could see tears welling up in his eyes, and he looked at me and said, "In Karenni State, on the mission, I am sorry. I am sorry, teacher. I don't have the words, but please, I am so sorry...". It was a nice moment of reconciliation and closure as I received his apology. But this nice moment was cut short when out of the corner of my eye I noticed the clip the bamboo raft is attached to dangling on the rope, without any raft attached to it any longer. I quickly broke eye contact with Kwar Kwar and looked around him to see we'd somehow come untied from the clip and were now floating down river towards the big rapids.

I yelled, "Kwar Kwar!" and pointed to the rope. He turned and looked and in his limited English said, "Oh shit..." I turned around now, looking at the big white water rapids we were quickly approaching. I had enough time to put my phone into my Karen bag and then jump off into the water and swim to shore before the bamboo raft went into the rapids, smashing into pieces as it slammed into big boulders. Kwar Kwar and I swam to shore and stared for a minute in disbelief. Slowly our eyes moved from the river to each other and then we died laughing. I gave him a big wet hug and said, "I love you, brother. You are forgiven!" And he hugged me back and said, "Thank you, teacher. I am so sorry." I carried on my way to get my load, laughing out loud a few times as I replayed in my mind the slapstick of the moments that had unfolded. For some reason, the absurdity of it seemed normal and fitting for life in the jungle. The next day Kwar Kwar got his first task at camp: go and build a new bamboo raft.

I have a Ranger friend that I call AK47. His initials are AK and he's an Arakan soldier who often trains with an old AK-47 rifle, so I felt AK47 was a good nickname for him. He laughs every time I call him that. When I visited his base I called him AK47 so often that now even his commanding officer will refer to him by that name. I like coming up with nicknames for the guys, because love requires a word that belongs just to us, and I have seen AK47 be totally transformed by love this year.

The Arakan are a very serious and dedicated army. They are strict and strictly keep to rank and structure. Discipline is of the utmost importance to the Arakan. They accept no nonsense from anyone in their army. At their parade ground that I visited they have racks built along the side of the parade ground with sticks leaning in the racks. I asked what the sticks were for and learned that they use them to beat the soldiers during PT or other training. Love is never demonstrated to subordinates - the seniors may beat them but they won't show love.

This year I tried to make my home at our training camp an open place, where students felt welcomed to come visit, hang out, play a board game, and be loved. The Karenni adopted this home almost before I had arrived at camp. They knew where I would be sleeping, and already had all their stuff set up there waiting for me. But slowly other students would see them hanging out and stop by, interested in hanging out with the foreigner. But AK47 kept his distance. He would pass by my house, hearing other students inside laughing or playing games or listening to music, or drinking hot chocolate. He'd glance, but then keep walking. He didn't have a category for this type of thing, so was standoffish.

As the weeks passed at camp and we all settled into a routine and got comfortable with each other, I could see AK47 getting closer and closer to coming inside. He would stop and stand at the bottom of my steps and maybe watch, or talk to someone inside, but no matter how engrossed in the conversation, he didn't come inside, even if I invited him in. After about a week of that, he would come and sit on my steps, and after several weeks he was fully inside, playing games and laughing with the other students. I always welcomed him, but never tried to push him to come. Once he was inside, he was still shy towards me. I was seen as a leader and teacher for him, so he didn't know what to make of the fact that I was laughing and joking with the students. Slowly, with Htwar translating, I would ask a question or two to AK47, getting to know him, and showing him that I was interested in him and his life.

AK47 was only twenty years old, born in Arakan State on the western edge of Burma. He went to a Burmese school until grade eight and then said he realized he hadn't learned anything up to that point, so why continue, and dropped out. His father died when he was young, and his mother had a new boyfriend who would hit him a lot. AK47 bounced around odd jobs after that, trying to find his place in the world, and then eventually joined the Arakan Army, which is fighting daily with the Burma Army. They shipped him to their training base on the opposite side of the country in Karen State. Every year their training captain selects a handful of students to come and attend the FBR training program and he was one of the soldiers selected as part of his indoctrination as a soldier.

He had never heard of the Free Burma Rangers and wasn't sure what to expect from it. I think for AK47, and many students who attend FBR training, it is a place where they experience love in a way they have never experienced it. The staff aren't perfect at FBR, but they try to embody and demonstrate servant leadership to the students. This is not a common practice or concept among ethnic armed groups who focus on a disciplined, top-down approach to leadership. At FBR, leaders don't hit the students—for us in the West that might seem like a no-brainer, but I can assure you it is not the norm in many Asian cultures, including Burma, where discipline is often taught with a sturdy bamboo cane. To be motivated, encouraged, and disciplined without physical abuse is a new concept to many who attend FBR training. It can be disarming. And it shows that FBR is and does things differently. For AK47, who hadn't seen his family in over six years, there was something strange about attending FBR training. It was not what he was expecting. It was almost like being adopted into a new family, and he knew he liked it.

He came back a second year—requesting from his superiors to come again as an Advanced Ranger—and then slowly became friends with a crazy foreigner who wanted to know more about him and his story. Over the weeks that I was at camp I tried my best to love AK47 and all the Rangers as best I could. I often don't know what I'm doing as a leader or missionary, and I don't have an amazing skill set that transfers to the training or jungle life, so I try my best to love everyone as my skill. This is what loving the nameless, faceless people is all about.

AK47 was a great swimmer and he and I played a game during group swimming lessons. The game came about naturally, but was a great joy for me during the long hours I'd spend down in the river. In our small fifteen-meter swimming hole we'd often have thirty to fifty students swimming, or some attempt at swimming, all at the same time. They all look the same: shaved heads, green t-shirts for all the new recruits, grey shirts for the advanced, and a handful of staff scattered into the group trying to pull people off the bottom of the river. AK47 would dive under the water and swim up next to me. When he'd pop out of the water he would push me away with his legs, laugh hysterically, and then dive under the water, disappearing into the crowd. Then the game was that I would have to hunt for him. He seemed to be a master at disappearing. He'd shield himself behind other students. He'd crawl out of the water behind big boulders and hide from me, knowing I was hunting for him. I would search for him through all the students, scanning their faces, trying to find him in the crowd. Then I'd get out of the water and search along the shore for him. Sometimes I'd search for nearly ten minutes. I'd be smiling the whole time, partially amazed at how good he was at hiding, and partially because I knew he could see me from wherever he was hiding and laughing to himself as he watched me search for him. After about ten minutes he would sneak himself back into the water, swim across to the cliffs on the opposite side and climb up. He'd clap his hands twice, a sound I came to recognize from him, and I'd turn to find him dying with laughter. He'd hoot and holler and then jump into the river and disappear again. It seems silly and simple, but it was great fun and allowed AK47 and I to become friends.

One morning I was asked to lead a devotional for all the students at training. I prayed and decided to share about how Jesus, God incarnate, creator of heaven and earth, came and washed feet. I called up three students from the class of 120 and sat them on the stage. AK47 was one of them. I explained to the students that no matter how hard I try in the jungle, I can't seem to keep my feet clean. Even if I take a bath or shower, as soon as I walk five steps in my flip-flops I've got dirt on my feet again. They were never clean, no matter how hard I tried. I had a wash basin of warm water prepared, and I brought it out and then I explained that Jesus was perfect, but the lives and feet of his disciples weren't, but Jesus knelt down and washed their feet anyway. I explained that my heart is dirty like my feet. No matter how hard I try to keep it clean, and even if I ask forgiveness, it doesn't take long for it to be dirty again. But Jesus would wash my feet and my heart. I started to wash the feet of the three students. AK47 was the last. As I washed his feet, I explained through my translator to the class that sometimes we're called to love and serve people who are in a different ethnic group or religion from us. I explained that AK47 was Buddhist, and he was Arakan, while I was Canadian and Christian, but still I should love him and serve him.

As I lifted his foot out of the warm, soapy water, I placed it on my thigh where I was kneeled in front of him, to dry it off. I looked up at him and to my shock his eyes were welled up with tears and I could see lines on his face where tears had cut through the dust on his cheeks. It was as if love had broken through and reached some place that had been hidden away for a long time. I was amazed to see the power of love. AK47 couldn't fathom a leader getting on his knees in front of him, taking his dirty, gross feet, and then, with love, washing them. It was too much for this young man to handle, too much love, and it broke through to his heart. When I saw the tears on his cheeks I was taken aback. It's not in their culture, especially the Arakan, to show that kind of emotion. I stopped mid-sentence and immediately had to fight back my own tears.

Later that morning I left camp to head back to our HQ, but before I left, AK47 came up to me and gave me a big hug. He wiped away a tear as he held my embrace, and said, in English, "Bye." I told AK47 that I would come to visit him at his army base if I could.

A few months later, in a small boat, very early in the morning, I putted up to a sandy beach and parked the boat. I got out and was quickly greeted by two Arakan soldiers. They don't get many visitors to their training base. In fact, I was only the second foreigner to ever visit it. I hiked up to the base and got the formalities out of the way with the commanders of the base, and then I asked where AK47 was. We hiked all the way up to the top of the mountain where their PT ground was, and where the PT training team slept—AK47 was part of the training team. They were all still sleeping when we walked up. It was Sunday, so they were taking advantage of the free day. Their leader barked something and they all lazily rolled over and sat up. When AK47 saw me standing there, I could see he wasn't sure if he was dreaming or if it was actually true. He rubbed his eyes, his hair was a hurricane of mess, and he smiled. I smiled back and shouted, "AK47!" He climbed out of his blanket and stood up. I came over and gave him a big hug and said, "I told you I would try to come and visit you." He smiled back and wouldn't let go of me.

There are small ways to love someone: being interested in them, welcoming them, listening to their story, showing up for them, being patient and gracious towards them, pulling them off the bottom of a river when they're drowning, forgiving them, washing their feet. These small acts of unrelenting love break down hard, crusty hearts. They shine light into darkness. AK47 had an attitude that he didn't need anyone. He could survive this life on his own. He wouldn't let anyone in and he put a wall around his heart. But slowly, love broke down that wall, and it was amazing to watch these moments where he allowed himself to receive love. Where he felt safe, and comfortable, he could let his guard down, and soak in love, just receiving it. It was like his heart was taking a warm bath and wanted to stay a minute or two longer to let the warmth wrap itself around and penetrate deep inside.

Chapter 16

Name

The sun had set about an hour ago as we snuck our way into the edge of the refugee camp by headlamp and the flashlights our phones offered. The hike was harder—and hotter—than I had anticipated. I had done that hike a few times in the past but the first hike of the year is always the hardest. It wasn't until the sun was setting when I learned that my three guides had never done that hike before and didn't know the trail. Despite all the new growth after rainy season and doing it in the dark I somehow managed to find my way. I was happy, but felt stretched navigating the trail in the dark, and I was tired. Then they told me I'd have to drive my own motorcycle to the base we'd be linking up with the team at. I had done that ride on a motorcycle before as well, but only on the back, and never paying attention. Now it was dark, and I was tired, and I wasn't confident I could do it. I casually suggested we could stay in the camp for the night and go at first light if they were too tired. They weren't. Then it started raining.

My heart had felt fed and full as I had entered the old familiar roads a few hours earlier. Joyful memories with my Karenni friends came as I got closer and closer to the town near the camp. This is the checkpoint where I learned their hand signals to indicate if it was manned or not. This was the place we went night fishing and waded for a few hours up the stream catching a basket full of small fish for a midnight feast. That's the spot where I went to a birthday party in the river and my motorcycle fell over, totally submerged in the river. A few kilometers further and that's the spot we would go and drink beer and have an afternoon picnic. That's our favorite shop where the owner takes care of us and always opens up for us and cooks us something special. There's the house where we hid from the village headman when he wanted to kick me out, and up there is the big waterfall that we head to in the hot afternoons. This team had welcomed me, and they had become my friends and my family. I was happy to be back. It was always an adventure with them.

Now the rain was slow but steady, and I was shakily climbing onto a small 125cc scooter to ride the forty-minute goat trail to meet my friends, back from a mission. I did my best to keep up with the dim taillight of the bike in front of me. There were at least a dozen or more forks in the road and I had no idea which way to go. The trail was tight and overgrown. The jungle grabbed at me from the darkness like long claws reaching out to wrap around my handlebars or feet as I bounced along the trail. The rain softened the mud so my tires slid around as I worked the engine in first gear to get me up the steep mountain. I tried to see which ruts my guide put his wheels in and then tried to go into the exact same ones, assuming his experience growing up on these trails was guiding him. I prayed my usual prayer in these circumstances: "Jesus, keep me upright." Fear lurked outside of the glow of my headlight. Like the jungle I could sense its caress as I drove by. I didn't know if I was a skilled enough driver. I didn't know if the bike would get me there. I didn't know if I could do it. If I lost my way I had no idea where I was. I had to keep focused on the task at hand. Any slight distraction or lack in focus would immediately lead to a crash.

I fought off fear and distraction as I fought to keep up with the bike in front of me. There were a few points where I thought I recognized where we were: the place where Htwar crashed with me on the back and I rolled down the mountain, the place where I knew a small house was where I first ate red ants, a recognizable tree you had to duck under or it'll take your head off. Small things that were familiar in the dim glow of my headlight. At one point I sensed a great drop-off to my left and I hugged as close as I could to the right side of the trail, only watching the rear wheel of my guide's bike. Spider webs matted my hair as the spiders were out in the night making new traps in the low bushes. I didn't have time to worry about them though. I had to stay focused on staying upright.

Eventually we came over a small hill and I knew where we were. We were at the base of the mountain I had fallen from the previous spring. We pulled the bikes into a small hut where the owners came out to see what the noise was. They recognized me and smiled. I felt comfortable there. I felt at home almost. They invited me up to eat and drink with them. Normally, knowing my friends were on top of the mountain I was on, I'd feel in a hurry to go see them. But this time I wasn't. Something in me had changed. I was relaxed and in no rush. I took off my mud-caked shoes and climbed the ladder up to their house. They served me a plate of rice and some broth to season it. It wasn't delicious, but it was appropriate and what I needed. It was calories, and it was offered with a flavor of love. We sat for a few unhurried minutes trying to make a conversation but basking in the language of love, before saying goodbye and hiking up the final mountain.

I felt relieved to be back on my feet, but was soon winded as we went straight up the mountainside by headlamp. Twenty minutes later we crossed through the bamboo gate into the base and made our way to the huts. The team was all scattered around. Some sleeping in hammocks strung up. Others eating in the kitchen. Others talking on their phones after having been without cell signal for nearly a week. Slowly, as they recognized who had stumbled into their camp, the buzz of the camp grew into a celebration as we were reunited. "Rue Reh!" they would shout with joy as they would see me. Old friends.

Teammates. Brothers. As Rangers made their way out of their hammocks and came to say hi, time stopped. Eternity, it seemed, began. We laughed and drank and ate together. Guitars came out and we laughed more and sang together. I have no idea what time it was when I finally flopped onto a bamboo mat to sleep for the night. It didn't matter. I was home.

What a strange thing it seems, to feel at home sleeping on the top of a mountain, on the floor of a bamboo hut, the jungle and half a dozen young refugees all crowding around you, sometimes both a bit too close for comfort. What a strange place it is to discover love, in the midst of a war zone in Burma. What a strange group of people to see reflecting Jesus, a bunch of rough-around-the-edges teenagers who smoke and drink and swear and grew up in a refugee camp. And yet, God. I tried several attempts to finish that sentence, describing God and his higher ways, but each attempt fell short, so all I can say when it seems like I am in an impossible situation or an unbelievable place, and yet, God...

Have you ever eaten fresh mangos right off the tree? After I had my accident, Beh found a mango tree in the jungle and would climb the tree in the morning and, with a bamboo pole, knock fresh mangos from the branches down to the ground. There were so many mangos, bags full, so many that we couldn't eat them all. They were going rotten. We had an abundance. They were coming ripe, starting to turn yellow from green. We would bite into the wild mango, like eating an apple, skin and all. The sweetness, the juices, the textures and taste brought me right back to the garden of Eden. I think it's impossible to eat such a thing and not know goodness in this world— not know the abundant love and blessing of a caring Creator. Words escape me when it comes to describing the mango and why it moved me so much. Each bite felt like getting a B12 booster shot, an overdose of vitamin C, surging sweetly into your system. I think it moved me so much because it made me think of the feast that is being prepared for us in heaven. All the things I fear will be gone. My friends and brothers will be there, and we will remember each other.

We will remember our adventures, no grief or pain or shame between us. Everything that is precious to me will be there, family and pets too. And there will be an abundance of goodness, so much that even writers far greater than I have failed to be able to put words to it.

And it's in these moments of love and celebration, where time seems to stop, that we get small glimpses of eternity. For a moment, and for an eternity at the same time, it seems our hearts are full and whole. Feasting and food abounds and the mood can only be described as celebration. Campfires glow, guitars out, laughing, singing, drinking, dancing, stories, family. It's a glimpse of heaven. All things made new, a new name for us, the Bible says, written on a white stone.

"Rue Reh!" they shout as they see me, my Karenni name, bestowed on me by a Karenni General. What a beautiful thing it is to be given a name. The team calls out to me in Karenni and I hear "Rue" in the mix of words I don't understand, and I know to respond. I know they are calling me by name. Rue Reh isn't the first ethnic name I've been given. At FBR we all have animal names that we sometimes use in communications when we don't want to use our real names for security sake. But we don't get to pick our animal names. They are given to us, bestowed upon us. I was in a village in Karen State on a mission when I met the village leader. He asked what my animal name was and I told him I didn't have one. He asked me where I was from, and I replied, "Canada." He thought for a minute and said, "You will be Tah Thu Wah. It means 'white bear.' We don't have a word in Karen language for polar bear, so we will call you white bear." And thus my Karen animal name was given to me.

On a mission that I did with the Arakan, the Arakan commander took me before all his troops and in a speech full of bravado and too many compliments, he announced to his company of troops, "He came to us David Small, but he will be known as Kai Nee, which means strength of the sun." Slightly embarrassed by this name, because I am so familiar with my weaknesses, I blush each time that AK47 or any of the Arakan team calls out to me, "Kai Nee! Kai Nee!"

And then there is my brother Naw Kham up in Kachin State who adopted me into their clan. All Kachin people belong to one of several "clans," and when you meet someone new it's often asked what clan they belong to, and if they are part of the same clan as you it's almost like meeting a distant relative. You open your home to them and take care of them. Naw Kham bestowed upon me his clan name, adopting me into the family, and giving me a proper Kachin name: Lahpie David Naw. "Naw" because I am the second-born male in my family, and Lahpie is the clan name that identifies me as part of his family. And when you share a name with someone, a nickname, a clan name, an ethnic name, you also share a bond with them, a connection like that of your family. And you'd be willing to risk it all for them.

One New Year's Eve, I had crawled into my sleeping bag in my hammock. Everyone else was already asleep in their hammocks around me. I lit a candle before I got into bed. I'm not sure why, or what symbolic gesture there was behind lighting a candle, but I thought I'd like to go into the new year by candlelight, in a hammock, with Rangers snoring softly all around me.

I wasn't asleep yet when AK47 showed up to inform me that our Arakan team invited me to a late dinner. I thought it was a kind gesture for them to show to a teacher on New Year's Eve, but I was wrong. December 31st is not a night of celebration for them. Nor is it a random night to invite someone to dinner. I learned that Arakan State—on the western edge of Burma—used to be its own separate kingdom. They were invaded by the Burmans, and it was on December 31st when they lost their country, when they had to surrender to the Burmese. December 31st is known as a "black day" in their history. You don't wish an Arakan "happy new year." Instead you mourn with them.

AK47 led me through the jungle, much further and deeper than I thought. We walked quickly and quietly by headlamp: across a rice field, climbing over a fence, balancing on a bamboo log across a river, over a steep hill, deep into the jungle. The whole team was busy cooking a feast when I arrived. I was still confused about where he was taking me, and surprised by how many of them were out there so deep in the jungle. They served me a hot drink and we huddled near the fire. It was cold on this December eve. When the food was ready they also began their remembrance ceremony. It was totally dark except for a few headlamps and the glow from the fires, yet the team formed up in perfect military ranks, and then performed some of the finest drill I've ever seen. On command of their leader they snapped to attention in unison, then on the next command, as one unit, saluted and held their salute for a minute or two as we stood in silence. After they were told to stand easy there were four speeches given. They talked about the past, the present, and the future. They talked about unity and their current fight for freedom.

The all-Buddhist team requested if "Kai Nee" would end their program by praying for them and for the food. I don't know why, but the thought of losing my country and being forced to become a part of another country brought tears to my eyes. I looked at the faces of all these young Arakan soldiers. Their country was lost decades ago, and as one year folded into another, they pause to remember why they're still fighting. And the Karenni are in the same boat. What used to be known as the Kingdom of Karenni, once a vibrant country, has been lost, abdicated to the Burmese, and now caught up in a long fight for their freedom.

I think part of my candle lighting that night was for the Arakan and for the Karenni. I want to be with them. I want them to have peace and freedom for their people. I think the other part of my candle lighting was because I want more Jesus. I can feel my eyelids getting heavier and I know sleep will take me soon. But tomorrow when I wake up in a new year, I want the opening movements of my heart to be for more Jesus, more hope for the coming future I have promised to me. Hope that all things will be made new, that death is not the end of the story, we get a new name. So I light a candle for that.

These teams have given me a new name in this life, one that

symbolizes my place among them, and with that, their fight has become my fight too. Risking everything to be with them, risking jail, illness, falling from mountains, landmines and even death, I won't leave them. Because like my boss says, "Even if we die trying, we won't leave you. Because you count." You have a name that I know. We have an inside joke that only we laugh about. It's stupid, yes, but it's ours. And when the Burma Army comes again, which they will, they don't burn down your home, they burn down our home. They don't take away your freedom, they take away our freedom, because even though I can run away and get on an airplane and fly back to safe Canada, I will forever see your face in my heart and never be free of that.

The name of my past, bestowed upon me by the Deceiver, was "Shame." If there is one name that I have given power over much of my current life, it's Shame. Shame for what happened that night so many years ago in the tent, shame for my inability to break free of that identity: the identity of abused, broken, hidden, used. Shame for all those dirty little secrets that I try so hard to keep hidden, those sins that keep my heart dirty no matter how hard I try to wash it clean. We make agreements with the name Shame, and it seems easier to keep on hiding, to keep things secret, to stay in the darkness, than it does to break free and try to start a new life – one of healing and wholeness and community and light. One that comes with a new name as you cast your old name down at the feet of the devil.

We listen too often to that voice that tells us we're behind: behind in our relationship, behind in our devotions, behind in our fitness goals and behind in our life goals, we're behind in our maturing, behind in our careers and communications. That voice that is always telling you that your development is behind, your body is behind, everything is late, is the voice of Shame. And for some reason we listen. We give room to shame and fear in our lives, and there is comfort, or at least an illusion of comfort, in the life we live trapped in the refugee camp. But the name that God calls us by is not that of refugee. It's not of slave or orphan. The name that God calls you is daughter or son, beloved, forgiven, chosen, friend. You are on time.

That voice of Shame spoke to me for most of my life. It told me I needed to fear everything. It told me that everything and everyone was out to get me. It taught me the lessons of betrayal, pain, and loss. It encouraged me to make agreements to "doing it all on my own" because no one else could be relied upon to come through, especially not God. I gave so much control of my life over to Shame. I walked in so much fear. There was nothing good in me. And God has seen me at my absolute worst and never held it against me.

The names bestowed on me in this wild and crazy life—Tah Thu Wah, Kai Nee, Naw David Lahpie, Rue Reh—are, like the feasts and celebration moments we share together, only a small glimpse of the heaven we can look forward to. What an amazing feeling of belonging, of being a part of something bigger than yourself, to be given a new name. A tribal name. A name that lets you know that these people will forever feed and fight for you. You belong to them and they belong to you. You are chosen. And what will it feel like when Jesus returns and comes before you, looking you straight in the eye, taking your hand in his and putting a smooth white river stone into your hand. You open your hand and look down and see your new name etched into the stone. I don't know what yours will be, but when I look down in my mind's eye now, I read "Beloved Son" on mine. I'm sure Jesus has another name for me too. He will bestow it on me when he's ready, and I will go to pieces inside, to be chosen, selected, part of his tribe, picked proudly for the team.

And I think about the song lyrics that go, "And what a beautiful name it is, nothing compares to this, what a beautiful name it is, the name of Jesus."

Chapter 17

War

I wonder if we make coffins to keep our hands busy because we don't know what to do with our hearts. The workers empty out all the sawdust and shavings and even spend time sanding it. It seems a bit unnecessary, but at the same time totally necessary to keep the hands and mind occupied. They wrap the wooden coffin in a silver tarp. The corners are tight like a department store Christmas present, wrapped perfectly and stapled into place. It looks beautiful. As I survey the wooden box I can't help but think it's going to be too cramped. Once they put the lid on and hammer it shut, there's not going to be enough space or oxygen in there. I don't know why I think these things but it's the first thing that comes to mind. I feel a bit of panic rise up in me as I think of Saw Gay Ku's final resting place.

His body lies ten feet away. Candles burning around him. Someone has brought his plate with a full meal prepared on it. As if he is taking a nap and will wake up from this whole ordeal with quite an appetite. But he won't. He won't wake up. And I can only hope that he is feasting with Jesus now in heaven, so full of joy. But I don't know. I don't know.

I am angry towards the people who taught me first aid and CPR. It's an irrational anger, but I need to direct my feelings somewhere, and since I don't know how to process these other feelings well, I turn to anger. No one told me that CPR was so violent. When I learned CPR it was in a temperature-controlled classroom. We had nice mats to kneel on when we did our chest compressions on the dummy they so carelessly called Annie. Annie had no limbs and was clean and sterile. Annie didn't vomit into your mouth when you gave breaths. Annie's limbs didn't flop around with each compression and need to be moved and adjusted as you kneeled over her body. The room we learned in was so clean and everything I needed was right there within arm's reach. The instructor was there talking into my ear telling me what to do, and I only did enough to prove that I knew what I was doing.

They didn't tell me we would need to do compressions long after my strength has failed, long after it makes sense. They didn't tell me that we would be kneeling in vomit and blood and fluids and dirt. They didn't tell me that the casualty would most likely have soiled himself. It seems in class everyone was able to get a pat on the back and told they were able to save Annie. But that cough and gasp for air from the casualty, that thought of "Phew, it's all going to be okay. It's like TV," never came. Instead you keep doing compressions. You look around pleadingly at the eyes of the crowd that has gathered around you, desperately hoping someone will have an idea of what to do, but all the eyes confirm what you're afraid of: "It's time to stop." But you don't stop because you think "one more compression, one more breath, and then he'll cough." You think stopping is quitting on his chance of life. That if you stop too early you are giving up on him. You wish there was a doctor to take over, to tell you what to do, but there is no one. The body you're kneeling over was alive and laughing only an hour ago. Now it's cold and lifeless.

They've packed up all his things. His backpack is ready right beside him, as if he is going on a trip somewhere. His canteen is full of water, and someone's even bought him a Coke and a few cigars. His shoes are neatly put together below his feet, socks in each shoe ready to slip on, and his flip-flops side by side right next to his shoes. One of the other teams has made a sign saying he's part of their family. The other teams all follow suit and soon his body is surrounded by beautiful wreaths made from jungle flowers. Each team naming him as one of their own, as part of their family, as part of the FBR family. There is something healing about the beauty of the flowers and the wreaths. A small reminder of goodness and new life somewhere.

As the body hardens in rigor mortis, fluids start to leak out, a brownish fluid coming from his mouth and nose and ears. Students take turns all night sitting beside him and dabbing the fluid away with cotton balls. I sit beside him. I hold his hands, which are folded together over his chest. I pray that Jesus would have mercy on his animist soul. I don't know how this works, but I ask Jesus for mercy. I pray for his family who sent him here, to a training from which he won't return. I sit for a while with him, holding his rock-hard hands as if to comfort him. I keep expecting him to stir and slowly yawn and stretch and open his eyes as if he is only sick and coming out of a deep sleep; I feel that he'd be comforted to see me sitting beside him holding his hand, that he'd smile his beautiful smile at me. Like the words written on his coffin are true: "Rest In Peace," as if he's only taking a rest now. But he doesn't stir. The rise and fall of the chest, that motion we take for granted, is noticeably missing.

I think about the pronouns I use to describe him as I write, constantly having to go back and rewrite. Him. His. A man. A person. A brother. And I wonder when it shifts in my vocabulary, that he stops being a him and starts being a body. The body. The coffin. A corpse. Separate from the being, separate from the man. The coffin is finished and placed next to him.

We have laid his body in the classroom, center stage. One blanket was rolled up and given to him as a pillow, another covers his body, only his face showing. Slowly the students started to filter in. I am surprised when a group of students sit down on the stage not far from his body and start to play cards. It seems an odd time and place for a game of cards, callous almost. Students go back to their dorms and one by one bring hammocks and blankets back with them. They are going to sleep together one last night with their fallen brother. Hammocks are strung up all around the classroom, in windows and rafters. Every student is there. Then, what I can only describe as a party begins. A full celebration. It starts with us all standing and singing our Ranger song to him, and then our guitar player starts taking requests. Demoe plays his guitar with such passion and bravado, the best I've ever seen him play, only pausing momentarily to choke back tears.

A large speaker is soon brought out and loud karaoke begins and doesn't stop until 4:00 a.m. the next morning. All night we shout out the joyful choruses to our favorite songs. Movies start playing, food and drinks are brought out, campfires lit, gamers gaming on their phones, laughter, dancing, stories, running around. Everyone celebrating. Everyone smiling and laughing. Everyone takes part. It is beautiful crazy chaos. When they were ready, each student and staff would go and sit beside his body, the only relatively calm place in the room. They would light a candle, clean his face, hold his arm or hands or sit quietly keeping him company. At times the celebration was so raucous that people were tripping over his feet and legs. I know he would have laughed at that. I know he would be smiling at the whole celebration.

We gather all the students together and hold a ceremony for him the next morning. I am asked to say something, but no words come. What can you say in this moment? It seems no words will comfort. I muster to tell them I am sorry and that I love them. When everyone has had a chance to share, we lift his body into the coffin. We have to unfold his hands and force them to the side of his body so we can get the lid on. It is a tight fit. The coffin is attached to bamboo poles and on the count of three we lift together and raise him to our shoulders. I am standing in the middle, right next to a photo of him fixed to the coffin, his hopeful young eyes staring at me as the procession slowly leads us through camp. "I am sorry," I whisper to him.

We carry the coffin from one side of our camp, right through the middle, across the bridge and through the other side. We cross the river again, this time wading through the waist-deep water and then through the jungle to where some of the students have dug a hole for him. I think about the students who dug the hole, how they are often told to dig holes, but this hole was different. It wasn't for a trash pit, or a fence post, or a toilet. This hole was a grave. I wonder if it felt different, not like work to dig this hole. They picked a beautiful spot in the jungle, not far from the river that took his life.

It starts to rain as we rest the coffin on pieces of bamboo laying across the hole. We open the lid one last time, shielding his face from the rain, and place in his canteen, his backpack, and a few of his possessions. His plate of food, with the meal still on it, is placed in as well, on his stomach. We read out a proclamation from FBR, then tear the proclamation into pieces and place it in the coffin. We seal it and hammer it shut. Up until that point it seemed there was still some sort of hope that he could sit up, but with each bang of the hammer, like a gun salute, finality sinks in. Using ropes we lower the coffin into the grave and each student takes turns picking up a handful of dirt and dropping it into the hole. The wet dirt sticks to our hands like his life sticks to our hearts. We fill the hole with sand and rocks and place all the wreaths around him and a FBR flag. Then we silently make our way back through camp, each consumed with their own thoughts and feelings. And like that, it is finished. Yet my heart feels unfinished. Grief will take time.

I don't know if this is true or not, but it feels like in the West we have a fear of the dead body. Like we don't want to touch it or get too close to it, as if death was going to be somehow contagious and we might catch it if we get too close or hold his hand. But to sit for as long as needed, touching the body of our brother, is healing, a loving good-bye, if not for him, then for us. Still, in one sense, we might be right in thinking that death is contagious. Inevitably one day we'll all catch it. We don't have a choice in that. We do however get to choose how we live each day, how we pour out our love and our grief and our tears and our laughter into the lives, and souls, of those God brings in front of us, for however long he chooses.

There are some things that I don't want to write about because I don't know how to explain them and they are too scary for me to think about. To write about them means that I must experience them again and feel them again, and I hesitate in doing that because I don't want fear to have any more exposure than it needs. But this is a story about how God has taken a young wimpy boy who was afraid of everything and thrown him into a war zone to learn and grow and experience God. After Saw Gay Ku drowned in our camp swimming hole, fear invaded our camp.

I have a friend named Wilma who said to me the other day, "Your life feels like it's part of a movie." And sometimes it feels that way. It feels like I have been cast in a role in a great epic movie. I feel wildly underprepared and out of place, and yet I've been cast in this role. And sometimes, as life unfolds, the movie can seem more like a horror movie than anything else. The kind of movie that I hate to watch because I don't think we need to entertain evil or demonic ideas.

I don't have much experience with spiritual warfare or demon possession, and up until this point in the story, I hadn't paid too much attention to it. But after some of the things I have now seen, I don't know how else to explain it.

After the death and burial of Saw Gay Ku we moved on and continued training. The death was on Monday, the funeral on Tuesday, and on Wednesday morning one of our team members took some of the Ranger's possessions and started to make his way back to his home to give the possessions back to his family. On Friday, we were training as normal when suddenly I got a call on the radio that there was something happening up by our rappelling tower. I ran over to see what it was. When I came around the corner, one of our female students was standing with a circle of people around her. She was crying and moaning and yelling and pointing. Her face seemed unrecognizable. I wondered if I had seen this student before or who was she? I asked someone what happened and they said she got scared on the rappelling tower and suddenly started to have a meltdown. She started freaking out and yelling and screaming, even though she had already gone down the tower a few times. I had seen scared students before, and students who didn't want to do a certain activity, but this was different. Something else was going on here. She was pointing at all the instructors and yelling, "I hate the instructors. I am angry at the instructors." Her eyes were narrowed with a look I can only describe as evil. It was as if death itself was staring out of her eyes, trying to kill with each glance.

We brought her away from the crowd and back to her dorm to calm down. At one point it seemed that the girl we knew had returned and we asked her what happened. She said she couldn't remember anything, only that a black darkness entered her and then she doesn't remember after that. We prayed with her and when we did she jolted back into whatever was possessing her. Joseph, one of our medics, said her name and she interrupted him quickly, saying, "That isn't my name."

He responded, "That's what it says on your name tag."

With pure evil in her eyes and voice she looked him in the eye and said, "You know who I am." She started to thrash around and yell and moan. We decided to remove her from her dorm and bring her to the clinic where they could take better care of her and keep her safe.

We carried her across to the clinic and there they gave her a dose of medicine to help her relax and fall asleep. It did nothing. She kept yelling, and this time the focus of her yells and anger shifted onto the swimming staff. She kept yelling that she hated the swimming staff, myself included. They gave a second dose of the medicine. No reaction. It took five students to hold her down as she thrashed around on the floor of the clinic. Another dose of medicine, still no reaction. What should have totally knocked her out by now seemed to have no effect at all. Whatever was going on inside of her was strong and hated that we wanted to calm it down. A fourth dose of medicine was given with still no result. All night the students and medics tended to her and listened to her yelling and moaning.

One of our senior leaders came over to the clinic to help and stay with her and pray with her. He was the leader in charge the day Saw Gay Ku drowned at the start of the week. When he walked into the room her eyes fixed on him and she yelled, "Why did you let me drown? You said you would protect us, but you let me drown." I don't know how to explain it, but what I could gather was that it seemed like the spirit of the Ranger that had drowned was still hanging around and had taken hold of this girl. I don't know how to explain this kind of stuff. I had no category for it. Of course I had read about it in books and maybe seen it in Hollywood movies, but when you stand face to face with someone acting like this you try your best to reason it away and make sense of it any other way possible. But I couldn't deny that this seemed like textbook spiritual warfare.

By the next morning she seemed to exhaust herself and started to calm down. She kept pointing down to the river, nearly exactly to the location where we had buried the Ranger and saying, "Why did you leave me there? Don't leave me there." By mid-morning she drifted off to sleep. By now news of this girl's demon possession had spread around camp and the spirit of fear was having a heyday with the students. We gathered the staff together and read some scriptures, sang some hymns and prayed together. I felt that truth needed to be proclaimed in that meeting, and even though some of our staff are Buddhist and some are animist, I felt like I needed to tell them what I knew about Jesus. The animists and Buddhists wanted to make an offering to the spirit, bananas and coconuts and juice, and light some candles. Their idea was that they wanted to appease the spirit and make it calm and happy and then maybe it would go on its own. I opposed this idea and said that Jesus, and only Jesus, destroys any spirit that is not loyal to his spirit. There are no neutral spirits, spirits are either loyal to God, or rebellious. But when I invited Jesus into my heart, my personal spirit swore loyalty to God. We don't want this rebellious spirit hanging around our camp. We want it gone, destroyed, banished, and the way to do that is with the name of Jesus, boldly and loudly proclaimed. We also each had a responsibility within our own lives and hearts to cleanse our spirits, to ask forgiveness for our sins.

We walked through camp down to the swimming area where our Ranger had drowned. We sang a hymn there, read some scripture, prayed together and consecrated that river and area to God. Then we moved to the rappelling tower, climbing ropes, monkey bars, and finally classroom, repeating that process of worship, scripture, prayer and consecration. We wanted to be sure that this land and ground was holy ground. Meanwhile, across at our clinic the girl was continuing to react to anything about the Bible or Jesus and continuing to be held in tight possession by this foul spirit. I was encouraged and emboldened by our morning prayer time and thought I would go across to see the girl at the clinic.

As I walked over I rehearsed in my head everything I knew how to do. To use the name of Jesus, out loud, and command the evil spirit out. I knew about proclaiming the authority of Jesus, and that it was going to take some battling. Everything I had ever read about spiritual warfare I pulled out of the files in my brain and laid them out in my imagination to do. I walked into the clinic and as soon as I walked in, the girl, who was surrounded by other students trying to take care of her, snapped her head around and made instant eye contact with me. Her eyes were so evil. I immediately shrank. I tried to act like everything was normal and that I wasn't afraid. One of the staff came over and said, "Do you want to pray for her?"

I said, "Yeah, I will, but in a few minutes." I was afraid to get too close to her, and her death stare continued to glare at me. I stood back across the room and watched for a while and at one point I managed to whisper in the smallest voice, "Jesus come." But that was it. I left the clinic feeling defeated and ashamed at my cowardice. I had had all these big ideas and thoughts of how I would cast out the demon and save the day and do it so boldly, but then when you come eye to eye with the devil you better bring more than some daydreams of courage and Sunday school lessons. This young girl had taken the wind right out of my sails without saying a word, by the evil in her eyes. I had toppled. Whatever was inside her was not going to go away because I timidly hoped it would and because I wanted to be the hero.

The next night we gathered all of our students and staff together for a prayer service. We read the story in Mark 5 about Jesus facing off with Legion and casting the evil spirit out into the pigs. We sang a few hymns and read different scripture passages. We then opened up the room to let anyone pray who wanted to pray. A number of the staff and students took their turns praying and I finished the prayer by proclaiming Jesus' authority and dominion in the camp. It felt better to be surrounded by strong and faithful Christian staff members. I thought that of course I needed backup. I needed others to help me with this. We need to do it together as a community.

Almost as soon as we had finished our prayer service one of our staff members, and friend of mine, Htee Ku, came over to me and our chaplain and said, "I felt fear come into me. I am afraid. I don't want to sleep in my house tonight. I can't be alone." We laid hands on him and prayed for him. I prayed more boldly for him, and it helped him, but he continued to feel symptoms that we couldn't explain. He said it felt like his head was on fire, not a headache, but a burning. At one point he asked me if his eyes were bleeding. He said he felt fire burning inside of him. We brought him to our chaplain's house where we continued to pray for him and try to help him. We gave him the Bible and some scripture passages to read and he read them over and over and over, saying them out loud. Over and over, for hours, he repeated Psalm 23 to himself.

The next morning we all felt confused and exhausted. Htee Ku was still struggling, and the girl at the clinic was doing better but still having fits whenever a Christian would enter the room. We asked for prayer from our team all around Burma and the world, and encouragement, scriptures, songs, and prayers flowed in, but it still felt like we were in the middle of great battle, one I didn't know how to make sense of. That evening I got called over to the house of one of our leaders as he was trying to get the satellite phone working. I asked him what was going on. Our staff member who had gone to return the possessions of our fallen Ranger was supposed to be back by now, but wasn't. This isn't unusual. Things like that happen a lot in the jungle, but we wanted to follow up. We reached his mother, who seemed concerned. She said he was still there at home. He had gone to the animist funeral celebration, to return the items to Saw Gay Ku's family, and when he came back he wasn't himself. He was saying strange things. He couldn't control himself. He was afraid. He didn't even look like himself. He was possessed by the same spirit that was in Htee Ku and in the girl. When we got this news we stopped right there and whoever was in arm's reach we held hands and prayed.

There seemed to be a strongman in our camp. Something was happening in the unseen world around us, and we were all a little afraid. I want to say that we were all mighty warriors and cast out the spirit at the whisper of the name of Jesus, but we didn't. We bumbled our way through it. None of us wanted to admit it, but we were afraid. As I held hands with our chaplain and prayed, I sensed his fear through his soft grip. We prayed more in those days than I had ever prayed in my life. It seemed every turn someone was asking for prayer, or clearly in need of prayer, or afraid, so we prayed. We prayed at the start of every class and then praised God at the end of every class. It was the only weapon we knew how to fight with.

I started to sense that God was growing me up through this as prayers became more natural and bold. I had a steadfast assurance that God had already won, but we still needed to fight, and he was using this experience to grow some of us up. After days of praying and reading scripture over the girl, the spirit possessing her seemed to leave. She snapped out of it after a long prayer time over her and she just began to weep. She seemed exhausted and weak, but more like herself, she even looked different. She asked if she could leave training and go home, so we sent her. Htee Ku never fully recovered, he constantly seemed to struggle with fear and eventually also asked to be sent home. While the war in Burma was ramping up to new levels, we were also being trained to fight spiritual battles. This wouldn't be the last time we'd see this, and the next time we saw it we'd be better equipped to handle it.

Chapter 18

———————

IDPs

T he mosquitoes were merciless, but that seemed less important than the fact none of us were sleeping as we formed a perimeter around camp to watch and listen for a Burma Army patrol. The patrol had broken away from a larger resupply column and gotten lost in the Karen State jungle. A Karen army unit was tracking them, and the last heading had them coming directly into our camp. The Karen sent us security units, and our Rangers filled gaps in the perimeter. We all swatted at mosquitoes nervously as we waited for the Burma Army to walk into our defense.

Around 1:00 a.m. the first gunshot rang out. Not from our position, but another Karen position about 500 meters south. Our eyes widened and those with weapons gripped them tighter as we listened to the fight unfold. Machine guns opened up. A mortar round or two. Lots of small arms fire. The pop of grenades and whistle of RPG rounds echoed through our camp. Radios chattered and we sat tensely waiting to hear the outcome. The mosquitoes seemed to have disappeared—or at least we didn't care anymore. Soon we got word the Karen had ambushed the Burma Army patrol, killed a few, and the others ran south.

That night sitting beside my Ranger brothers, listening to the fight, seemed surreal. I'd trained for several years as a soldier in the Canadian Army but never deployed. This was the closest to a real gunfight I'd come, but I didn't know it was only preparing me for what was coming in the next weeks and years.

In the morning we packed up camp and checked on the nearby villagers who, the day before, had been laughing and singing at our Good Life Club program in the jungle. Then we moved to a new location.

One thing our Ranger teams do on mission is recon Burma Army camps and positions. We document them and what they're doing, to shine a light on what reality looks like in Burma. There was a mountain near our new position where we could perform a recon on the Burma Army camp, but we needed to pass through a landmine field to reach our vantage point. The mountainside around the Burma Army camp had over 400 landmines on it. We had one Karen soldier who agreed to guide us through—he'd memorized where they were.

This is crazy to me. Remember where 400 landmines are? I can hardly remember where I put my phone, let alone 400 landmines. No map, no GPS location, just this soldier's memory.

He started guiding our line through the landmine field. We couldn't talk because we were close to the Burma Army camp, so all communication had to be by hand signals. Our leader would walk through the jungle, turn to me, make the signal for a landmine, then point to the spot on the jungle floor. I was supposed to turn around and repeat that process to the person behind me, and so on down the line so each person who passed that spot knew where the mine was.

The problem is when the leader pointed to the spot, I couldn't make out anything that looked like a mine or out of the ordinary or like the dirt had ever been disturbed. The jungle floor is a tangled mess of vines, leaves, roots, rocks, and bugs. The place he pointed looked like everything else. I did my best to point to the exact spot, but as the signal passed down the line, the line and the spot being pointed to would drift until they weren't pointing at the same spot anymore.

Dave, my boss, first recognized the danger of the drift. He used a hand signal to halt our movement, then signaled me to come stand by him. When I reached his spot he whispered, "There's a mine right here"—pointing to a tangled mess of jungle floor—"I want you to straddle this mine until the last person in line has passed you. That way we can be sure the line-drift won't become a problem." He patted me on the shoulder and signaled to keep the line moving as I nodded and stood over the spot he'd pointed to.

As our team slowly passed me and saw me standing over the landmine, the absurdity of the situation dawned on me. "What the heck am I doing?!" This is crazy. This was definitely one of those moments where I wondered, "How the heck did I end up here, in the jungle of Burma, sneaking up to recon a Burma Army position, and straddling a landmine...".

I've seen many images of landmine victims. Our Ranger teams send incident reports to me almost daily, and it's not unusual for them to report on landmine victims. Landmines are horrible. If the person survives the explosion, they're a mangled mess. They usually lose a limb or two. I pass by a lot of soldiers with prosthetic limbs out in the jungle.

Landmines are not like Hollywood shows them in the movies. Ninety percent of landmines explode on contact. There's no stepping on the mine, hearing the click, then trying to figure out how to put a log or rock onto the trigger sensor so you can dive to safety. When you step on a mine, your leg is blown into a thousand pieces before you even know it. This is the information I tried to force out of my head as I stood in the jungle over one of these mines.

As the last of the team passed me, the line paused while I carefully made my way to the front to where the next mine was so I could repeat the process. "Jesus, I can't do anything here but trust you. Please guide my feet. Each footstep, I give to you. I trust you, Jesus." I prayed silently as I stood over the mines.

We made it to the vantage point and got good footage of the Burma Army camp and soldiers. The next thing we needed to be careful of was not getting seen. If the Burma Army saw us and started mortaring us, we'd need to run, trying our best to backtrack our exact footsteps through the minefield. One panicked misstep could mean stepping on a mine. I prayed again, "Jesus, blind the eyes of those who want to do me and my team harm. Help us to do good. Help us not to be foolish, but not be led by fear."

I want to live a life where if God doesn't show up, I'm hosed. I've bet it all on God being my provider and protector—literally my life—and if God doesn't show up, if God isn't who he says he will be, then I'm screwed.

When I lived in the West, God seemed like the insurance policy we deposited into every Sunday morning. The rest of the week our lives were designed around trying to meet our own needs and be our own protector. We got good jobs, made money, put money into retirement (usually more than we gave away or to God), bought toys for our pleasure, and kept a little money for a rainy day. We buy locks for our doors, fences, security systems, and video monitoring systems so we can watch our possessions anytime anywhere from our smartphones. We even buy guns to protect ourselves from fellow citizens who might be mentally unstable. Our capitalistic culture has designed our lives so we don't need God. He's just handy to have in your corner, like a good life coach.

As I move through the jungles of Burma, I'm humbled and thankful my life requires prayer. My life requires God. It's not a Sunday school or youth group lesson that sounds like a nice concept, but it's truly a requirement.

Our team continued its mission. We took an epic eight-hour motorcycle ride through a goat trail of jungle tangles to reach a village currently threatened by Burma Army. It was the hardest riding I'd ever done. The handlebars were wider than the trail and would constantly get tangled in the bushes, slashing your hands and pulling your bike either to an abrupt stop or right over into the jungle. Each time I put the bike down it seemed to get heavier to lift back up and mount again. The riding was technical—over rocks, through rivers and streams, straight up steep mountain hills, around corners so tight you'd have to lift the back end of the bike around. We'd hired local boys to help porter our supplies and teams. I was impressed by the courage and skilled riding of these young guys as we all navigated the trail together. By the end of the day we'd all become friends as we'd all helped push each other up a mountainside or lift a fallen bike off each other.

The people still remaining in the village were surprised to see us. They were in such a hard-to-reach place, a forgotten village on the edge of a Burma Army-controlled area, and it seemed to mean a lot that we'd even found them. I think some wondered if we were lost. But we weren't lost. We were exactly where we wanted to be, with the forgotten people who were about to get shot at.

We made camp for the night, hanging our hammocks near a stream and bathing in its cool waters. The cold water felt good on my exhausted muscles and cleaned the scrapes and scratches from the day's journey. The next morning we went back into the village and talked to villagers. We met with the village headman and prayed with him. I started goofing around with children gathering around watching us, making them laugh as I made faces and played simple games.

Suddenly a boom from a mortar could be heard in the distance. Eyes widened and people exchanged worried glances. The round impacted about a kilometer from us, but subsequent rounds began creeping closer. At about 400 yards the villagers decided it was close enough and began to quickly pack whatever they could carry and run into the jungle—new Internally Displaced People (IDPs). We stayed in the village as mortar rounds kept moving closer. Small arms fire could be heard as the Burma Army patrol shot randomly into the jungle to clear their path. Once we were sure no one else was in the village, our team packed up and followed the IDPs into the jungle.

Coming up the mountainside about an hour outside the village, we came across our first set of IDPs. I wish I was a better writer and could describe the feelings I had and the sights I saw as these scared villagers made shelters in the jungle. "Shelter" is an optimistic description of what they were building. Some lucky ones had a tarp they could use as shelter. Others who'd been there a week or two had collected leaves and woven a roof. But most lived on the ground—maybe some dried rice grass as a bed, or a hammock. Children roamed around and parents had a resigned look on their faces that showed this wasn't the first time they'd run for their lives.

There was a disabled boy whose grandmother was taking care of him, and an elderly woman who couldn't walk and had been carried on someone's back when they fled the mortar rounds. She lay still in a small hut they'd constructed for her. I wondered how many times she'd run over her long life. They said she was over eighty years old, and this war has been going on for over seventy years. Would she die out there on the run, hiding in the jungle?

Nearly a month later I was back at our training camp, safe in my house, when suddenly a huge rainstorm blew in. Fierce winds, torrential rains—and in the dry safety of my house I couldn't help but weep as I pictured my friends in that IDP camp, knowing some still had no tarps, no shelters, thinking how miserable it must be. My heart broke for them. I wanted to go sit outside in the rain in the middle of the storm, to share in their misery and to yell prayers into the storm for them.

We stayed with those IDPs for nearly two weeks. We did a medical program for them, checking on the elderly and sick each day, and also did a Good Life Club program to help them all laugh and forget their circumstances for a few hours. I was asked to speak at Sunday morning church with them. They set up a tarp on the ground for their church and they all gathered together—and despite the distant sound of gunfire and mortars, had a worship service in the jungle, complete with communion.

I got choked up when they passed the communion elements

around. These symbols of the body and blood of Jesus were a sign that we were family. As I sat next to my new friend San San Poe, we took the elements together, and I seemed to understand more clearly what it meant to be part of the body of Christ. San San Poe and I were connected through the sacrifice of Jesus, and as we took the cup and the bread I fought back a tear at what a powerful and beautiful symbol it was. Even there, sitting in jungle church, I felt connected to all of my friends and supporters and prayer warriors who support me back home. Those who sit in the pew at Sturgeon Alliance Church, or Lakeside Baptist, or Oromocto Baptist, or Offlake Church or City Church in Winnipeg, are connected through the blood and body of Jesus to the IDP who sits next to me. We are in this together. We are not alone.

While we were with the IDPs, we got word through the Karen security unit posted near us that the Burma Army 77th Division was moving our direction. The 77th is known as the death unit in Burma. Wherever they go, lots of killing follows. They were active in Kachin State offensives, they were part of the genocide against the Rohingya, and their reputation is that when they move in, something bad is about to happen. We began making plans for if we had to help the IDPs move again, and what kind of defense we could put up to give them time. Then suddenly we got word that the 77th had turned around and gone back to the capital. It seemed strange. We didn't understand what had happened.

The next day there was a military coup in Burma.

In the first action of the coup, Aung San Suu Kyi and most of the prominent members of parliament were snatched up and arrested in a well-organized and executed theft of power. We heard later from one of Suu Kyi's advisors that she had an idea the coup would happen and she had enough time to scribble a note on a piece of paper and hand it to her aide to pass onto a friend. The note said, "Rise up. Start the Civil Disobedience Movement (CDM)."

We said loving goodbyes to our IDP friends. We'd organized

through a donor to provide enough rice to get them through the next few months, tarps for all of them, and medicine as they needed it. As soon as I got back to camp I would begin procuring these things and getting them delivered. But for now we were heading to a secret meeting of the top Karen and Karenni leaders and politicians to discuss their response to the coup. It's not normally our place to engage in political-type meetings, but we felt if we could go and pray for the leaders while they met, it could be useful.

The meetings were interesting and fruitful. It also gave me time to head south of the meeting location to visit my old friend Wah Shee, who was about to graduate from technical college. It's always such a joy to see him. He's the most sarcastic Karen I've ever met, and he always enthusiastically greets me by saying, "Hello, brother! You are so fat!" and then pinching my love handles.

Just north of where the meetings were taking place was another set of friends. My friend AK47 and his Arakan team had a small base nearby our meeting place, and it was a sweet reunion with him too. It was amazing to have this feeling that whenever I travel around Karen State now, I know people. I run into people I know, people I love and who love me. I get to keep praying for them and encouraging them, making them smile and pointing them to Jesus. What an amazing gift this is, and there's no other way to explain the feeling except gratitude. I'm grateful for this amazing life, for these amazing friends I have across Burma, and for all the adventures we've had together as we try to bring help, hope, and love to oppressed people.

Our meetings ended and we headed straight to new IDPs that had run from Tha Dah Der over the few days we'd been in meetings. We stayed with them for a week as the Karen Army began preparing to try to take one of the Burma Army camps. We talked and prayed about whether we should stay for that. We decided we would stay for two primary reasons. First, we had highly trained medics with us, so if someone was wounded in the fighting our medics could treat them. The second reason was we could document and record the situation and show that this war was still going on.

We met with the platoon leader who was going to be responsible for the attack. They had three plans. First was to lay mines all around the Burma Army water source and cut off their ability to get water. The second was to shoot all their heavy weapons—mortars, RPGs, and machine guns—from one hillside facing the hilltop Burma Army camp. The third plan was to send one smaller unit led by a special forces sniper named NineStone around behind the hilltop to the backside and cover the flank. They would need to sneak across a Burma Army-controlled car road, behind the front line, and then come up the backside of the camp. It was a dangerous maneuver that would mean having to constantly be on alert for Burma Army.

As we were discussing the details of their plan I suddenly raised my hand and asked, "Can I go with the flanking unit across the car road?" Even as the words were leaving my mouth I wondered what I was thinking. It almost felt like someone else was talking because my brain was saying, "Are you crazy? This is stupid. This will be very dangerous. What are you doing?" My question was translated and followed by a few seconds of silence. Everyone looked at me, and then some serious discussion between the ethnic leaders and then NineStone. He looked at me and nodded.

I selected a small team of Rangers to lead on the flank mission with me. One of them was Beh, who wouldn't let me go alone.

We set out early the next morning. We would take one day to move to a hideout, do a recon of the trenches and sniper positions, and then the next day do the attack. As we moved through the jungle we stepped quietly and only spoke through glances and hand signals. Anyone who had a weapon had a round chambered and on safe, aiming it at known or potential ambush points as we silently made our way across the car road and to our sleeping spot for the night. I'd been given an AK-47 with two magazines, a hand grenade, and a 9mm sidearm by the Karen Army. I had the AK loaded and on safe as we moved. I'm a soldier. I have training in this—no experience, but at least a little training. If things go bad, I hoped and prayed my training would kick in.

The evening before the attack we were all going over our plans and kit, cleaning and oiling weapons and making sure everyone had tourniquets and QuikClot and gauze. NineStone came up to me carrying a yellow oil jug. He said, "The night before a big fight I like to have a drink of whiskey. Would you have a drink with me?" He motioned to the contents of the oil container. I agreed and he poured out some homemade rice moonshine with an oily film on top. We toasted each other, clinked our bamboo cups together, and I coughed down the liquid. It burned all the way down. He laughed and refilled my cup. We clinked our glasses together once more, I winced as it went down the hatch, and then we retired for a night's sleep.

Everything about war is violent. That may sound obvious, but maybe you've never experienced violence to that extreme in your life. Everything about it. The explosion of the rifles, always when you're not expecting it, not ready, causing your body to violently jump as fright grips you, and shame is right there instantly telling you you're a wimp for flinching. The sound of the bullet cutting through the air is violent. It rips through the sound barrier making a sound like a knife ripping through thick fabric. It seems unnatural to be able to hear and be the cause of the tearing of the sound barrier. The ghostly echoes of the explosion and trajectory of the bullet echo back off the mountain walls, coming back on you from all directions, wrapping you utterly in fear. And then if the bullet hits its target it doesn't pierce or sting or prick or cut, but it shreds. It destroys. It goes through skin, muscle, and flesh as if it weren't even there, causes bones to shatter, and then keeps going.

The soul-shaking booms of the big guns reply to the bullets. Mortars explode randomly around you, sending jagged pieces of steel whipping through the air in all directions, slashing through trees, dirt, and human bodies indiscriminately. The rockets fired out of RPGs shriek through the air as if the most ghastly demons were riding the projectile, exploding in a devilish harmony with the mortars. And what war does to the body is violent. Invisible snipers surprise the silence with their perfectly placed bullets. The target collapses to the ground before you can even hear the sound of the gun—the bullets moving faster than sound. And as you crouch in a foxhole or trench or behind a tree, your mind's eye can't help but imagine you in the sniper's crosshairs. You shudder at the thought and must force yourself not to think that way or you'll never move again. If you have to shoot back, you must stabilize your violently shaking hands and panting breath, otherwise you'll never hit anything. You can't see anything. Your targets are not clearly in front of you, but you must bob and weave your head and body around branches and trees, hoping you can spot them before they spot you.

War brings out the most violent evil of the heart of man. The perfectly crafted death weapons shouldn't be something we're proud of as humans. The technology in the weapon is never an advancement, but always a backward step, illustrating only the evil of our hearts. And even after the shooting stops and you're back in a safe place, the war continues to play in your mind. How can it not? The way a body that once was standing or running is, in an instant—an instant—no longer alive but crumpled in a pile on the ground. The way a body looks when it's been shredded by shrapnel. The insides of the body on the outside. And the ethical questions you ask yourself in the quiet moments between battles: Can I take his life? Can I kill? There's no going back from that. Can I inflict that violence upon another soul? And I can't help but know that each target at the end of the crosshairs is a soul. And while I may try to justify my place in a war zone by helping the oppressed, I know that by taking up the instrument of death I have the capacity in my heart for as much evil as the person on the other end.

I believe in the cause. As Isaiah said, to "Seek justice, help the oppressed, defend the cause of orphans, fight for the widows." Fight for them, God said. I also think about King David, who wanted to build a temple for God but wasn't allowed because he'd killed so many people in violent war. But I can't help but feel disgusted and shocked at the utter violence of the fight. At the capacity for evil within a man's heart.

Before I went into the fight this morning I prayed, "Jesus, should I shoot if it comes down to that?" And in my heart I felt the heart of Jesus say back to me, "I hate war. I hate it. But I will help you." And as I scan my memory of the countless interviews I did with the Rohingya, the unimaginable evils inflicted on them—the countless widows and orphans among them—as I think about my friends who are now IDPs hiding in the jungle from this war they didn't choose to be a part of, as I think about the lifetime of violence inflicted on people I love here in Burma, I think I could bring myself to taking the life at the other end of the crosshairs, but I hate war.

I want to cry as I write this and I know I hate that part of me that is willing to participate in the violence of war. I know if the soul at the end of my crosshairs crumples as my ears violently ring, I will forever hate a small part of me. And as the battle unfolded over hours that morning, Jesus did help me. He helped me not have to shoot. To not have to hate. And I'm alive and whole for another day. But I'm sad that tomorrow's menu could easily be more of this violence, and as long as I choose to help people here, help my friends in this war zone, then I will need to wrestle in the deepest places with this evil violence.

I spent two nights and three days with NineStone and we became friends over that time. We shared our life stories together, we shared photos of our families, we laughed together, and I got to pray with him a few times. He's animist, but as I put my arm around his shoulder and prayed for him and his platoon, and then said the Lord's Prayer together, he was able to say some of the words to the famous prayer and hugged me goodbye after we were safely back across the car road and linked up with the rest of the team. We've since stayed in touch and see each other every chance we're in the same area. Before he goes into a fight he tries to let me know so I can pray for him.

These little relationships formed throughout this war zone, with NineStone, AK47, Wah Shee, San San Poe, and the many IDPs, are the beautiful part of the job. Year after year getting to go back and see the same people, to continue to build relationships with each other, to continue to point them to Jesus and pray for them—it means something to them.

To not be forgotten means something. To stand next to a person in the worst moments of their life, means something.

Chapter 19

———

Disobedience

Each New Year I try to ask God what word or theme he has for me. At the start of 2021 the theme I sensed God had for me was "obey." One word, and it kept coming back over and over throughout the year. I want to be obedient to God, to my leaders, to those in authority over me, and to those who host me in their country. And as I softened my heart to obey God more, the Civil Disobedience Movement (CDM) began to unfold across Burma.

After the coup on February 1, many civilians stood up and protested against the military coup. The Burma Army responded the way it always does when someone stands against it—they kill. Hundreds of protesters were killed in the cities and hundreds more disappeared from their homes in the middle of the night, never to be seen again. The people in the cities began to feel what the ethnics in the mountains have felt for the past seventy years, and thousands began to flee out of the cities into ethnic-controlled areas, looking for safety and protection from the ethnic armed groups, or looking to join or get training so they could continue their fight for freedom.

An old Ranger and famous Karen leader, Htoo Htoo Lay, came to meet with Dave Eubank and our staff out at our Ranch HQ. He explained how groups of fifty or sixty protest and revolution leaders from the cities were begging him for training. He wanted to know if Free Burma Rangers would train them. We didn't know much about protests, and in Burma none of our work had been done in cities, only in the jungle and mountains. We weren't sure if it was our mission, but we prayed about it as leaders and decided we would train one group. We would not try to be something we weren't, but we would train them like we train our Rangers and focus on three key ideas: love God, love each other, never surrender. It would be the first time we trained a primarily Burman ethnic population and the first time we were involved in the CDM.

We had fifty-five Burman students arrive to attend our first training. Our training staff was the best training team I'd ever been a part of. Dave Eubank was our overall leader and was running a lot of rescues out of the cities for people being hunted by the Burma Army. I was the team leader for day-to-day team decisions and training. Adam is a former US Army soldier and has been our FBR training officer for the past eight years. Kevin is a former US Special Forces sniper and is our head FBR chaplain. Sky is a former US Marine and has worked almost every mission FBR did in the Middle East. And finally Blake, a former Navy SEAL medic and sniper, rounded off the experience of our team. I was humbled to be a part of such an amazing team while we were getting ourselves involved in a unique situation training members of the CDM.

As we were about to begin our training, the Burma Army stepped up their offensive in Karen State and began bombing with fighter jets. In their first two nights of bombing they bombed villages all around our training HQ and attempted to bomb our HQ but the bombs missed. All of my friends that live at our training HQ had now become IDPs and were hiding in caves. The town we do most of our supply shopping in had become a ghost town—the high school had been utterly destroyed by cluster bombs, as well as the clinic and the army base. Thousands of people fled the village into the jungle. They bombed the building that Dave Eubank and I had been at for our secret meetings after the coup, and hundreds of people attempted to flee across the border into nearby countries.

I was going crazy. I wanted to be at our training camp. I wanted to be with my friends hiding in the caves. We all did. Dave had to talk me down a few times, telling me that unless I can shoot down an airplane there isn't a lot I can do right now. We had to take time to pray and decide if we should continue to run the training or if we should abandon it and go north to our main training HQ. It was not an easy decision and a lot of emotion went into the conversation but in the end we decided to honor our commitment to train and then head to the HQ as soon as we were done or if it got worse. I would wake up in the nighttime and start praying for my friends who were being bombed. I longed to be with them, if for nothing else but to sit with them as the bombs fell, to hold their hands, make them smile, and pray with them. But we'd agreed to the training and when we prayed we all felt we should stay.

The training was one of the most incredible trainings I'd ever been a part of. Each team member was such a passionate man of God, and each one so experienced. Every minute we spent with the students they soaked up knowledge like sponges. They were so passionate. We shed tears together, we sang together, we did a lot of physical training together, and we learned a lot of skills together.

Midway through the training I got word from northern Karen State that one of our Rangers, and a friend of mine, had died. Baw Mu was in his mid-twenties and had suffered from an episode of epilepsy. Normally with proper treatment and medicine, available at the nearby hospital, he would recover, but since the coup the Burma Army had made it nearly impossible for people to travel from the villages into the towns to get supplies or medical help. Baw Mu died before he could even reach the hospital. I'd been with him two months earlier. We'd taken a picture together on the edge of a soccer field, and I'd asked him about his health and he told me not to worry, he was fine. Now he was dead. I cried.

Baw Mu was Buddhist—as far as I knew. He'd been a basic

Ranger, and then came back as an advanced Ranger. He'd heard the gospel message presented clearly while he was at our camp. What decision he made in his heart, I will never know, but could only pray that Jesus would have mercy on his soul. His family held a traditional Buddhist funeral for him and sent me pictures. The weight of his loss, in the light of all that had happened only a few months before at our training camp losing Saw Gay Ku, was heavy for me.

That night I was walking around camp and wandered by one of the student dorms. They were all sitting together singing. I walked in and sat down to listen. They were writing songs. It was brilliant. They were revolution songs, anthems of hope, of change, of democracy, of a future in Burma. They sang so passionately and beautifully. They fully believed in the hope in the lyrics, for a new country, a future without war. I wondered about the songs of the sixties, the famous songs the African Americans wrote about freedom, and the songs calling for an end to the Vietnam War. I wondered if one day these songs would be remembered as the songs that shaped and changed a country. Their hope buoyed my spirit.

I shared with them about Baw Mu and his death. As I was sharing I could feel a tear slip from my eye and fall from my cheek, but I wasn't looking for sympathy from them, and I wasn't intending to be dramatic. I was matter-of-factly telling them about my loss and when I finished, the guitar player, Thit Sa Lin, said something in Burmese to the group, and then started to play a beautiful song of mourning. They sang for a future hope in their country and remembered the ones who were lost in that fight.

To become a Ranger you can be a man or woman, young or old, from any religion or have no religion, as long as you can read or write in at least one language, do it out of love of your people (because we don't pay our Rangers anything), and have courage to not run when other people can't run. During Ranger trainings, one thing we do is share what we believe with them and encourage them to think about their lives in a more holistic way: body, mind, spirit. We train the body with morning PT, we train the mind as we learn new skills and information to help people better, and we train the heart and spirit by having morning devotions each morning. Usually when we start out with a new class of Rangers we don't jump straight into Jesus stories and Biblical texts. We've found that doing that usually causes the Buddhist or animist students to check out. So we start by introducing them to topics of the heart, things like courage, love, hope, peacefulness, resiliency, forgiveness, and start to slowly ask where these topics come from. Eventually we start to share our own testimonies and stories with the students and what we've come to believe, and then move into the gospel presentation.

A few days after Baw Mu's death I woke up early and he was on my mind right away. I was feeling sad that he was gone, having been laughing with him a few months before. But the images of his Buddhist funeral kept coming into my mind, his body lying in front of Buddhist monks as they performed ceremonies. I felt a burden on my heart for the students we were now teaching, that I'd come to love, and the gravity of their personal situations. Many would return home after our short training and be hunted by the Burma Army. Later we would hear stories of them crawling out of second-story windows as the Burma Army rushed up the stairs of their house, narrowly escaping. And for some of them they would be killed during protests, airstrikes, or clashes with the Burma Army.

I suddenly remembered what I'd learned on my long Karenni mission years before: if you do all this but don't share the gospel, it's a waste. If I taught these young guys medical and security and communications and other technical skills, they could go back home and fight bravely and die quickly. But if they don't know Jesus, or at least have the opportunity to know Jesus, then it would be a loss.

It wasn't my turn to share for morning devotions but I went and asked Kevin if he'd mind if I took the class. He didn't mind and I prepared myself to share, clearly, the gospel story with these new Rangers. When I was younger, and before I walked away from my faith, I used to love preaching to a crowd, being on the stage, and sharing a gospel message and doing an altar call. As an adult, I've come to know the power and influence my words can have. I know that I can convince someone to say a sinner's prayer, whether their heart is in it or not, by fancy stories that touch the heart. It's with this knowledge that I've become cautious when I share the gospel. I don't want to force anyone to believe anything—that never worked for me. I don't want to exploit my friendships or influence over people so they will believe. I don't want to be like that person who takes you for coffee and tries to get you to join their multilevel marketing company. I only want someone to respond to God.

So that morning I shared with them about Saw Gay Ku and about Zau Seng and about Baw Mu, Rangers like them, who I knew and loved and lost. I outlined to them the gospel story as I believed it: God created the earth and man and it was all good. Man took a path apart from God and sin and death entered the story. God loved man so much and wanted to be in relationship with him that he sent Jesus, fully God and fully human, born in a barn to a virgin mother, and eventually killed by the religious leaders of the day, in order to take on sin once and for all. Through his death and resurrection, and through believing in him, all of humankind can return into a life and relationship with God. And the last part of the gospel story is the response. God will never force himself upon someone. He will never kick in the door. Rather, he will knock gently, giving each of us the dignity to decide for ourselves.

So when I got to the response portion of the morning devotions, I told them I would pray a prayer and Doh Say would translate it. I told them that if they felt God was nudging their hearts, if they felt that God was messing with them, and they wanted to give their lives to God that morning, that they could repeat the prayer that Doh Say translated. I told them they didn't need to pray out loud, they could pray it quietly in their heart or in their mind. I didn't want to cause embarrassment or shyness to be a stumbling block for them, and I was also worried if I asked them to pray it out loud that no one would respond.

I started my prayer, the first line, and Doh Say translated it, and then much to my surprise, causing me to open my eyes and stop for a second, more than half of the students repeated his prayer. Not quietly in their hearts or minds, but boldly, loudly, out loud. I continued the sinner's prayer, and they prayed it along with me as tears welled up in my eyes. When I finished I asked them if they wouldn't mind putting up their hand if they'd prayed the prayer and thirty-four of our fifty-five students put up their hands. I put out a box of Burmese Bibles at the front of the classroom and told them if anyone wanted a Bible they could take one. The box was emptied immediately and those that didn't get a Bible asked if we could get more sent to us.

This gospel message felt more pure than those of my past. This gospel message was all about building up Jesus and had nothing to do with me or manipulating words or stories. All I could feel was gratitude, grateful that Jesus would let me be a small part of his kingdom. Grateful that from Baw Mu's death, others could come to life in God. Grateful that despite being a bumbling fool most of the time, God would still choose me to be a part of the story he is writing on earth. As part of our graduation ceremony after a Ranger training we offer to baptize anyone who wants to get baptized, and at this training two of our students said they wanted to get baptized. We would see many of these students a few months later and to our joy and surprise many of them still had their Bibles we'd given them, verses underlined and pages turned down, a sign that the Holy Spirit was speaking to them through the Bible. What an incredible thing to be a part of.

As word of our training spread through the ethnic groups we started to get more requests to lead similar trainings. Immediately after graduation we lovingly said our goodbyes to the students and made our way to northern Karen State where airstrikes had become more sporadic, but still were causing over 100,000 people to hide in the jungle now. We had two long days of walking, much of it at night, sometimes without headlamps, and a lot of it without any drinking water, to reach our link-up spot to meet the rest of our headquarters team where we were able to get into trucks and travel on to our training camp.

On the way to the camp we stopped in a nearby village to visit the sites that had been bombed. First up was the high school. An awed silence fell upon our group as we got out of our trucks and walked up to the high school. A concrete-walled building, with separate rooms for each grade, desks, tables, chairs, chalkboards, and all the equipment that would almost make it like a Western school. It was completely destroyed. We saw the craters where the cluster bombs had landed about fifteen meters from the school wall. The walls for the 100-meter length of the school were littered with holes where the shrapnel had blown through the concrete. The tin roof was nearly entirely gone; pieces of tin lay crumpled like balls of paper all around the school grounds and hung dangling from the rafters. Windows and doors were blown completely off the hinges and we stepped over and around them as we silently took in the scene.

As I entered into one of the classrooms I got choked up at the devastation the bombs had made. Every wooden desk and chair in the classroom was covered in tiny jagged pieces of shrapnel. I shuddered at the thought of these pieces of metal ripping into a young high school student's body, and I thanked God that this bombing had happened at night when the school was empty. The destruction looked like something out of a superhero movie.

Next we moved onto a house where nothing remained except a black charred square on the ground. No posts or beams or furniture survived, and neither did the family that took the full force of the bomb through their roof. After that we moved to the nearby Karen Army base and looked at the craters left by the bombs dropped there. Doh Say climbed down inside the crater and his head was below the ground level, it was so deep.

One of my Ranger friends, PaLu, had been sleeping in the army camp the night it was bombed, in a house five meters from the impact site. In the last six months PaLu had been baptized and then got married and his new wife was now expecting their first child. PaLu had gone into the town to buy some things and visit some friends on the army base for the night. He heard the first bomb land on the school and the sound of jets overhead. In the dark of night he ran as fast as he could to where he knew a trench was and dove in. Seconds later, before he'd even picked himself up off the ground, the bomb landed on the army base, ripping apart the house he'd run from. Thankfully and miraculously he was unharmed.

A few weeks later the Burma Army attempted to bomb our training camp. The way our camp lies in the valley means the planes have to come in low and make a sharp turn, so when they dropped their bombs on our camp they missed and the bombs landed on the mountain opposite the camp. But it was enough to cause the village to flee, including PaLu's pregnant wife. She would later have a still-born delivery, much to do with the stress of the months hiding in the jungle and fearing for her life. I was heartbroken when PaLu told me they'd lost their baby. He was looking forward to being a father. I wondered how many residual casualties, like this baby, war causes. Even months after losing his baby I would be sitting with PaLu, looking at photos on his phone and he'd come across the picture of the stillborn and stare at it saying, "My baby, this is my baby...", I could tell by how he looked at the picture that this was a hard loss for him.

We ran another modified Ranger training at our training camp and then moved up into Karenni State to run another one. I was up visiting Beh Reh and Htwar Reh and one of their generals asked to meet with me. He told me that sixty-five Burma police had abandoned their jobs and surrendered themselves to the Karenni Army. They didn't want to be on the side of the dictator. They wanted to be on the side of the CDM. They wanted some more training and then to go back and help the protesters. Would we train them? For years we've been praying that the Burma Army, police, and government would have a change of heart, that their consciences would be convicted and that they would turn from evil. Right in front of us were sixty-five answers to this prayer. Of course we would train them.

I felt confident about this training with the Karenni. Beh Reh and Htwar Reh and many of the Karenni Rangers had become like family to me. I'd visited them dozens of times, done missions with them, and being around them and around the refugee camp felt like home. I encouraged our HQ staff to come and be part of this training, to see what it's all about, and that if they had families, it would be a great opportunity to bring their kids. One thing I've grown to love about FBR is that we are a family and do things as families. If we're going on missions or sneaking across borders often the staff who have kids will bring them along. Two families and a few other staff signed up to be part of our training team.

There's something about a beautifully organized movement that gets me excited. In the army they say the "link-up" is one of the hardest tasks to perform in the field, yet at FBR we make multiple link-ups, with a Mr. Bean type plan, during a single movement. Htwar Reh relied on me and my experience moving in that area so he could focus on the second half of the movement that would be done on motorcycles. As the sun started to set I led our team off the road, through a rice field, and then onto a trail that disappeared into the jungle. We hiked for a couple hours, the kids doing an awesome job hiking or being carried by Rangers. With perfect timing, in the perfect location, we linked up with Htwar and Beh and a dozen motorcycles that would move us through the refugee camp, out the back gate, down a goat trail in the jungle, and then across the border into Karenni State. I was happy to be bringing our headquarters staff up to Karenni State. It felt like I was bringing my friends to show off how awesome my family was. To have a chance for all our headquarters team and their families to see how amazing our Karenni team was felt like such a gift. I couldn't stop smiling as I sat on the back of Beh Reh's motorcycle as we zoomed through the jungle. Over an hour later we were in Karenni State and on our way to meet up with our next group of trainees.

It was another beautiful training. One morning Blake led the group in a gospel devotional, and more than forty of the students prayed to receive Christ, asking God into their hearts. I thought back to the beginning of the year, when God had told me simply to obey. We were now part of training a movement of people in Burma who were disobeying the dictators—choosing to stand for freedom, love, and democracy, even if it cost them their lives.

Chapter 20

Combat

I've often wondered if every man wonders how they would do in combat. I wondered that. I've seen all the famous war movies and I've read some great books about the Korean War and the Second World War. I've read accounts written by some great war heroes and I've wondered what I would do, how I would react if I was in their shoes. It was many years ago now that Dave, my leader, told me that he would trust me with his life, but I often wondered if another person's life was in good hands if they were my responsibility.

Baw Mu.

Zau Seng.

Nay Tho.

Saw Gay Ku.

Elizabeth.

Ree Doh.

Hsi Hsi.

Saw Black.

Day Chit.

I could go on and on with the list of names of my friends who have died in the war.

I may be in the wrong line of work with FBR because I have a hard time with death. I'm not brave. I'm not courageous. I don't like blood and guts. I feel all these things deeply. One night in Karenni State on a mission a Karenni soldier was going to clear an area for me to set up a rear Casualty Collection Point (CCP), and as he was clearing the area he stepped on a landmine and blew his leg off. His foot was still in his shoe, and the shattered bones of his leg were sticking out the end as blood squirted out with each heartbeat. Blake and Joseph were on him right away with tourniquets and wound packing, but it only took a glance of that scene for it to be stuck in my head. The image of his face littered with dirt and shrapnel wounds, relatively calm but eyes wide with shock. He lay, half propped up in the back of the truck in the middle of the night, his life changed forever. I tried not to spend time looking at the amputated leg. I don't like looking at these things. And yet, I seem to be surrounded by them. I've noticed recently that I don't like Hollywood movies that have excessive amounts of war or killing or death in them. Even the silly "superhero" movies that seem to be the only thing that comes out of Hollywood these days make death and destruction and violence seem so easy. And I feel like I have enough of that in my life. It's not entertaining.

When I was in the army I quickly learned about the "grey man." A grey man is someone who goes on course or training and at the end of the course the staff see his name on the roster and have to ask themselves, "Who is this guy?" A grey man doesn't stand out. They are neither amazing nor terrible. They disappear among the soldiers. Saw Black, despite his name, was a grey man.

I live a hidden life. In many ways, I have exiled grief. So when someone like Saw Black gets killed by the Burma Army, I don't know how or where to begin to feel it or grieve him. I don't cry well. That's far too exposing. Saw Black was my friend, but we weren't overly close. He was a grey man. A grey Ranger. A grey friend.

Saw Black was a true superhero. He came to our first ever CDM training. There was so much energy and emotion in that training. The area around our Burma headquarters had been bombed by Burma Army jets, and this gave us a feeling that everything we taught was relevant and important and we had a sense of purpose as we taught. Our students were amazing, motivated, engaged, passionate. Saw Black went home after the training and never stopped fighting. He never surrendered. He didn't need to be colorful. He needed to fight for what was true. He didn't need to be remembered, or helped, or messaged regularly to be motivated. Truth and justice motivated him. The rest of the colors didn't matter. He never sought attention or money or fame. He built bombs. He employed them strategically. He made a difference in the revolution—he did. And he'll never be remembered. No one will know his name. He'll never be celebrated as a hero. One day when Burma is free, Saw Black's name will never be read out as one who gave his blood and life for that freedom.

He was left to die in a ditch.

The Burma Army closed in on him and his bomb-building team, and as they fled, shot Saw Black in the leg. He fell to the ground, unable to run anymore. They put another round in his chest. Even still, he tried to crawl away, tried to escape, tried to live to fight another day. The Burma Army walked over to him and slit his throat.

He died alone in a ditch.

What kind of life is this I have chosen, or that has been chosen for me, where this kind of occurrence is not surprising, but rather regular? That coming to face death is not uncommon. Trying to grieve a friend and teammate is hard every time. Every death is as unique as every life that is lived. Every life of each teammate and friend is precious, unique, and beautiful. Saw Black was a superhero to me. He lived a quiet, hidden life of service to others. His death is tragic and hard, but it's not the first. There have been many this year as a front line emerged in Karenni State while we were there on mission.

It's hard for me to write about the Karenni mission. I don't know how or where to start. So much of it is details. So much of it is death.

It seemed that all hell was breaking loose around Burma. After the February 2021 coup, A resistance government was stood up in the shadows called the National Unity Government. They issued a public proclamation, calling on all people, in all corners of Burma, to arm themselves with whatever they had, and fight the Burma Army wherever they could. Soon militias were raised up in nearly every neighborhood across Burma, armed with pitchforks and machetes, .22 rifles and slingshots and old muskets from the First World War. Any weapon they could get, they would use. They would fill sandbags and dig bunkers and secure their streets and neighborhoods. And when the Burma Army would pass by they would fight bravely, and many would die quickly. All across Burma the revolution turned into the bloodiest fighting Burma had seen since World War II. Thousands died and continue to die as nearly the entire country stands together with a common enemy.

For me it all began with Elizabeth crying.

We'd finished a short training mission in Karen State and we were trying to decide where our headquarters group should go next. There seemed to be fighting happening everywhere—in Kachin, in Chin, in Karenni, in Karen State. Elizabeth was one of our newly graduated Rangers who was from Karenni State. Dave and I were talking logistics about where we should go next when Elizabeth came walking past. She'd been in a prayer meeting, praying for Karenni, and she burst into tears as she walked by. "The Burma Army just burned down my home. My parents are now IDPs. Please, please, come to Karenni and help us," she begged. I looked at Dave and knew at that moment we'd be going to Karenni.

Elizabeth was an embodiment of everything good in the world. She was the garden of Eden manifested in a person, in a smile, in a personality, a faith and a laugh. She was strong, she was a ball-buster, she was hilarious, and she loved her Karenni people. As she wiped the tears from her eyes, we all agreed we would go.

I'd been on two Karenni missions prior to this one and had spent the previous four years building relationships with the Karenni leaders and our team. But once we arrived in Karenni, outside of Loikaw city, this was a totally new environment and area for me. My previous missions in Karenni were jungle missions—hiking for days, hammocks in bamboo, cooking over fires. Now we were in a city. We were driving in trucks along paved roads. We had electricity, cell signal, shops and restaurants. It was as if I was in a totally new country from the Burma I'd encountered on all previous missions. I remember going for a run on one of the first days there, along a paved road, under the power lines, with trucks passing me constantly, and it felt surreal.

The second day we were there we went down to Demoso to meet with some leaders. While we were there the Burma Army started to shell the town from their camp. We could see smoke rising from burning houses in the distance and decided we would go to help if we could. Dave often describes FBR to people like the volunteer fire department. We aren't the fire marshal who goes door to door and checks people's fire alarms or teaches in the elementary school about fire prevention and safety. We are the ones who are at home doing our thing when the alarm gets sounded, something bad has happened, and we'll come and do our best. As we all piled in the back of the pickup trucks and headed towards the billowing smoke I pictured the volunteer fire department in my mind. We would go and throw some buckets of water on the burning house, literally, and then we'd go home or move onto the next fire.

Then the sniper fired a round from the tall blue building down the road.

Our team heard the crack of the round and moved off the main road. The resistance fighters were everywhere and pointed to where the shot had come from. "There is often a sniper in that building," one soldier told us. We didn't want to turn around so we decided to recon and see if we could get around the sniper. One by one we ran across the road. We wanted to see if we could see the sniper or find him in a window. We climbed over a wall and into an empty house. Every house in Demoso town was empty. My heart was pounding as we cleared the building and went up the second floor. We would quickly pass by windows and then lean over to try to get a vantage point of the six-story hotel a few blocks down the road from us.

We never could see the sniper. We ran around the area for about an hour, but all was quiet, and we eventually fell back to our trucks. The adrenaline of the day was still pounding in my chest as we went back to our camp for the night. Many of our team had been involved in the FBR Iraq and Syria missions, but I'd always felt that I should stay focused on Burma, so I never went. Now as I reflected on the day, I couldn't help but think to myself, "Wow, there's something kind of exciting about these urban missions." Jumping over walls, running through abandoned houses, seeing the fragments of the lives that everyone left behind as they fled. These feelings would quickly fade.

We stayed in the Loikaw/Demoso area for a few weeks doing children's programs and medical programs. We would go visit and encourage the resistance soldiers in their dug-in positions. Our team made our home base halfway between Loikaw and Demoso and would go out every day to a new place and meet with some of the thousands of displaced people across Karenni. We had some journalists with us and one day I was asked to take the journalists around and try to meet some people.

We got news about some Burma Army soldiers who'd been captured as defectors. The journalist wanted to go and interview them and so Htwar and Thit Sar Lin and I took her down to try and find the soldiers. As the journalist was trying to find out more information about the captured soldiers, Thit Sar Lin and I wandered out to the street. At first it was one lone motorcycle loaded up that passed by, but that seemed to be the opening of the floodgates of people and vehicles that soon were streaming past us. I stopped one vehicle and asked what was happening. "Burma Army is taking our town and starting a ground assault. Our homes are gone," the villager answered before starting to flee again.

I texted Dave right away to let him know something big was happening. He rallied his team and headed to the front lines. We didn't know at the time, but this was the start of a major offensive that would rock Karenni State and cost hundreds of lives. Typically in Burma there is not a geographical "front line" that one could go find. As is the nature of guerrilla warfare, the front line is wherever two opposing groups happen to turn a corner and run into each other. But now, in Karenni State, a front line was beginning to form. As the Burma Army took Mobye, the resistance groups began to dig into rice fields and ditches to prepare to stop any further advancements.

The next day we returned early to the front line. The resistance was still organizing itself, but it wasn't much later than 9:00 a.m. when the sky seemed to open up and mortars began falling around us and didn't seem to stop for the next several days. The Burma Army began shooting mortars from their bases several kilometers away and spent the whole day adjusting their rounds to try and kill as many of us as possible. I knew about mortars and artillery fire. When I served in the Canadian Army I was an artillery officer. I'd trained a lot calling in artillery fire, but never had I been on the receiving end of indirect fire.

For those of you who have seen the HBO docuseries *Band of Brothers*, you'll remember the episode where they're in the forest and keep getting targeted by indirect fire. It's like the trees explode as a shell lands nearby. There's nothing you can do but get in a hole and pray the round doesn't land directly on your hole. Point-detonating rounds—which is what the Burma Army was firing—explode when the point of the round impacts the ground, sending a spray of shrapnel upwards and outwards in a cone shape. The 120mm mortars that the Burma Army was firing have a range of nearly 12 kilometers and a blast radius of 40 meters diameter—anything within 40 meters of that round landing will be picking shrapnel out of themselves.

In conventional armies like Canada, you never fire indirect weapons without a forward observer. This was my training in the army. The forward observer goes to the front line with the tanks or infantry and then calls in the artillery rounds. Once the rounds start falling then it is the job of the observer to adjust the rounds onto the target. The observer is responsible to make sure that the rounds aren't landing on civilians or schools or churches or other sites designated by the United Nations as protected sites. The observer, who is watching the round impact through his binoculars, will call back to the gun line and tell them to either move their round up or down, or left or right until there are rounds landing on the frontside and backside of the target. Then there is one final adjustment and a call for "fire for effect" and the next volley of rounds will land on target, closing the bracket procedure.

In Burma there is no forward observer. The Burma Army fires the mortars indiscriminately, aiming towards a grid where they have troops in contact, but they don't care if they hit civilians or children or people fleeing. They fling the mortars like terrorists, crushing morale with each round. We tried to keep count of how many rounds they were firing at us, but we lost count at 150 rounds, and it wasn't even noon. Each round that impacts contributes to a slow fraying of your nerves. There are benefits and pitfalls to not having any observer guiding the rounds in. The benefit is that a trained observer will inevitably hit the target he is intending to hit. So if we are that target, and there is an observer bracketing us, then it's only a matter of time before the rounds find us. The pitfall to the hail of mortar rounds without an observer is that it becomes random. You hear the distant thump as the round is fired from the Burma Army base and then you start counting in your head. You know you have around twelve to fifteen seconds before the round lands. And without the observer you have no idea where it may land, and statistics from World War II come to mind that tell me that half the casualties in the war were from artillery and mortar fire.

Thunk. 1, 2, 3, 4, 5... BOOM! Thunk. Thunk. 1, 2, 3, 4, 5... BOOM! BOOM!

All day the rounds landed around us. We formed a makeshift CCP about a mile back from the newly formed front line. There was a train track that ran along one side into Mobye where the Burma

Army wanted to start their push to reclaim lost ground. The tat-tat-tat of machine gun fire filled the lulls between mortar rounds. All day we used our trucks to shuttle wounded soldiers back from the front lines, bouncing along the train tracks, praying a mortar round wouldn't land on your exposed truck, trying to turn the truck around on the train tracks, put the patient in the bed of the truck, and then drive back to the CCP. Several times throughout the day we had to wash the blood out of the bed of the truck as it was pooling from all the casualties.

There were gunshot wounds, mortar wounds, grenade wounds, and bodies so mangled and disfigured it was hard to know how to carry them or what part belonged where. My friend Hsi Hsi and I stayed at the CCP for most of that day, unloading patients, ducking when mortars would come in, and using our vehicles to shuttle patients back to any hospital or clinic that still had medicine behind us. Around dusk I began to wonder about Dave and some of our team who were still on the front lines. We'd lost contact with them for a few hours and I didn't know what to do. The resistance groups began to fall back and even most of our Rangers began to fall back, walking down the road in a daze. A group came with explosives and said they were going to blow up the bridges leading to the train tracks—I told them our team was still out there. If they blew up the bridge, any vehicles would be stuck on the other side. They paused and talked for a few moments but then the urgency of their orders took over and they continued to set the explosives.

We prayed and decided we'd fall back a mile and wait there for Dave. As the darkness began to set in, it also brought the Burma Army jets. The jets come in and make a few strafing runs, firing bullets from their cannons at whatever may be down there. Then after a few runs with the cannons they switch to bombs and begin their bombing runs, dropping 500-pound bombs, explosions that shake the earth. Soon Dave and the rest of his team drove down the road and we were reunited. Everyone was alive, for today.

The battle of Mobye lasted weeks as the Burma Army wanted to reclaim all the ground between Demoso and Loikaw. Every morning when we would go back to the front line, we were one kilometer back from where we'd been the previous day. The Burma Army soldiers were now in the trenches we were in the day before. All day we would get pounded by the Burma Army, carrying out the dead and wounded, and then we'd go home at the end of the day knowing we'd lost ground. We'd been pushed back. Back at our camp we would walk around like zombies, going through the motions of showering and washing our clothes, rinsing the blood out and silently being thankful that it wasn't your blood. We would sit around the small campfires and silently stare into the flames. The flames would flicker in front of our eyes like images from the day. We'd eventually climb into hammocks or beds, a rifle always within reach.

It's the sound of war that is hard to describe. I think it was Mark Twain who said "When you see an adjective, kill it." And I think about my limited vocabulary to describe the sounds of war. The adjectives are so cliche. "The mortar thundered into the ground." Thundered. It's what everyone says when they write about mortars. And it's a start, but it doesn't do justice to the actual sound of the mortar. I don't have the prose of Buechner or Berry or Twain to use my words to paint the picture of the sound of terror.

It started a few days ago when we were visiting the front line on the outskirts of Loikaw. We crawled our way forward through the rice field to get a vantage point to recon the Burma Army. Shortly after we got there, we got mortared. These weren't big mortars—they were small 60mm mortars—but they were landing close. One of our ethnic team, someone who's been fighting the Burma Army his whole life, someone who's killed dozens of Burma Army soldiers, ducked down behind the berm as the round impacted 100 meters from them. He is a big guy, and my respect and admiration for him matches his huge size. A few rounds landed around them but no one was hit. Our team moved back to our rally point.

After we were all safely back in our vehicles and heading for home my big friend chuckled to himself as he imitated the sound of the mortar coming in: "Shhhhrrraaaappp-BAAAAM." And then he would laugh and shake his head at how close it had been. And for the next two days he would walk around making that noise, "Shhhhrrraaaappp-BAAAAM," saying it to himself, over and over, the noise of it stuck in his head. I imagined it was his way of communicating the disbelief that it was a close call. I noticed how he would be sitting in his hammock or building a fire and he'd make the noise. Sometimes he'd chuckle afterwards, and sometimes he would stare silently into the crackle of the fire after the "BAAAAM." I didn't realize the significance of this until this morning.

It was past 3:00 a.m. and the cold of the morning was laying down upon me. I was stirring on the ground, adjusting my blankets, rolling over to get a few more hours of sleep among the creaking bamboo trees. I don't know how long it was after I fell back asleep before the first round impacted. "Shhhhrrraaaappp-BOOOOM." I went from sleeping to instant terror. At first I thought we'd been bombed by a jet. The sound of the round cutting the air before it hit the ground made me think it was the roar of a jet engine. I knew that often when the Burma Army bombs with jets they use two jets, so I listened to the darkness for the approach of the second plane. Then as my brain caught up with me, I realized it wasn't a jet, but a 120mm heavy mortar. Moments later the second round impacted. I can't describe the sound. It was the sound of all death and all evil charging at you with their full force. When the round impacted, dirt and debris sprayed over me. The sound of terror could be felt like cancer deep in my bones, a rotting dreadful sound.

Run.

But which way? Where? Where will the next round land? What if I run right towards it? What do I do? How long do I have? Are there troops nearby? Can I turn on my headlamp? Jesus. Help. As we jammed our feet into shoes and tried to grab everything we thought we needed, the third round came in. If you listen carefully to terror you will hear the scream of death coming for you. It's enough of a warning that you can drop to the ground wherever you are and hope the round doesn't land near you. We dove for cover under a big abandoned bus. Then the fourth round came shortly later.

We had no casualties among our team, but two neighbors got hit with shrapnel. One we helped stabilize and move to a nearby clinic. The other we treated in our house. And as shaken as I was by the violent wake-up call, the sound continued to echo in my head. The sound that my big ethnic friend walked around imitating for days has a way of finding its way inside of you.

It's a sound that unfortunately the people in this village—and all over Burma—have become accustomed to. One of the rounds impacted about 70 meters from where I was sleeping. It landed in the backyard of a family's house, next to their outhouse. It blew holes through the concrete wall of their outhouse and blew the wooden door clean off. Shrapnel hit the family home, but amazingly none of them died. Once the mortaring stopped, the family went back to bed. About an hour later I was at the site investigating the crater by headlamp and the family woke up and stuck their head out the window wondering what all the noise was about now. I couldn't believe they were still there, but the sound of mortars, jets, bombs, landmines, machine guns—the sound of terror—has already made its home in these people's lives. A few hours later at dawn the man in the house did what I've seen him do every day we've been here: he led his cows out. I was struck that this was such a normal thing to do. He walked behind them, swatting them; the sound of their bells clanging and the animals mooing and burping and grunting as the herd made its daily move out to pasture was a sound of normal life. But the normal sounds of life here also include the sound of terror: Shhhhrrraaaappp-BAAAAM.

I began to notice that my team all began to do what my big ethnic friend did. I'd notice each of them in their own way trying to imitate the sound: weeeeeeeaaaaaa-BOOOM, sssssssssssssss-CRAAAM, zzzzzoooowwaaaa-DDUUNG. Each person's noise was different from the next, each person trying their best, but falling short, to imitate the sound of terror.

Chapter 21

Alone

The rattle of machine gun fire formed the background noise as we stood at a T-intersection outside Demoso. The resistance group was planning to attack the Burma Army camp in Demoso. We would follow them to support with medical evacuation and document with videographers. Dave decided he would follow behind the assaulting element and Blake and I would follow the flanking element.

As our group stepped off I glanced at my watch, making a mental note of the time. We'd learned by now that when a big attack like this was happening it took roughly ninety minutes before the jets would arrive and start bombing. I reminded myself that in about an hour I'd need to start listening to and watching the sky as well. If we last an hour.

Since I don't understand the language, I'm often following along without much information about what's going on or what the plan is. I've learned to take my cues from the ethnics. If they're relaxed and nonchalant then I know it must not be too dangerous in the present moment. But when their eyes start to get wide and tense, and when they chamber a round in their weapons and walk with the guns at ready, I can be pretty sure it won't be long until we run into trouble.

On this particular morning the flanking group I was walking behind was casual, relaxed, joking with each other as they slung their weapons over their shoulders and sauntered up the alley. I remember the image of one soldier strutting up the middle of the lane with a large machine gun over his shoulder and the belt of bullets wrapped around his torso. He looked so calm, so casual, so relaxed. I was about twenty meters behind him. I looked around the alley we were walking up, a tall wall along both sides, only opening up into people's abandoned houses. It was as the thought occurred to me—that we were walking into a funnel, something the army trains us not to do whenever possible—that the Burma Army ambush opened up on us.

The machine gunner who'd been strutting up the road in front of me was suddenly gone. All hell broke loose, and all our supporting soldiers were gone. I dove into a thicket of bushes that ran along the cement wall. I could hear the crack and whiz of bullets as they passed by me by the hundreds. I crawled along the ditch until I reached the entrance to a house and ran into the backyard. Thit Sar Lin was with me and trying to capture everything on film. We jumped over the fence and climbed through a house to a more protected spot. Thit Sar Lin sat on the wall filming when suddenly a mortar round landed in the rice field behind him. I don't know how he didn't get hit with shrapnel. It was so close. He grinned as I yelled at him to get down off the wall. The sniper was back in his perch in the big blue hotel, taking shots when he could but, more deadly, calling in the mortar rounds, using his scope to find our location and report it back to the base.

Blake and I crouched behind the house panting, taking a minute to get our wits about us and figure out our next step. We were on our own and we didn't know what was happening. LayKay, our medic and one of my best friends, had gotten separated from us in the initial attack, but everyone else was with us and no one had any holes in them. "We can't leave LayKay," I said as we ducked from more mortar rounds coming in. I knew we couldn't leave him, but I didn't know where he was or how to find him, and it seemed like sure death if we went out searching for him. I prayed, "Jesus help us, help LayKay."

We decided we would bound back three or four houses to get ourselves out of range of their machine guns and sniper fire and then try to make a new plan. We jumped over the walls between the houses and ran through the yards. We finally got to the end of the houses and knew we'd need to run down the street for a few yards to finally get out of range. We took turns sprinting down the road. My puffy jacket that I'd been wearing for warmth that morning had been ripped as I dove into the ditch and as I ran down the road the final few meters a cloud of down feathers trailed after me. I was panting and sweating and had down feathers stuck all over me. "This is a Mr. Bean moment," I thought to myself. We jumped into a ditch and I looked around and realized LayKay was with us now. He'd seen us run back and, from his hiding place, had jumped up and run back with us. I thanked God he was okay and we were reunited. We could now get out of there.

We took turns bounding back down the road, back to where we'd originally started from. It's exhausting work, sprinting, diving into a ditch or behind a concrete wall, then up again a few seconds later and doing it again. The final push I made I could hear bullets cracking around us and I remember a sound of deep grunting panic coming out of me as I made it over the final wall to a safe area.

It's hard to say how close I came to dying that day. God knows. There were a few casualties from landmines and mortar fire that Dave's group helped treat and evacuate. As soon as we got back to a safe place we reported what had happened to our base camp. Adam headed down to help us as soon as he got the news. When he arrived at our location he stepped out of his truck and came walking over to us. We all looked shell-shocked by what had just happened. He walked out into the street to look and see if he could see anything happening down the road. As he did, a bullet from the sniper whizzed down the road not far from Adam's head. He ducked and came back over to us. We all laughed for some reason. I think it was the relief of being alive still.

Our team stayed for nearly two months in Karenni, trying to help as best we could in the intensifying battle. Dave and the headquarters group would continue to go back up there every chance they could, but our ethnic Rangers mobilized in an incredible way, taking charge of all the battlefield relief. It seemed that anytime there was a battle happening, anywhere in Karenni State, our Rangers were there, ready to put on a tourniquet, ready to pray, ready to help bury the dead.

As I left Karenni State and began the journey back south to Karen State and eventually back to the headquarters, I remember the surreal feeling of saying goodbye. I remember hugging Ree Doh and taking a picture together. I remember the sounds of the battle in the distance. I remember thinking I had to say goodbye to these Rangers as if I will never see them again.

While I was in Karenni I remember the feeling of wanting to be anywhere else in the world except there. The feeling of excitement I'd had on the first day, jumping over walls, running through abandoned buildings, had faded. In its place was a feeling of dread—every night that we got home and went to bed we knew we were lucky to still be alive. We got into the trucks that would take us the two days back to Karen State and as soon as they started to drive away from our team I remember an intense feeling of wanting to stay. While I was there, I wanted to leave, but as soon as I was gone, there was nowhere else in the world that I wanted to be. I wanted to be with the team. If they were going to die, then we would die together. And if they were going to live, then we would live with a common understanding of the battles we'd faced.

My brain and heart were in a fog as we slowly made our ex-fil from Karenni. It would take us three or four days to get back to the headquarters, a long time to sit and think about the team I'd left behind there. On day three of the ex-fil, we stopped for a break at a checkpoint, now back in familiar territory. I switched on my Zoleo messenger to see if there was any update from the team in Karenni—there was. One of our Rangers had been hit by a Burma Army airstrike and killed. "Who?" I asked. "Ree Doh," came the message back a few minutes later. I couldn't believe it. I felt like I was going to throw up. I walked away from our group into the jungle and collapsed in the forest and cried. Waves of rage and shock flooded over me. I couldn't believe he was dead.

We got back into our boats and continued our ex-fil. We had to hike the final few hours, and as we began the hike I paused the group and asked to have a moment of silence to remember Ree Doh. We stood in the silence of the jungle for a long time and then I said a prayer and continued to walk. I cried silently as we walked the final hour.

Reintegration back to life in the headquarters and the city was hard. I still had a lot of anger and grief about losing my friend Ree Doh. But it felt like no one understood what we'd been through. How could they? This feeling that no one understood created isolation in my heart and from our group—they hadn't been through what we'd been through, they hadn't seen the things we'd seen. Life in the city seemed surreal. Every time an airplane would take off from the international airport my ear would hear the roar of the jet engines and immediately start to go into survival mode. My eyes would scan the sky each time a jet would take off, trying to find it and analyze its path to see if it was a threat or not. This reaction would stay with me for years.

It was only a couple of weeks since we'd been back in the headquarters that we got even more devastating news. Elizabeth had been hit by a mortar and was in grave condition.

Elizabeth and some of the other girls had been back at the camp when they heard an airstrike happen at a nearby village. They immediately decided to head towards the bombed area. They wanted to help anyone who was injured, like they'd been trained to do. They were able to help some people evacuate and some others get medical treatment. Elizabeth wanted to document what had happened so she got one of the other girls to film her as she explained to the camera about the airstrikes and destroyed buildings behind her. Then the Burma Army started to mortar the area. One of the rounds landed near Elizabeth, shrapnel hitting her in the back of the head.

She was rushed to a nearby clinic and the doctors did several operations on her throughout the night, trying to save her life. The next day she died of her wounds. Her death was a blow to everyone. She was loved by everyone who met her. It was as if a light had been put out when she died. My heart didn't know what to do.

In Karenni we would end up losing many of our Rangers—and at the time of writing this—continue to lose Rangers. My dear friend Hsi Hsi who gave me courage to drive along the train tracks and help evacuate casualties in the battle of Mobye would be dead within the year. I have a picture together with him. We'd both been awarded FBR medals during a ceremony and we posed for a picture together— a week later he was dead.

What is a heart supposed to do with so much death?

One evening back in the city I met up with a friend of mine from Karen State who'd come out of the battle to get a break. We went out for Mexican food and it felt like I was finally with someone who understood the horror of war. His name was Myo Htet Aung, but I just call him MHA.

"Most nights I can't sleep well. But on the nights I do fall asleep I often wake up because of my dreams," MHA said to me as we sat at dinner.

"What do you dream about?" I asked him. "Sometimes I dream about dead bodies. Sometimes I wake up and I'm almost still holding my gun. Sometimes I dream because I can hear the airplanes from the international airport while I sleep. And sometimes I dream about playing games with my friends." He pulled out his phone and found a video to show me. It showed a group of young men carrying each other piggyback, running around a kickball court, all laughing. "Whichever team loses has to carry the other team around the court by however many points they lost by," he told me smiling as I could see the memory glistening in his eyes.

"You know, we weren't friends before we joined the resistance. None of us knew each other before. But we got put on a team together, and now..." he trailed off searching for the vocabulary to describe the brotherhood he feels towards them.

"What did you do before the coup?" I asked him. "I was a university student. I was doing a master's in mechanical engineering at Mandalay University." I was surprised by this and asked three or four clarifying questions. I'd only ever known MHA as a soldier. I didn't know him in his life before the coup. "I'd already completed four years and have two more to go to get my degree as an engineer," he told me. "I want to work on ships."

"Ships?" I asked, wondering if I heard and understood him correctly.

"Yes, marine mechanical engineering. On big ships. I want to go out to the ocean and around the world."

I always get excited talking with young people who have dreams like this. It inspires me when I listen to MHA talk about the world and the things he wants to do in it. He wants to sail the seas, he wants to use his hands to fix things, he wants to conquer small parts of the world.

"But everything changed the day of the coup," he said. Within days of the coup happening MHA had joined with the other students from his school to march as part of the Civil Disobedience Movement. They protested and chanted antigovernment songs at the wall of police waiting for them. One day he heard about some people going into the mountains and becoming part of the resistance and he thought he should join.

"Before the coup I never dreamed of being a soldier. That thought was so far away from my mind. I wanted to finish school and get a job. But like that," he said, snapping his fingers, "I was learning how to shoot and carry a gun and become a soldier. I was put on the team and sent to 6th Brigade in Karen State."

MHA's team was involved in almost all of the early fighting in 6th Brigade. They took control of the Burma Highway and fought many bloody battles along it. "I have killed Burma Army soldiers now. I didn't want to do that. I wanted to be a student. Now I have done things..." He again trailed off. This time he wasn't searching for the vocabulary. The things he's done he doesn't want to talk about. They play in his dreams.

"Three months ago my best friend on our team—you know, we've been together almost two years now, every day together. We fight together. We eat together. We play games together. We train together. We do everything together—my best friend, they killed him. He died in front of me. They shot him in the head. He was right beside me. One second he is alive and fighting, the next he is dead. I've never met his parents before, but I had to be the one to tell them he was dead... After that I needed to take a break. So I came here."

MHA, like many in his situation, snuck across the border in the middle of the night. He borrowed money from a friend of a friend, with a promise to find a job in this new country to repay him. With the borrowed money, he hired a smuggler to bring him to the city. They packed him in the center of a truck full of cabbages. He was lying on cabbage and had hundreds of cabbages around him and above him and on all sides of him. I could picture these trucks clearly as I'd seen them many times on the road here, and then I could picture a young, heartbroken, worn-out soldier buried under all those cabbages.

"I spend my days reading books, or talking to my friends or team-mates who are still back inside fighting," he told me when I asked what he fills his days with. "I've found a job. They pay me a little bit to clear tables and wash dishes, but they only let me work on the weekend. The rest of the week I'm bored." He paused for a minute and pushed around the scraps of food left on his plate then said, "I feel so useless." He didn't expand on that.

When I dropped MHA off for the night I gave him some money and told him it was toward his debt. I could see him getting squirmily uncomfortable because emotion was welling up in his eyes. He quickly broke eye contact and then gave me a hug. "Thank you, bro," he said into my ear. I reminded him that he's not alone, that life isn't meant to be done alone, and that we'll try our best together. I said a prayer for him and said goodnight. As I drove home, my heart was full and heavy. I prayed and asked God to reveal himself to MHA, to guard his heart and mind and dreams, and unfold a beautiful plan for his life.

As I lay awake that night thinking about MHA and my place in this war zone, I got a message from a soldier who's still in Karenni. He wanted to say hello and thank me for helping him. His message brought me back to when I had met him.

We were at the CCP as the battle of Mobye raged on. We got word that an ambulance was on the way bringing some patients so we quickly got things ready. Two vehicles came racing into the parking lot and before they even stopped the doors were open and they were unloading several patients. Dr. Myo quickly went to work triaging the patients. One man he gave pain medicine to, but looked at me and shook his head. "I'm trying to make him comfortable, but he will be dead soon," he said. The other boy, a young boy, had a bullet hole going through his calf and hadn't had any pain medicine. Dr. Myo didn't want to waste the pain medicine on this through-and-through bullet shot, so instead he took a roll of gauze and put it into the boy's mouth and told him to bite on the gauze when he was in pain. Dr. Myo started to cut into the calf muscle with his scalpel, removing some fragments and cleaning the wound. He stitched several layers of the wound as he worked.

I feel useless in these moments. I'm not a medical guy and I often feel like I don't know what to do and don't want to get in the way. In that moment I sat next to the boy while Dr. Myo operated on his leg.

The boy was biting hard on the gauze and reached his hand out. Instinctively I grabbed his hand. He squeezed my hand as Dr. Myo did his work on his leg, the boy's long fingernails digging into the back of my hand as he winced and bit on the gauze. I was in awe of the boy's strength. For twenty minutes I sat with him and held his hand. Finally the worst of it was over and he was able to spit out the gauze and take in his surroundings. It seemed this was the first time he noticed me, a strange look coming over his face and he quickly let go of my hand.

I spent some time talking and joking with him before he was transported back to a clinic for follow-up care. We exchanged our contact details and took a picture together. After dropping MHA off and getting a message from my friend, I was reminded again that we don't need any special skills to be here. We need God's love in our heart and a hand to hold, and we have a place. And the funny thing is, that often through these small, simple acts of love, holding someone's hand while you feel totally out of place and useless, opens up a door into that person's life. It is these small acts of love that move people out of the category of stranger and into the category of friends.

I've found a strange brotherhood with many of these warriors here in Burma. As we crouch in a trench together with explosions happening around us, or as we hold hands during the pain of wounds or malaria or amputations, or as we imitate the sounds of war, we find a common ground that goes beyond ethnic lines or religious lines or racial lines. When we bleed together and cry together and laugh together, we are not alone.

Back at our training camp a few months later I was immersed in the training of new teams. One of the advanced students who I've been on mission with is named Moses. He's only nineteen, but he's tough. He had malaria and was having a hard time. Very high fevers, convulsive chills, body aches, and a headache that laughs at migraines. The other night with tears streaming down his face from the pain of the fever he said two heartbreaking things. First he said he feels like he's dying and doesn't want to die. And second, which I suppose is closely followed whenever the first one is uttered, he said he misses his mom. It's hard for a heart not to shatter a little bit when you see someone in his state.

Last night we were all camped out in the jungle to avoid any airstrikes on our camp. I'd had my winter hammock sent in as it was getting cold at night. I was looking forward to a cozy sleep and because I'd had a poor sleep the night before, I was exhausted. LayKay had returned from another village and set his hammock up beside me. It had the makings for a great night: cooking over the fire, a warm hammock, good friends all around, and even a shot of jungle whiskey each.

But Moses was sick and as I visited him I could tell he was dreading the oncoming night. Having had malaria a few months ago I could relate to his feelings. I would have a stack of towels beside my bed. In the morning they'd all be soaked through with sweat. All night my muscles would take turns cramping as I tossed and turned. Sweating, shivering, convulsing, aching. It's miserable. And as I said goodnight to Moses and walked back to my hammock I couldn't help but think that I shouldn't leave him. He shouldn't feel alone tonight. A few minutes at my hammock and I knew I had to go back and stay with him.

He had thrown his tarp down on the ground. He didn't care about the boulders, rocks, roots, and shoots that he lay down on. He curled into a ball under two blankets and shivered, but as I lay down next to him he reached his hand over and in the dark managed to find my hand and squeezed and mumbled thank you the way only a teenager can.

It's funny how your body remembers things.

As I squirmed and sighed trying to contort my body into a spot with no rocks or branches under it, my body suddenly remembered the last time I slept on the ground like this. Almost instantly the night of the mortar attack flashed through my mind. I was sleeping on the ground, only a small tarp between me and the ground. I could feel the cold of the earth below me. Ants and other night crawlers tickled me as they explored the new warm presence. All night I would toss and turn trying to stay warm and find that perfect spot to sleep. Then at 3:00 a.m when the first mortar round came in with such violent force that it sent dirt spraying over us, I realized we were being targeted in a mortar attack. The next round crashed in so close that its roar came from hell itself.

As I lay on the cold hard ground next to Moses all these memories soaked through my body. The memories were almost as uncomfortable as the ground itself. But as I drifted in and out of the memories and sleep, I noticed that something else was present there too: love.

On the mortar night, LayKay lay next to me. When the first round of death crashed in he instinctively found my hand in the dark. I rolled over top of him in what, to an outsider may have looked like bravery, throwing myself over him to protect him from the shrapnel and death, but was a fear-reaction to cling to love in the face of death. And as I lay next to Moses, his body fighting off the parasite of death, his hand clinging to mine, I couldn't help but also miss my mother.

Growing up, my two brothers and I all shared a bedroom. But at one point I remember saying I wanted my own room, so my parents prepared one in the unfinished basement. There wasn't much reason to go down to the basement in those days, and when I saw my new bedroom it felt like Siberia. I wonder if any soldier has ever requested a transfer to Siberia? And I wonder if they miss their mothers when they arrive there, their request fulfilled. I remember being so scared the first night I slept in my new room. It might as well have been an entirely different house. But my mother stayed with me. She sat in a chair as I fell asleep, reading or doing the crossword under a lamp. Her presence there helped me fight off fear. I remember waking up a few hours later and she was still there, the warm glow of the lamp still illuminating her book. Then a few hours after that, I rolled over and barely opened my eyes to see her still standing guard over me. Satan could have unleashed the fury of hell that night and my mother would have fought it off. Even though she never spent another night down there, for me, she never left.

Each time Moses would moan or toss and turn or sit up to change his sweat-drenched shirt, I would sit up, find his hand in the darkness, and squeeze it a little bit to let him know I hadn't left. I'd say another prayer for him.

We aren't meant to be alone.

Chapter 22

Beauty

I sat on the beach staring out into the ocean. The gentle crash, crash, crashing of the waves lulled me into a trance, the riptide playfully pulling the sand from under my feet as I sat on the sand, still warm from the intense sun of the day. Each wave seemed to creep closer to me as it washed ashore. I felt small as I looked out into the vastness.

I can't believe I'm still alive.

The thought came to me totally unexpectedly. It was a slow, unhurried thought that came like a beach drink, mixed with the salt and sand of the ocean to make it almost relaxing. I'd been out of the jungle for only a few days, and the reality of being in a safe place was only starting to wash over me. For the past four-and-a-half months I'd been in the jungle and faced some serious threats. There is no safe place in Burma anymore. I used to always feel safe in our camp, but not this year. This year I felt like I was living in the bullseye of a big target, lying on my back, looking up to the sky, arms wide open, ready to catch the 500-pound bombs the jets were carrying and dropping on all our neighbors.

I was surprised when the thought popped into my head, I can't believe I'm still alive. I didn't realize how close I felt to death and how accepting I'd become of living in that space. But after only a few days of safety my soul took a deep breath and whispered a sigh of relief. My ears still perked up every time an airliner took off. The obnoxious roar of the jet engines would send shivers down my spine, and my heart would skip a beat or three before my brain would say, "It's only Thai Airways..." This reaction to the sound of airplanes would haunt me for years to come.

Burma Army jets are designed to be silent on approach. You can only hear the dragon-roar of their engine once they're directly over you or past you, already too late. The Burma Army bombs in the middle of the night between 11:00 p.m. and 3:00 a.m., the most vulnerable time of our lives, when we've succumbed to all the events of the day and lie prone in our deepest sleep. The jets have no red and green or white lights that flash in the darkness to allow you to spot them. They come as an angry roar. They come as evil in the sky. They come as Smaug, an angry beast hellbent on consuming and destroying anything in its path. There's nothing you can see, nothing you can spot, track, or pick out of the sky. It's only blackness that envelops you and the growl of death prowling around.

I remember the night when I frantically sprinted into the jungle. It's unwise to turn on your headlamp in the middle of the night when the jets come, in case it catches the eye of the pilot and he changes course. So we ran in total darkness, me and LayKay and Htwar, straight up the side of the mountain as the hungry growl of the jets prowled overhead.

We crouched in the jungle in the middle of the night, listening to the sky as the jets made wide swoops, lower and lower, angrier and angrier with each pass. I began to shiver. To this day I don't know if it was the cold of the December night or the intense fear of death hunting me, but my body shook as I sat in the dirt. No insects crawled on me. Nothing stirred. It was as if all creation were crouching in a trench waiting for the boom of the impact.

We heard distant booms of the bombs landing.

And it's here that I must pause and ask forgiveness for using the word "boom" to describe the sound of the bombs. It isn't a boom. I can't describe how the tinny bass sounded as it echoed off the mountains that I shivered on, because at the moment it wasn't a sound at all, but only a feeling. I have difficulty describing how sound mixed with darkness and temperature to create a noise that my ear told my brain must be evil. It was only the thudding footstep of death stomping on something, shaking the ground from miles away.

But that night it was not stomping on me or my camp. It was stomping on my neighbors. A strange feeling came over me, one of thankfulness and relief that I was not the one in the thermobaric vacuum the bomb causes, ripping the air from you as it collapses your lungs despite the walls of your trench or bunker protecting you from the shrapnel. But the thankfulness for the air in my lungs was thin with sadness, knowing that the bomb landed on my friends, our neighbors, and in the darkness I could only hope and pray they were breathing still as I was.

How do you fall back asleep after all that?

Yet I did. Three months of this had conditioned me to know that for tonight, Smaug was satisfied. He'd had his fill of destruction for the night, and it's almost surprising how quickly I could fall back asleep, clutching the radio to listen again for the early warning signal to pass over.

My soul seemed to sigh out these memories as I sat beside the ocean on my break.

I can't believe I'm still alive, my soul whispered, to whom I'm not sure—maybe it was a prayer of thanks, maybe it was letting my heart and brain know that I was safe now, that I didn't need to worry about the sound of the jets anymore. Or maybe it was whispering to the waves and ocean as the beauty of the sea playfully and powerfully whispered back.

Beauty heals us. The dark colors of the water at dusk and the bold colors of the clouds as the last of the day's light disappeared were helping me heal as I sat there and drank in the beauty. There is so much beauty in Burma. It takes my breath away all the time, and it's a paradox that among all the death and destruction is beauty that heals and restores. I let my mind drift back to some of the beauty I'd seen over the past few months.

The timpani of mortars made a background soundtrack as we were led up the river only a few weeks earlier. Despite the sounds of war in the distance, I couldn't help but wonder if we'd somehow stumbled into the Garden of Eden. The river seemed to flow directly through the forest rather than in one channel. Clumps of trees grew right out of the crystal-clear water. Mini waterfalls stepped down like stairs, wide platforms of water stretching between each step. Sometimes there was a bigger drop—waterfalls descending into deep pools of crystal-clear water. Beautiful, big trees were scattered throughout the flooded ground, forming a canopy that let the intense sun through in gentle streaks. The water was cool but not cold, and the rocks along the bottom had a grip of calcium on them so you could step anywhere without fear of slipping, as the water pedicured your feet.

"You're the first ever white person to visit this spot—at least, as far as my memory goes," the village leader, who was one of my guides, said to me as we settled on a picnic spot beside a small waterfall. I had a hard time believing him. Surely other foreigners had been here and seen this. But he insisted and tried to back up his claim with all the history of white people visiting his village during his lifetime. There weren't many.

I sat on top of the small waterfall, my legs dangling over the edge as streaks of sunshine warmed my body, and I tried to take a moment to soak in what my guide had told me. There are over seven billion people on this planet. I make Thailand my home base, and it sometimes feels like there isn't anywhere you can go in Thailand that doesn't have some tourist roaming around taking selfies in the sun. But here, deep in the war zone of Burma, was a piece of the Garden of Eden, and even though I'd never been here before, my soul somehow recognized it.

What do you do with such a gift as this? I pondered. Why me?

How can I be so lucky to be the first ever foreigner to see this magical place? So I slowed myself down. I did my best to drink in each detail of the beauty. I swam in some of the deep pools. I took off my flip-flops so my feet could feel the rocks. I didn't rush. I prayed, "Jesus, I receive this beauty and your love into my soul." I let the beauty soak my tired heart like a warm bath, because that's what beauty is supposed to do, isn't it? I sat for a while and let myself be mesmerized by the ripples of sunshine dancing off the water onto the canopy of jungle leaves above. I let the white noise of the rushing water drown out the sounds of war in the distance, and for a few minutes every detail of life seemed to be perfect.

I let my imagination wander back to Genesis. Is this what every moment of every day would have felt like in the Garden? I imagined that the beauty I was soaking in was only a shattered glimpse of what an untarnished beauty was like back then, and will be once again when it's restored. As a writer, I sat and stared at small snippets of the scene before me and wondered, how can I use words to describe this? How could I use my simple vocabulary to paint the way that tree leaned over that deep pool of water, and the white water from the waterfall mixed with deep blues and greens and yellow streaks of sunlight to form colors that I could feel but not describe. When colors become feelings no amount of vocabulary will do justice to the description. God is like that too. I think of the attempt that John made in Revelation to describe the indescribable. And as I sat and lapped in the beauty, it filled my heart with a hope that what was to come would be even better than anything I could describe now.

I'd experienced beauty in Burma that soaked deep into my weary bones and heart to restore and heal. I'd also experienced beauty in relationships as love shone brighter than fear or war.

It was almost two weeks ago that Htwar came back to our camp with a bag of flour. I laughed as he carried it into our house, and I asked him what he was going to do with it. He told me, "Mee Mar's birthday is coming up, and I want to make her a cake." We had a bag of flour—this was a good start for a birthday cake for his girlfriend's birthday. We found some baking soda in a Tupperware container that was probably a few years old. We had a rice cooker we could use as an oven. We had eggs from the chickens this morning, and we had some sugar. We had sweetened condensed milk and lots of bananas in the jungle trees. Surely this was enough to make a cake.

We found a recipe on the internet and did our best to follow it. We didn't have butter. We didn't have buttermilk. We didn't have two cups of sugar or vanilla extract. But we had a desire to celebrate our friend, so we used that ingredient as a substitute for the things we were missing, and we made a batter. We plopped it into the rice cooker and hit the cook button, shrugged, and then forgot about it for a few hours. When we remembered and checked on it we were blessed to find a beautiful cake.

There'd been so much death that year. So much mourning. So much loss of life. So much fighting against joy. And even that day, with a bag of flour and another birthday, there felt like so much against this. Htwar and I had no idea what we were doing. Neither of us had ever baked a cake in a rice cooker. We were missing ingredients. We were lazy. But somewhere deep in both of us we felt that celebrating his girlfriend, celebrating her life, celebrating life itself, was worth trying. So try we did.

When the cake was finished we brought Mee Mar over. We'd put candles into the cake, but it was still too hot, and the candles melted and fell over. No problem. We blindfolded Mee Mar and led her upstairs as we replaced the candles. We sang "Happy Birthday" as we removed the blindfold. We had a piece of paper we'd folded into a simple card, in which we each wrote a little note or drew a picture. As we performed our rendition of "Happy Birthday," many of Mee Mar's team members heard and started to come join us. Soon there were over fifty people crammed into our small house. Most were friends who knew Mee Mar, but some had only just met her. They wanted to be a part of a celebration. In a place where celebrations are rare, where life is hard and scary, this celebration was a magnet to pull in all the hungry souls within range. But even as we tried to celebrate, the enemy seemed intent on crushing the celebration.

"Airplane! Airplane! Airplane!" came the call over the radio. A call we all fear and dread hearing, but one we'd avoided hearing for the past 48 hours. It's a radio call that always sends shivers down our spines and stops whatever is happening. But that day, for some reason, we all felt that celebrating was more important than running for the bunkers. Even I, a generally fearful person, thought, "If a bomb lands on us as we're celebrating Mee Mar, then that's an okay way to die." We simultaneously fell silent for a moment—only a moment—to all listen to the sky. Then Hte Reh strummed a familiar chord on the guitar, and everyone began singing celebration songs again.

Helena got down on her knees as the song ended and folded her hands and began praying a blessing over Mee Mar. As I listened to her prayer I couldn't help but think of the friends Helena had lost that year: Elizabeth, Hsi Hsi, and Ree Doh, to name a few. I couldn't understand her prayer, but I could feel her celebration of Mee Mar's life, despite all the death we'd faced that year. Finally. Finally, we could celebrate.

Mee Mar stood up at the end. She'd been celebrated more than ever before, and more than was necessary, and not nearly enough, all at the same time. She started to make a thank-you speech, as she looked out on all the faces packed into the room, but was overcome by tears.

But isn't that how it's supposed to go? Isn't the ultimate purpose of a simple bag of flour, not to produce cookies or bread or cake, but rather tears of joy? Even Jesus—we celebrate his life and death and resurrection each month with bread. Of course, it's not about the actual product the flour and sugar are baked into, but rather it's the act of remembering. A life, a birthday, a death, a crucifixion, a new beginning, an addiction freed—flour is transformed into something sweet enough to celebrate a new life.

It started with a bag of flour. I'm not even sure where Htwar got it, but somewhere in the jungle of Burma he found a bag of flour. He didn't know what to do with it, but he knew that girlfriends need celebrating on their birthdays and birthdays need cake and cakes need flour.

What a beautiful thing it is to be celebrated. What a great thing it is—a heavenly thing—to celebrate extravagantly those we love.

Celebrations that heal and restore our tired hearts.

Chapter 23

Missionary

More than eight years ago was the first time I snuck across the border into Burma. When we got to the border, which was marked by a river, we were about to start unloading our trucks—two trucks full of supplies and medicine—when suddenly a border guard patrol was upon us. They'd been in the bush and we hadn't seen them. Our boat that we were going to meet was waiting across the river on the Burma side, watching the scene unfold. The border guard troop, about ten strong, raised their guns as they formed a circle around our two trucks. I knew that crossing into Burma was no joke and that there was potential for risk, but I had no idea that risk would find me so soon. I was crammed in the back seat of the small club-cab pickup. Our driver turned around and said, "Don't get out of the vehicle." And then he himself cautiously got out.

The rest of us in the vehicle started to pray that we wouldn't be arrested or worse. Our driver talked to the leader of the border guard for ten long minutes, and then motioned for all of us to get out of the trucks. We looked at each other and got out. They lined us up and one by one took our photos, then took photos of us as a group and with our truck. Then it seemed the official business was over and the mood suddenly changed. While they've got this group of foreigners they might as well snap a few selfies with them. So after our official photos were taken, we posed for a half-dozen hero-shots. Their commander confidently said something to them and after one more quick selfie with the foreigners, walked down the bank of the river, got into a boat, and disappeared up the river. What had happened? I have no idea. I have no idea what our driver said to them or what they did with our photos. But I sighed a big sigh of relief. It wasn't time to stand around—we waved at our boat waiting across the river, they came over, and we quickly unloaded the supplies from the back of the truck, got into the boat, and crossed.

I don't know much about being a missionary, other than I believe that all Christians are missionaries. Some just travel farther from home to live and work than others. In my first couple years living on support overseas, on what most would commonly refer to as the "mission field," I wouldn't have referred to myself as a missionary. I felt like I wasn't deserving of that title. Growing up, whenever an overseas missionary would visit the church they always seemed to have it all together, almost like they were super Christians, the finest selection from the congregation, chosen on their merit, to go and share the gospel with the world.

I definitely didn't fit into that category. I occasionally enjoy smoking a nice cigar, and I've been known to have a drink or two of alcohol. I like to listen to loud music and occasionally let out the odd cuss word or two. I have a problem with authority and being told what to do, and I am not a super prayer warrior or Scripture memorizer. I am afraid of everything, super selfish, and don't like being uncomfortable or dirty. I don't seem to fit the typical image or idea of a missionary. Like one friend of FBR said when describing us, "You are an island of misfit toys." Maybe that's why I've found my place here.

One thing I learned early on about being a missionary was that the most important thing was my personal relationship with God.

Nothing else mattered outside of that. Jesus said, "I am the vine, you are the branch." But too often we're like cut flowers, sheared off, and desperately need to be grafted back to Jesus. I realized quickly that if my relationship with Jesus was on track, then all those other missionary things that supporters like to read about in newsletters, and hear about in the seven minutes churches give you to update when you're home, fall into place on their own. The conversions, the baptisms, the healings, the miracles—all that stuff will take care of itself as long as I "seek first God and His kingdom."

Sometimes I charge ahead in the humanitarian cause of FBR, fighting for widows and orphans and for justice, but through that I forget to invite Jesus along. I need to put my priorities straight, and it's been helpful for me to remind myself, and give myself permission, to know what my priorities are for the day. I occasionally have an early morning meeting, or if I'm on mission, a village move that starts before the sun rises, and I skip reading my Bible and talking to God that day. But if I remind myself "this is the most important thing I will do today"—spending time talking with my King—then it gives me permission to slow down. I can even be late for a meeting, I can be super inefficient with my life, because the most important thing is that I get myself right with God. If I don't start in my own heart, the rest of it is wasted movements.

The next thing that I know for sure about being a missionary is that it's about loving people. Everyone. I'm not good at this, but step by step I'm trying. Dave often paraphrases Mother Teresa by saying, "God does not look at the greatness of the work, but at the love in which it's performed." It is possible to sneak across borders, avoid landmines, hike through jungle trails and help someone in need, without love in your heart for them. I did it. The first couple years I was in the jungle it was mainly selfishly driven. At first I would live in constant fear of everything in the jungle, so my days were not full of love—they were full of trying to make myself comfortable and create a bubble of safety for myself within the jungle. But slowly as I learned the jungle ways of life and got comfortable with spiders and the creepy crawlies, my motive shifted, but still wasn't led in love. It was now led by adventure. I wanted an adventure, so I would push for the mission, I would push to go somewhere new, but it wasn't out of love. Over time something happened in my heart. I fell in love with these ethnic Rangers I work alongside. Through the adventures, through the fears we faced side by side, we became brothers. I wanted to be with them through thick or thin. I wanted to go visit their villages and put on programs there, because those people meant something to them, and they meant something to me.

I look at the work of my boss, Dave Eubank, and he's done a lot of incredible things in his life. He loves the unusual and unique and has lived the missionary life in a unique way. I respect him and I'm thankful to be part of his team, but one of the things I think is his greatest achievement in the past twenty-five years of Free Burma Rangers is that he never left. He heard the call of God to help the people in Burma and that's what he's been doing. He hasn't wavered from his mission. He hasn't gone off chasing the next best thing. When we decided to move to international missions it was led by and attended by our Burmese ethnic leaders. They were right there with him and even when he wasn't physically in Burma, Burma was with him. I think a skill my generation is lacking is staying power. We will have dozens of careers (not jobs, but careers) throughout our lives. We change our interests as quickly as we can change the channels on TV. But Dave has never left the people in Burma. He's shown them he has the staying power to not give up on them. He has loved them through thick and thin, when it's hard and scary, and when it's boring and easy.

I'm still learning how to love people well. It requires a lot of giving up my selfish desires and living in grace. But when it boils down to it, working as a missionary is easy, whether it's in Burma or in your backyard—love God, love others. And that's it. If you call yourself a Christian, you are also a missionary. You don't need to go to Burma to love people there, but you do need to leave your house, leave your computer screen, and go love people. I hope our church can be known for outlandish amounts of love that it pours out on the community around it. All I have to do is consider the amount of grace that Jesus pours out to me every day, and if that grace was a commodity, how can I match the amount with the love I give to others? Unfortunately, I often require more grace from God than the amount of love I give to others. But slowly it's changing. Slowly I'm finding it easier to love people I wouldn't normally choose to love. And through that love, I can share my Jesus with them, point them to the cross, and walk with them.

When I first went onto the mission field I didn't have a clue what I was doing. I had no money in my bank account, I had two supporters—one was my mom—and had no idea even what it meant to be a missionary. But I knew for sure that God was telling me to go, and when God tells you to go, then you have to trust him that he'll take care of the rest, because his Bible says he will. I was not, and am still not, a superstar Christian. I attend a church sometimes not far from our headquarters that is full of missionaries like me. I was asked to preach there one Sunday and I told them that I felt intimidated to stand in front of them, the real missionaries, the Bible translators, the scholars, the church planters, the ones who must have been the all-stars in their home congregation. It might have been a joke, but I was feeling this intimidation as I stood in front of them. I gave my sermon, and afterwards a man came up to me and took me aside and said, "I was pastor of this church back in the nineties, and I'm back here visiting, and what you said at the beginning of your message, I felt that feeling every single Sunday."

But one reassuring place for me is in the stories of the Bible. Not a single person that God used in the Bible was a superstar Christian. Not one of the characters in the Bible that did amazing things were Ned Flanders. More to the point, they sometimes drank so much they passed out naked (Noah), they despised other ethnic groups and tried to run away from God (Jonah), they had people killed so they could sleep with their wives (David), they were terrorists going place to place burning down churches and killing Christians (Paul). God uses broken people to bring his message and kingdom to the world. Because broken people understand grace.

Recently I've been asking God about the amount of alcohol I consume. And I must confess to you, dear reader, that this issue sort of snuck up on me. It started in Karenni State. Our mission was the bloodiest mission FBR had been involved in in Burma since the organization began. Every day we were carrying the dead and wounded from the front lines back to safe areas. By the end of the day, I was exhausted. I would go home, wash the blood out of my clothes, and get ready to sleep. Every day I would find two beers in my hammock, placed there by one of my teammates. Slowly I began to rely on those two beers to help me relax before I fell asleep. They became the crutch I needed to shift my brain off the images of the day.

I don't have a moral problem with alcohol or drinking. I do think it's sinful to get drunk, but I felt fine sipping my beer next to the evening fire. But slowly, alcohol crept into my life. I would get this feeling as I entered a meeting or visited with a friend that having a drink or two—not getting drunk, just a glass or two—would help me relax and say what I wanted to say. And that's a problem. I look to the cold beer or glass of wine to give me comfort, to give me confidence, instead of looking to God to fill that need.

I've been learning that our legacy is our pattern in life. If I let this pattern of alcohol continue it would eventually become my legacy in life. If I let the pattern of shame continue in my life, shame would be my legacy on this earth. And as broken as I am, if I let brokenness be my pattern in life, brokenness will be my legacy. Dave's pattern has been to go to the war zone and help and love people as best he can. That will be his legacy that he leaves behind. So I choose grace instead of shame day by day. I choose healing instead of brokenness, through God, through counseling, through living in community. I choose to try and become a better man, more like Jesus, each day that I can. Salvation happens that moment you invite Jesus to save you, but Jesus doesn't leave you in that place. He wants to bring bits of heaven to you now. Healing, restoration, deliverance from addictions—it's all available through Jesus, but it takes time and relationship.

I'm a big believer in what John Eldredge calls the three keys to the masculine soul: a battle to fight, adventure, and beauty. When I don't have these things in my life, as a man, I feel lost, floundering or untethered. Working with Free Burma Rangers has been one of the greatest gifts of my life, something I've been honored to be a part of, because every day that I go to work at FBR I experience all three of those things. This book is a few of the adventures that have filled my life over the past decade, but I can assure you there are many more. And we have a big battle to fight, sometimes physically, but often for the hearts of the people we love and serve. And walking through Burma I've experienced some of the most breathtaking, untouched beauty on this planet. In the lives of our Rangers and in many friends in Burma, I get to experience beauty and love. It's sometimes hard for me to adjust back into the city life after a mission in the jungle. The concrete of the city is not beautiful like the jungle mountains.

The jungle is slow. Nothing happens quickly in the jungle. Things happen when they happen and no one seems to mind. No one is in a hurry. I think there's something about the nature of my heart that feels the urge to rush once I get on my motorcycle. I can pass someone, I can go faster than someone else, and find a more efficient route. Because I can get from place to place so quickly and without much effort, I tend to fill my days with too many meetings and people. And the rush from my motorcycle doesn't stop when I turn my bike off. The adrenaline continues to surge into whatever meeting or appointment I happen to come into. There are times in the jungle where everyone disappears into their hammocks and takes a nap. It seems crazy to do something like that when you're living in the city. There's something about the city that forces us to compete with the rush and technology. Our heart and soul wasn't designed to go the speed of a smartphone. In the jungle we rise and sleep with the sun. There's something beautiful about that rhythm. We have solar at our camp, but it usually has run out by eight or nine at night. The sun comes up at 6:00 a.m. and sets at 6:00 p.m. My body gets trained to the natural rhythm of life and nature instead of the lights that never shut off in the city, the noise that never stops, and the pace that doesn't slow.

In the jungle you bathe and wash your clothes in the river. Sometimes the water is muddy and often it's cold, but it feels like more of a connection to creation than throwing a pile of clothes into a washing machine and pushing a button. In the jungle on a mission I have three sets of clothing: one I'm wearing, one that is drying, and one I'm going to change into at the end of the day when I shower and wash the clothes I'm wearing. Fashion and style aren't as important in the jungle.

Slowly you make peace with the insects of the jungle: spiders, scorpions, snakes, centipedes. They have their place and you have yours. In the city I turn to chemicals and pesticides to kill any of these things I find in my house. These things may be predatory, but I am not their prey. They are there, created by the Creator in the same way I was. There's a rhythm to life and to death in the jungle. Death is fought against but with much fewer and different tools then we have in the west. It is sad when one dies, and we grieve, but then we move on, because death is a natural part of life in the jungle.

In the jungle I have found a place where my strength is needed, a place where I am loved and where I love my community. I have found a place where my knowledge and experiences are relied upon, as I rely on the knowledge and experience of my ethnic family.

The jungle, and following God, has been the greatest adventure of my life. It struck me this morning that of course you're going to grow up during an adventure. There's no other way about it. By definition, adventure means to enter into the unknown, and whenever we give ourselves permission to enter into the unknown, we will learn something, we will be tested, we will grow. When we enter into the unknown, our strength is needed. Our community needs our knowledge and problem solving and experience. And in many ways, God is an adventure. He is the Great Unknown, and when we cast off the ropes, push away from the dock, and venture into the Great Unknown, he will meet us there and he will return us to shore, changed. Having experienced him in new ways, ways we didn't have categories for before. But by stepping into the Unknown, he gives us a new category to receive him in. And it's beautiful, and it's what Christians would call sanctification, the process of being made whole and holy. It doesn't happen by staying put in the city or faithfully attending church every Sunday. It means facing fear, bankruptcy, demons, and even death. It means maybe freezing at night or heat exhaustion by day. It means cooking over fire, dirt under your nails, calluses on your hands and feet and sore muscles, muscles you didn't even know you had. It means wolves and bears and snakes and spiders and stings and scrapes and bites. And you won't die. And if you do, you'll be celebrated and missed here on earth, but be moving into a far greater adventure in heaven.

Dave has said to me, "You either have a religion or a living God," a thought I cling to whenever I find myself facing the unknown on a new adventure, when that false self in me screams as I leave my comfort zone and enter into a place where I don't know what I'm doing. Because if I have a living God with me, then why should I fear? And if I don't believe that God is a living God, then all I have is a religion, and I've never wanted one of those. I need to ask myself: God either parted the Red Sea, or he didn't. He either felled the walls of Jericho, or he didn't. He either walked on water and calmed storms, or he didn't. He either rose from the dead after being tortured and crucified, or he didn't. And if I believe that he did all that, and if I believe him when he says he is with me, and when I trust that he is the one leading me, then who and what shall I fear? Bring it on. Let's go. Green lights as far as you can see. Go for it.

Men and boys in the West are bored, lazy, and fearful. It's not their fault. They are a product of the safety culture they're raised in. They experience the diseases of affluence. The World Health Orga-nization did a study that found humans live ninety-three percent of their lives indoors. What's your gut reaction to that statistic? I've shared it with friends all over the world, of many religions and no religion, and not once has someone celebrated it as an achievement. Not once. Why?

I push one button on a machine, half asleep, and it spits out coffee at me. I don't need to chop wood, light a fire, go collect water, slowly and patiently wait for it to boil, and attempt to pour it over grounds without burning myself. I turn a dial and get a hot shower instead of the freezing river. I sleep on a mattress instead of bamboo and dirt. I push another button and air conditioning replaces the sweat and heat. Thousands of restaurants will deliver anything I want, any time, day or night—hot cappuccino, fresh fruit smoothie, whole pizza. Shouldn't all this convenience make my life and heart and soul happier? And yet, as I transition from jungle to city, the real to the artificial, I find it doesn't. I find I am living out the statistic of ninety-three percent indoors. I find adventure on Netflix or a video game. I find exercise in a climate-controlled gym with a trainer.

Somewhere deep down in my soul, that part of me that experienced something before I had memory or knowledge to experience, remembers being formed from the dirt of the garden of Eden, and it longs to return. Ecclesiastes tells us that God has "hidden eternity in our hearts". There is a deep part of all of us that knows that ninety-three percent of our lives indoors is not a statistic to celebrate, but to mourn, without needing to be taught about creation or the Creator. That deep part of us that comes alive when we turn off the pavement onto a dirt trail, when we shove the canoe into the water and leave the shore behind, when we gather wood to make a fire so we can hopefully eat something.

God is wild. His creation is wild. Our hearts are wild. We try so hard to tame them and teach the wild out of them, but they always remember. As a young man, God knew what I needed for my initiation, it wasn't a quiet monastery or sterilized office. But instead, I said yes to God. I said I would follow him and trust him wherever he leads me. And he took me onto the greatest adventure I have ever been on. He led me deep into the wild, into a forgotten place, to a forgotten people, with one task: try your best to love them. I didn't know what it meant to be a missionary, but God has shown me that part of it is making myself vulnerable by being willing to face the unknown and be changed by it.

And each year that I return into the jungle, each year that God wills me back, I think to myself, "There's no way that this year can be more of an adventure than last year was..."

And then God winks and smiles.

Chapter 24

Revolution

Ten years ago I stepped off a plane in Thailand, a naive kid from a small town in the middle of nowhere who thought adventure was the point. I didn't know anything about war. I didn't know anything about suffering. I didn't know that following God into the jungle would cost me friends, health, and pieces of my heart I didn't know I could lose. I didn't know that God would use blood-soaked ground and mortar-cratered earth to grow me up. I didn't know that love looks like holding a teenager's hand while a doctor cuts into his leg without anesthesia, or that joy tastes like rice-cooker cake with melted candles during an airstrike warning.

Now I know.

The revolution rages on in Burma. I was walking with Silverhorn one day and he said to me, "I'd rather that this becomes World War III, and I will fight and die, so my kids don't need to grow up and live their whole life in a war zone." For almost eighty years there has been civil war in Burma, and I fear that it will only get worse before it gets better. There is hardly anyone left in Burma who remembers a time before the war. Every person in the country has spent their entire lifetime in a country at war. Another villager said to me, "I will tell my children that war is terrible, but slavery is worse. They will not have to fight because I am fighting now." I walked and pondered that for a while. War is terrible, but slavery is worse. Having seen the horror of war firsthand, I wondered if it was true. I wondered about the things in my own life, my own heart, that I am slave to. War is messy, it is loud, it is chaotic, it is scary. As I walked and thought about the things in my life I am slave to, I wondered what it might look like to declare war on those things because war is terrible, but slavery is worse.

The ground in Burma is soaked with blood. The roots of the jungle plants and trees are growing out of the blood-soaked soil and the decaying flesh of corpses, many of them my friends. This is the cost of freedom. The people here are willing to give everything so that one day their revolution can succeed and their country can be free. I've had everything in my life handed to me. I've never had to fight for my freedom. And when it comes to my soul, Jesus has already won that war.

Last week I wrapped my arm around Htwar as we stood on the edge of camp, looking out at the jungle. We'd gotten word that the team was heading back into Karenni tomorrow. He'd be going. I wouldn't—not this time. My role was shifting, though I couldn't yet see to what.

"I love you, bro," I said to him. The words were almost as much a surprise to me as they were to him, but there seemed to be an unspoken brotherhood between us that made it an acceptable thing to say. We'd been through too much together for it to be anything but true.

After a brief pause to think, he said, "I love you too."

We stood there for a minute in comfortable silence, the kind only brothers can share. In the distance we could hear the sounds of the camp—someone laughing, the clang of cooking pots, the crackle of a radio. Normal sounds. War sounds. Home sounds.

"Be careful out there," I finally said.

He grinned. "I always am."

We both knew he was lying. Careful doesn't win revolutions. But love does. Love that's willing to walk back into the fire. Love that holds the line when jets scream overhead. Love that keeps showing up, keeps putting on tourniquets, keeps burying friends, keeps celebrating birthdays with melted candles, keeps fighting because slavery is worse than war.

I realized in that moment that I'd spent ten years learning how to love the nameless, faceless people. The ones we look at but don't see. The ones who wash the dishes or hold the general's coffee. I've learned that a smile can be magical—it can defuse a situation, make a new friend, invite someone to share their story, heal and give hope. I've learned that God is never boring. Sometimes I am boring, but God is never boring. Following God has been the wildest adventure I have ever been on. Every year has been more awesome than the last. Every glimpse of God's goodness is even more humbling than the one before.

I can't help but realize, as I live in the midst of this beautiful revolution, that the greatest revolution is the one that happens in my heart. I have been reflecting lately about my heart as the dwelling place of Jesus. My heart is God's temple, the Bible tells me. I think back through the Bible stories, about God first dwelling in the tabernacle, his glory filling the tent and leading Israel on. Then later when Solomon built the temple, God's glory descended on it and his glory filled it as he resided there. I also can't help but think about when Jesus went into the temple and saw that this place that was meant to house his Father's glory had been turned into a marketplace. He fashioned a whip and went to war. He overturned tables and drove cattle out. He scattered coins across the stone floor and cracked his whip as he fought with a vengeance—a revolution for the temple.

The greatest revolution is in my heart, a conclusion I come to with reluctance, knowing there are a few tables in the temple of my heart that I need Jesus to overturn, but I am still afraid of the pain it might cause.

I attended the Karen Revolution Day marking the 75th year of the Karen Revolution. A villager leaned over to me during one of the speeches and joked, "Can we call it a revolution if it takes 75 years? Shouldn't we use a different word by now?" I laughed at his joke, but his words stuck with me. The definition of a revolution is the "forcible overthrow of a government or social order, in favor of a new system." So I suppose with that definition the Karen are still in the midst of their revolution. What impresses me as I reflect on their war is that they haven't given up on their overthrow of the Burma government in favor of a new system. There is a feeling in Burma now that the end is near, that this most recent coup will be the last. The people dream that the dictator, General Min Aung Hlaing, will be killed and his body will be dragged through the streets as people celebrate their victory.

For me, on that day, I hope I am still here. I hope the country will become free and I can travel to every corner of this beautiful place. I hope to eat a meal and drink a beer in the homes of all my friends in all corners of the country.

I come back again to this idea of the greatest revolution is the one in the human heart. If my heart is the temple of the living God, and if at times Jesus needed to "forcibly overthrow the social order" of the day—turning over those tables of the vendors who had turned the temple into a crowded marketplace—then I need to reflect seriously on the revolution of my heart. The image of the Karen Revolution is a lifetime of work, with some good days and some bad days. It inspires me to a lifetime revolution of my heart. There will be some good days, and there will be some tears and maybe even some blood that needs to be shed, but I shouldn't get discouraged because my heart revolution isn't finished yet. If I have learned anything from the Karen, it's to not lose focus on the end goal—a peaceful life of freedom. If I have learned anything from a decade with the Free Burma Rangers, it's to never surrender in the fight for that goal.

That morning I sat on a hillside overlooking the valley where our camp sits. The sun was beginning to rise, painting the jungle in shades of gold and green. Mist was lifting off the trees. Somewhere in the distance I could hear the faint sound of mortars—the timpani of war that never quite stops. But up here, for this moment, it was quiet.

I closed my eyes and prayed. Not fancy words. Honest ones.

"Jesus, I don't know what comes next. I don't know if I'll survive another ten years of this. I don't know how many more friends I'll lose. I don't know if Burma will be free in my lifetime. I don't know if the tables in my heart will ever be fully overturned. But I'm still here. I'm still yours. I'm still saying yes."

And then, so quiet I almost missed it, I sensed his presence next to me. Not audibly. Not visibly. But as real as Htwar's arm had been around my shoulder. As real as the sunrise painting the jungle gold.

I sensed him looking out at the same view I was looking at. The jungle where I'd learned to make peace with spiders. The trails where I'd carried wounded soldiers. The rivers where I'd found pieces of the Garden of Eden. The villages where flour became cake and tears became joy and strangers became brothers.

"Isn't it beautiful?" I sensed him whisper.

And I realized he wasn't talking about the view. He was talking about all of it. The whole decade. The fear and the courage. The death and the life. The revolution happening in Burma and the revolution happening in my heart. The nameless, faceless people who'd become my family. The God who is never boring, who leads his children into the wild, who overturns tables and weeps with Mary and whispers "Isn't it beautiful?" over the broken, blood-soaked, glorious mess of a life lived in the jungle.

"Yes," I whispered back, tears running down my face. "Yes, it is."

The revolution continues. In Burma. In my heart. In the hearts of every Ranger who pulls on their boots and walks back into the fire. In every bag of flour that becomes a cake. In every hand held during surgery. In every moment of silence for the dead. In every choice to love instead of hate, to fight instead of surrender, to say yes to God even when the cost is everything.

War is terrible.

But slavery is worse.

And so the revolution rages on.

I opened my eyes. The sun had fully risen now. Down in the valley I could see movement—the team was stirring, getting ready. Getting ready to go back. To keep fighting. To keep loving. To keep being the nameless, faceless people who carry light into dark places.

I stood up, wiped my eyes, and started walking back down the hill.

There was work to do.

The revolution wasn't finished yet.

Neither was I.

Acknowledgments

Leaving the Free Burma Rangers was one of the hardest decisions I've had to make in life. For the past decade, FBR had become my family. I had learned and grown so much—at times it felt like God's hand was almost visible as he reached down to shelter us or provide for us. When I started seriously wrestling with the idea of leaving, I met another mentor-friend for coffee, and he gave me great advice: "If you're going to leave, leave beautifully. Keep your side of the street clean."

The process of leaving FBR was not easy. We had many meetings to discuss why I was leaving and if my new idea, to form the Jungle Discipleship School, could just be folded in under the FBR umbrella. I kept reminding myself, "Make it beautiful." I explained to Dave, who had fathered me through much of my initiation, that I didn't want him to consider this like a divorce, but rather that one of his kids had grown up and was ready to spread his wings and leave home.

"I will have some failures on my own, and I'll have some successes on my own, but I need to do it on my own," I explained to him as we walked around the lake next to his ranch.

"You have my blessing," he graciously said back to me. "If there is anything you need, just call me. If your new program doesn't work out, you always have a home with us here at FBR."

And with that, I was on my own.

As I drove away from that meeting with Dave, I heard the still small voice I'd spent the past decade tuning my ear to hear. "You can lose it all, but as long as you have me, we'll be ok," Jesus whispered to my fragile heart.

I remembered seeing a photo of Nate Collins many years ago. You could make out his silhouette in the jungle, and he was giving some instructions to a group of ethnics. He had camo fatigues on and an old-school chest rig. I remember seeing the photo and thinking to myself that Nate was the coolest person on the planet and I wanted to be him. It was that photo and desire that reminded me of the Free Burma Rangers a decade ago.

Adam was my first real friend at FBR, and he continues to be my friend to this day. Adam and Micah thought it would be a great idea to light an explosive outside my office window one morning. The small cherry bomb packed way more punch than they were anticipating, and I walked out of the office looking stunned, my ears ringing, wondering who I should strangle. Adam and Micah stood looking equally stunned, but with boyish grins on their faces. Adam would go on to marry Aimee, and because Aimee had about fifty bridesmaids, Adam's side needed an equal number of groomsmen. Adam only had about three friends at the time, so he scraped the bottom of the barrel and asked if I'd stand up at his wedding as one of his groomsmen. It was a beautiful wedding—Aimee was stunning—and Jonathan and I enjoyed drinking some expensive wine that was a special present to the newlyweds.

Jonathan was only with FBR for a brief period, but we became fast friends. Adam, Jonathan, Justin, Eli, and I all rented a house together—what is now called Olive's House—and it was the beginning of the "FBR Commune." Jonathan and I would have wine and Nutella nights where we'd sit and drink a bottle of wine and eat Nutella by the spoonful.

Olive's House turned into a bit of a frat house. Let's just say we weren't the cleanest. We were a bunch of single men, all slightly rough around the edges, living in a foreign land. We needed a dorm mom. We thought it was a great idea—and why wouldn't someone want to do that? We approached our dear friend Lucy and asked her if she would like to be our house mom. "You wouldn't have to clean up after us; you'd just need to tell us what to do," we pitched to her. I think at first she thought it was a joke—there is no way these guys are serious about this. When she realized we were serious, I think she may have let a curse word slip in her definite "no."

Barry and Lucy became dear friends. Lucy and I did a mission to her native Kachin State one time, and Barry once made me drool over the best Cajun-fried spam and risotto. They taught me how to do real food distributions, and I always feel so honored to call them my friends.

Eli married Amber, Adam married Aimee, Jesse married Benita. The old gang slowly started pairing off and having the coolest, strongest, most amazing kids. Finan came first, followed by Eden. I got to hold Eden about fifteen minutes after she was born. She was gorgeous. Later, more kids came along, including Quinn, Adam and Aimee's second.

People come and people go at FBR; there were not a lot that stuck it out long-term. Bailey showed up as a young college girl and found a new home with us. She is a perfect match for Aimee—the life of the party, often before (and after) there even is a party. She has become like a sister to me and is an aunt to all the FBR kids. Hannah and Jack aren't technically FBR, but they live in the neighborhood, and we've always tried to recruit them.

Sky is an ex-marine who is as tough and brave as they come, but a total teddy bear. But don't tell anyone I told you that; it's an FBR secret. He married up, that's for sure, because his wife, Noelle, is a total rock star. With her southern twang, she once offered me a glass of whiskey and ended up pouring half the bottle into the cup like it was no big deal. She is Sky's brains. She can coordinate and plan anything. Sky and I like to play the alphabet game. We'll name a topic and then go back and forth through the alphabet naming things within that topic. I think he now plays that game with his amazing son, Hawk, and their newest, River.

Then there is Hosie. Hosie was and is an FBR legend. She had been the longest-serving FBR volunteer, just slightly more than Jesse. Hosie is always the most intelligent person in whatever room she's in, but you'd never know it because she'd be somewhere in the background baking scones, washing dishes, or just doing some sort of chore that is way below her pay grade. But that's the thing about Hosie: she doesn't believe there is any job below her pay grade. She once told me, "Learning how to print certificates and laminate stuff is FBR job security. . . . Plus, when it's really cold at night, the laminator keeps me warm."

We boys would often be debating the best way to save the world, arguing back and forth for hours on end, and then we would suddenly hear Hosie chime in, and she would say one sentence that was smarter and backed with more experiences than all of us. She was nicknamed the Ant because of her tiny stature and ability to lift a disproportionate amount of weight. Hosie knew way more than I did, but she graciously let me lead the Rohingya missions. On many missions since those days, I've often asked myself, "What would Hosie do?" We wouldn't have a Rohingya team without her. Thank you Hosie for editing this book.

Sahale, Suu, and Peter Eubank were just young when I first started at FBR, and now they're all in or finished with college. I can't believe it. They had the most amazing upbringing in war zones around the world, and they turned out amazingly. They are smart, strong, bold, humble, and intelligent kids. Sahale can stun a room when she starts singing. Suu and I could sit and make jokes and wisecracks for hours, especially if there are some of her world-famous chocolate chip cookies to munch on. And Peter has grown up into a man that I'm proud to know. He will be a force within the US Army.

As for Dave Eubank, well, he also married up. Karen Eubank is the perfect yin to Dave's yang. There are very few people in this world that no one could ever say anything negative about—Karen is one of those people. She is tough, so smart, and has a huge heart. Every decision, every inkling in Karen's body, is geared toward what is the best way to love someone in this given situation. She is a total inspiration.

Dave Eubank has inspired me, pushed me, motivated me, guided me, prayed for me, yelled at me, sang to me, sat up late around a campfire in Karen State telling jokes with me, gone on walks with me, missions with me (or I with him), and ultimately fathered me. He is a legend. He is a hero. He is my friend, and it's an honor to call him that. I'm thankful that so many years ago he was willing to welcome me. I'm thankful that he let me be a small part of the FBR family.

There are many more people I could and should mention and write about. Kit and Kawsay. Jazz and Ratree and NooNoo. The Sheriff, Larry, who was my first supervisor at FBR. Sarah Z, who is no longer with FBR but did the job that is now done by about six different people. She had a capacity for work like no other. Mon, whom I fought with like cats and dogs. Dan S (who is now married to Hannah) is my favorite FBR Brit. Justin . . . oh, Justin . . . the guy is maybe one of the best huggers in the world. Kevin and Katie, James and Sarah, Blake and Sami—all relative newcomers to the FBR family—are now the ones taking the reins from Jesse. Jesse led FBR through difficult days and huge growth. Next to Dave, Jesse was my boss, and it was a real honor to serve him. I'm not always the easiest guy to work with, but Jesse was always willing to listen to my point of view and take it into consideration. He would make a decision based on his vast experience and big heart.

As for some of the nameless, faceless people I've mentioned in this book: Aman and the Rohingya team have put in hundreds of wells and toilets and continue to faithfully serve their Rohingya people. FBR continues to build up this team. Silverhorn and KLLS are still fighting the Burma Army, trying to make Burma a country where their kids don't need to fight.

Beh Reh is still my little brother and still by my side here in Burma. He got hit by a mortar in some of the fighting in Karenni; a piece of shrapnel lodged under his kneecap. We were side by side through it all. I left FBR and formed the Jungle Discipleship School (JDS), and Beh came with me. It was a great joy to baptize him last year. AK47 also came to JDS and, halfway through the program, said he was now a "Buddhist-Christian"; by the end of the program he declared himself a "Christian-Buddhist." God is still working in his heart.

Saw Ok, who I had taught to swim, also came with me and helped in the early days of JDS, but he had to leave to help his family during some of the intense fighting in Karen State. He later committed suicide, much to our shock.

Baking that cake for Mee Mar must have scored him some points, because a year later Htwar Reh married Mee Mar. They had a rough first year of marriage as Htwar's sister and brother both died. But they are doing okay. PaLu, who lost his first baby, ended up having two more healthy babies and is a happy dad. Wah Shee also got married and is starting a family of his own. LayKay joined an advanced medical program to learn how to be a physician's assistant. He wants to continue using medicine as a way to help his people.

Kee Reh, my personal security man, got resettled by the UN to Australia. It was a great pleasure to go and see him there, but I miss having him watching out for me here in Burma. NineStone left the war, like MHA, and eventually got married. He and his wife now live in Thailand. Naw Kham moved from Kachin State last year onto the JDS campus with his wife. The fighting in Kachin had become so intense he feared for the life of his wife. He has become my right-hand man here on our JDS campus.

The Jungle Discipleship School sits in Karenni State, about 30 minutes from the mountain that I fell off of many years ago. It is surreal to think back on all the memories and that God was preparing me to lead this program.

I'm grateful to all of my FBR family, foreigners and ethnics alike. Thank you for serving the people in Burma and war zones around the world, and thank you for your love and friendship. You are all heroes.

Finally, I'd be remiss if I didn't say thank you to my mom and dad —you guys are the best parents anyone could ask for. I'm so incredibly lucky to have you. And to all of my supporters, prayer warriors, and donors: you enable me to do this work, and I'm forever grateful.

Also by David Small

The Wandering Leader

The Wandering Beloved

Join The
Mission

This book reflects a calling
that did not end with the final chapter.

Dave's ministry is ongoing,
and support from ordinary people
makes extraordinary work possible.

$1 a day helps keep the work moving
where it is needed most.

WALK WITH US

Scan the QR code or visit
www.davidsmall.org

Publishing Books
That Matter

WRITERS:
We publish courageous, meaningful stories
that refuse to be forgettable.
If you have a manuscript that matters,
 we want to read it.

READERS:
Discover books that value truth, craft,
adventure and the long road of faith.
Follow us to find your next great read.

www.SmallRevolutionPublishing.com

About the Author

David Small comes from the small town of Kenora, Ontario, Canada where he loves spending the summer on the lake and running away at the first sign of fall approaching. David now calls Chiang Mai, Thailand his home. He is the author of *The Wandering Leader*, *The Wandering Beloved*, *Hope Project*, *Small Stories*, and *Nameless Faceless People*. He also wrote and produced the soundtrack to Nameless Faceless People available on Spotify.

David is currently the director of the Jungle Discipleship School in Burma and co-owner of Apex Fitness in Chiang Mai. David served for ten years in the Canadian Army Reserves where he reached the rank of Captain. He has a bachelor of science degree from Haaga-Helia University of Science in Vierumaki, Finland, but Finland was too cold.

He welcomes your emails if you want to send him a personal message: dave@junglediscipleshipschool.com

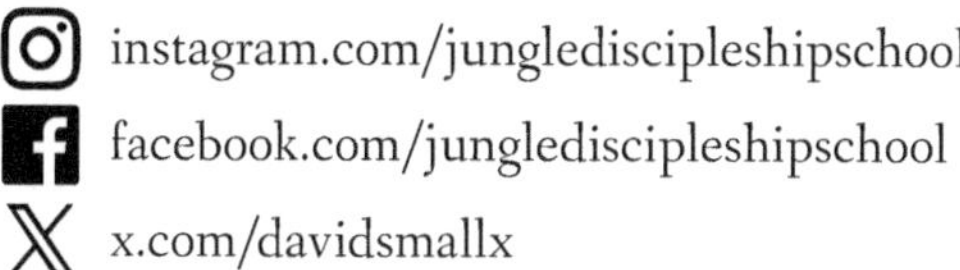

instagram.com/junglediscipleshipschool
facebook.com/junglediscipleshipschool
x.com/davidsmallx